THE DICTIONARY OF DISEASED ENGLISH

The Dictionary of Diseased English

Kenneth Hudson

Harper Colophon Books
Harper & Row, Publishers
New York, Hagerstown, San Francisco, London

This book was originally published by Macmillan Press Ltd.
in 1977. It is here reprinted by arrangement.

THE DICTIONARY OF DISEASED ENGLISH. Copyright © 1977
by Kenneth Hudson. All rights reserved. No part of this book
may be used or reproduced in any manner whatsoever without
written permission except in the case of brief quotations embodied
in critical articles and reviews. For information address
Harper & Row, Publishers, Inc., 10 East 53rd Street, New York,
N.Y. 10022. Printed in Great Britain.

First U.S. edition: HARPER COLOPHON BOOKS 1977

Library of Congress Catalog Card Number: 77-11529

ISBN: 0-06-090608-1

CONTENTS

Foreword   vii
Context of the Dictionary   xi
Introduction   xiii
Dictionary   1
A Note on Sources   259

FOREWORD

The last half-century has seen some powerful, and abundantly justified, criticisms of the increasing corruption of the English language. T. S. Eliot, F. R. Leavis, George Orwell and W. H. Auden come to mind at once. Earlier still, there was Ezra Pound's passionate assertion that when a language goes rotten the very substance of our thoughts and feelings goes rotten too. The same sort of impulse is behind Kenneth Hudson's fascinating and alarming *Dictionary of Diseased English*.

There seems little doubt that the virtues of decent, clear exposition in speech or writing are less sought at all levels of education today than they were a few decades ago. In such a climate jargon and its more publicly self-conscious relative, gobbledegook, can flourish almost unchecked and almost everywhere. It is virtually impossible nowadays to listen to a discussion among specialists in education without hearing again and again about 'the learning situation' or 'being in the classroom situation'; and no discussion on social work is complete without many references to 'the caring society' or 'the supportive society'. The only consolation is that phrases such as these have their day and thereafter fall out of use. Still, others like them take over.

It is important to distinguish jargon from proper professional and technical language. Specialists do need specialist languages for at least two good reasons: as forms of shorthand to speed up discussions between themselves and as safeguards against their analyses being misinterpreted because some of their words might be read in more than one sense. This is especially necessary in social-scientific studies; their language must be so far as possible cleansed of the ambiguities of subjective readings. It can be a pleasure to eavesdrop on conversations of this kind.

By contrast, jargon and gobbledegook are a special preserve of non-specialists and in particular of non-specialists who would like to be thought intellectually and socially up-to-date. They leap from one fashionable phrase to another, phrases which must, since this is their nature as expendable cult-objects, change from year to year. A quick ear for those words and phrases which are on the way out and for those just coming in can be a useful guarantee that we are keeping up with the right social-intellectual group. These can be called 'keeping out' words and phrases; they establish the idea of a sort of club from which most people are excluded. Another group contains language designed to embrace everyone who can be persuaded to read it; this is 'come in' or 'come on' language which has no real subject or substance; or, more exactly, whose substance is its tone itself. This is language which flatters, deceives, disguises, woos. The users of this group are specialists, but their specialism is linguistic persuasion.

I don't want to seem to suggest that all specialists always use their technical language in the pure ways I described earlier. There are some social scientists who use the language of their trade far beyond the needs of the occasion and in conversations with non-specialists. At its best, this is usually because they have fallen poetically in love with the apparatus of the discipline. They are like Scotsmen who walk round Central London in kilts. At its worst, they are often professionally insecure and using the jargon to establish their credentials. As both Kenneth Hudson and I know, since we have both worked in adult education, almost all of us can say almost all we ever have to say about our discipline in words accessible to a reasonably shrewd listener. It is chiefly a matter of being willing to come out from behind the protective wall of our specialist linguistic habits.

It follows that the current kinds of linguistic barbarism are more practised in some disciplines than others. We all know the prose-poem writing on menus, a practice which came over from the United States. My own experience is that in America, no matter what the preposterous claims of the menu, you usually get decent and tasty food at a reasonable price. In England, we have copied the prose-poetry but disregarded the food value. We are given, in most public places, awful food at inflated prices, introduced by entirely spurious claims. Then there are the worlds of advertising and public relations. I treasure a letter from the Customer Service Division Vice President of an American airline, to whom I had complained of careless and offhand treatment which had cost me several hours of exhausting shuttling back and forth. It began: 'Dear Sir, We are privileged to have shared your thoughts on the efficacy of our customer-relations procedures . . .'. Clearly, that kind of letter can be put on the computer for instant use with a facsimile signature. I enjoy remembering also the way a dour-looking Scottish grocer stopped in his tracks a salesman from Glasgow who was giving him fancy patter about 'customer promotions' and 'sales enhancing offers' and the like. The grocer said: 'Young man, give me no more of your inducements. Show me your bill of goods and I will tell you whether I will buy.'

Kenneth Hudson is right, too, to accuse the UN and its agencies of particularly awful linguistic practices. There is just one possible partial justification: sometimes they take refuge in gobbledegook so as to keep the boat steady until the danger of a futile political split has receded; plain speech might make such a split unavoidable. For all that, the UN system is a mine of internationally-deodorised, pseudo-intellectual and pseudo-scientific language. Working in UNESCO, I used to long for a day in which I did not hear about 'a fruitful dialogue' or an 'interface' or 'a viable objective'. And when we hired international non-governmental organisations to carry out parts of the programme we *always* referred to them in print as 'relevant NGOs' or 'competent NGOs', as though to assure our member states that we wouldn't really ask the International Music Council to carry out a study in world economic trends. It brought back the days when chimney sweeps in Leeds almost always described themselves, on little boards above their front doors, as 'practical sweeps', as though they reckoned we all had fears of sweeps so impractical that they would leave the house even more of a shambles than the 'practical' sweeps certainly did.

In politics, both the far Left and the far Right have their jargons, usually of instant abuse or instant package judgment. Kenneth Hudson, in his preface, quotes Rhodes Boyson on the ways 'the parties of the Left have been practising such (linguistic) destruction for years'. I wish Mr. Hudson had found another spokesman, rather than this pot calling the kettle black. Many of Mr. Boyson's own utterances illustrate how addicted those on the Right can be to this practice.

It is not easily possible and certainly not desirable to read a dictionary such as this from cover to cover. Mr. Hudson's discussion of any particular word is likely to set the reader off adding his own gloss, or recalling words he thinks should have been included. Since the process is a continuous one of invention, overuse and decay, such a book can in one sense never be finished. Perhaps the publishers would have done well to add a dozen blank pages, on to which readers could write their own most flagrant examples. It might all come to have the elements of a semi-intellectual parlour game . . . . if it weren't such a serious matter at bottom. For if we ourselves use language in these ways, and if we let ourselves be steadily battered by them (even though it is rather like being battered by pillows stuffed with cotton wool, in the end the process is numbing) if we put up with all this without objecting, we will surely blunt the edge of our own language and so blur our hold on our own intellectual and imaginative lives.

Richard Hoggart

THE CONTEXT OF THE DICTIONARY

'If the changes we fear be thus irresistible, what remains but to acquiesce with silence, as in the other insurmountable distresses of humanity? It remains that we retard what we cannot repel, that we palliate what we cannot cure. Life may be lengthened by care, though death cannot be ultimately defeated. Tongues, like governments, have a natural tendency to degeneration: we have long preserved our constitution, let us make some struggle for our language.'

Samuel Johnson: Preface to *Dictionary*, 1755

INTRODUCTION

What is Meant by Diseased English

Ignorant cooks, with no palate and no interest in food, can spoil the best of raw materials, so that what might in more skilled and more sensitive hands have become a dish to be recalled with pleasure, ends up as nothing better than a repulsive, tasteless mess. So it is with words. No language has better ingredients than English; no language has ever been more monstrously ill-treated and deformed by vandals and incompetents. The most beautiful instrument is always the most vulnerable to abuse and damage.

Linguistic abuse takes many forms. Sometimes it is sheer carelessness and clumsiness:−

'The telephone service in King Island has been characterised by the informality familiar to such services.'

Sometimes it is ignorance or indifference to the proper meaning of a particular word or phrase:−

'The game is riddled with such stories.'

Sometimes it is the kind of nonsense which results from the unthinking and indiscriminate use of a fashionable cliché:−

'The patented pulsing action literally dissolves stress from tired muscles.'

Sometimes it is the cult of the new, the ugly and the shocking for its own sake:−

'A good suit, fashionable and properly accessorised', or
'These can be souvenired overseas at bargain prices.'

Sometimes it is the immigrant's literal, but illiterate, translation from his own language, which strikes roots in the country of his adoption:−

'Pianist George Shearing', or
'He plays piano.'

Sometimes it is an inability to transfer speech to paper, with no realisation of what punctuation is for:–

'Another thing that attracted me to folk music was discovering Percy Grainger's arrangements, they are so subtle harmonically.'

Sometimes, and much worse, it is a conscious and cynical combination of iconoclasm and seeking after novelty, a professional job:–

'From the airline that brings you the world. A slice of luxury. This is jetting. This is Qantas. You're the star. Here impeccable service unfolds. Stewards and Hostesses are at your command. An iced drink, a hot towel, at take-off. Then some writing paper. A magazine. Or chess. Maybe a martini. Or whatever you wish. You chat. With your neighbour. Discover he's an Artist. Author. Diplomat. Banker.'*

Most frequently, the torturing and battering of our long-suffering but fortunately still breathing language stems from a longing for grandeur and advertiser's poetry. We therefore have such things as:–

'Fast, strong and perfectly shaped, the gondola embodies all the water-borne magic of Venice. And the agile, singing gondolier has for centuries been a central part of the Venetian legend, transporting sober citizens about their business, or lovers to their secret assignations.'†

Or, from the industrialist who, in his efforts to up-grade his simplest statements, has no fear or perception of the ridiculous:–

'We have a very good liaison with the Water Board and we circulate the people concerned.'

Or the unfortunate results of the Mayor's anxiety to make his words match the dignity of his office:–

'Poole is a very democratic place. The dinghy-sailors regularly cohabit with the people on the beach.'

There is nothing new or particularly frightening about the last two examples. They are in the English comic tradition of Sheridan's Mrs. Malaprop and Shakespeare's Dogberry, people who combine a

* Brochure, *It's a Woman's World with Quantas*, 1975.
† *The Reader's Digest Book of World Travel*, 1967.

fondness for fine language with the inability to use and control it. What has grown up in our own time is something much more sinister—a contempt for people who use language accurately and elegantly, and this attitude certainly did not exist in the days of Shakespeare, Sheridan or Dickens. It has now reached such a point of absurdity that, in many circles, the inability to write and talk well is taken as evidence of superior personal worth. Conversely, anyone who has learnt how to discipline his thoughts and his way of expressing them is regarded with the greatest suspicion. If he has a rich vocabulary and can spell and write grammatically, he is obviously a political reactionary and that most dangerous of all contemporary animals, an élitist.

One could, perhaps, tolerate this for a while, irritating and depressing as it may be, in the hope that it could amount to nothing more than the new power-groups flexing their muscles and letting society know that it has a fresh set of masters. Is it, after all, one might ask, so very different from what the Chinese were saying and doing during their Cultural Revolution? If the nation is to be democratised in a thorough-going way, then language cannot expect to escape the same cleansing and levelling process. Workers', soldiers' and peasants' Chinese must, by definition, be different from bourgeois or capitalist Chinese—or Russian, or German, or Portuguese, or any other language one cares to name. One must somehow arrive at a general use of the mother-tongue which will not make simple people feel inferior. National unity demands that the language shall be levelled down.

All one can say about this is that, plausible and commonly heard as the argument is, there is no evidence that either the Russians or the Chinese have ever believed or advocated any such thing. They may have introduced a new, crude and repulsive ideological vocabulary with which to abuse their enemies but, apart from this, their attitude to language appears to have been extremely conservative. Russian and Chinese children today are taught to handle written and spoken Russian and Chinese at least as accurately as their fathers and grandfathers were. Some no doubt succeed better than others, but there is certainly no officially inspired equation between sloppy semi-literacy and a People's Democracy, although the need to condition some responses but not others produces considerable psychological and educational problems. The split or two-level mind is an essential item of self-protection in any country with a totalitarian government.

In the West, however, things have been rather different, although one hesitates to say better. Our society, it would seem from the people its schools and universities produce, places a low value on literacy, if by literacy one means the ability to use the full resources of the language, to listen and read with comprehension and sensitivity and to speak and write easily and with clarity and grace. An unprejudiced observer might well consider, from the evidence before his eyes and ears, that today's Britain, America or Australia has a vested interest in semi-literacy; we want and we get people who are just literate enough to fill in forms, read street signs and see what is on the label of a medicine bottle, but not sufficiently at home with language to prevent themselves from being drugged and seduced by commercial and political propaganda. Much of this propaganda truly qualifies for the label 'diseased English', in that it is specifically and cunningly designed to work on the half-awake, half-informed mind. It aims neither at comprehension nor at clarity. Automatic responses are its measure of success.

'It has been claimed, [writes Dr. Rhodes Boyson,*] that the teaching of grammar is a bulwark of civil order. To this I would add that the debasement of the meaning of important words can help to destroy a free society. The parties of the Left have been practising such destruction of words for many years.'

Dr. Boyson, like George Orwell before him, has in mind such emotive, and now largely meaningless phrases as 'social justice', which is now a synonym for 'the creation of envy'—and, as John Stuart Mill said with complete accuracy, envy is 'the most anti-social of all passions'. He was also, no doubt, thinking of words like 'obscene', 'filthy' and 'indecent', which have been taken over by the Left as blunt, heavy weapons with which to attack anything it dislikes, such as private property, private rents and salaries which reward ability and hard work. 'Is this destruction and corruption of words by the Left,' he asks, 'part of the decline of knowledge in an egalitarian age, or is it intentional corruption? Either way it is a bitter commentary on the men who do it. Perhaps we should return to teaching grammar, spelling and meaning in our schools, instead of "social liberation" and "personal orientation" and such rubbish.'

Grammar, spelling and meaning, however, inescapably add up to a subject called English, and, throughout the English-speaking world,

* *Daily Telegraph*, 19th December 1975.

English appears to be losing its place to something much more modern-sounding and impressive called Communications, the concern of which is not literacy at all. The basic assumption of Communications is that language is just another means of communication, certainly no more important and perhaps even less important than television or films or popular music. This is the message of Marshall McLuhan and his disciples, who insist that print is dead, the days of the book are over, and that the prime duty of the citizen and of those who cater for his needs is to become expert in the mysteries of tape, film and incantation.

The consequence of this continuous barrage of anti-language propaganda is that we have become suspicious of those who speak well. We have come to prefer what has been well-termed 'mutter-language'. 'The verbal is out and the visual and the visceral are in. The result is students who take courses in "communications" and tell you that they sort of like, man, you know, dig their teacher.'*

It is possible that we are approaching a point at which the ability to use English with precision and sensitivity has become either the privilege or the burden of very few people. The rest of their fellow-citizens, in that case, will eventually be divided into three groups:—

1. Those who write nonsense without realising it.
2. Those who write nonsense in complete and cynical awareness of what they are doing.
3. The passive victims of (1) and (2).

This disastrous situation is not, however, inevitable and the present *Dictionary* reflects a belief that the worst can be prevented from happening, but that an essential part of any battle is the ability to recognise one's enemies and to identify their weapons.

The enemies of a free and democratic society are the people who are permitted and encouraged to write things like

'After a period of induction training concentrated on user and large account selling, you will assume complete responsibility for the export sales management control function which you will set up against marketing guide-lines and report directly to the managing director. You will recognise the company commitment to a philosophy of profitable sales attainment consistent with company marketing policy and production capacity.'

5   * Morris Wolfe: *The Globe and Mail*, Toronto, 31st January 1976.

and

> 'I don't think people are worried about employment. It's more a case of being concerned about the future.'

and

> 'It is untrue to state that two resolutions passed by the last session of UNESCO's General Conference deprive Israel of the benefits of belonging to that body. The Conference voted to apply sanctions to Israel and to withhold assistance in the fields of education, science and culture.'

The enemies of English use a small but superficially impressive vocabulary. They are fond of knocking the other side off balance with what is, to the ignorant and impressionable, indistinguishable from science. An American Christmas card, produced by one of the wittier members of the academic world, takes the form of three concentric and revolving discs and caricatures the pseudo-scientific style and approach in a masterly fashion. 'This structurally divergent communication,' the message around the extreme edge reads, 'conceptualises a wish that Christmas may bring a meaningful reinforcement of your specific predetermined behavioural patterns.' Each disc carries 24 words of this kind and by rotating the discs one can build up a large number of magnificent but totally meaningless phrases, of the kind that stops communication in its tracks. One can have, for instance, 'child-centred procedural dysfunction', or 'innovatory motivational maladjustment', or 'basic theoretical strategy'. The full range of socio-psychological rubbish is here, ready to dope and bemuse the unwary, and to entertain the privileged and dangerous few who have seen through it all. For those who would find it convenient to have this select vocabulary for reference, the words are:—

Outer disc Activities; communication; resources; synthesis; validation; techniques; consensus; maladjustment; sector; criteria; autonomy; analysis; polarisation; objectivity; strategy; situation; over-involvement; evaluation; components; dysfunction; methodology; quotients; reorganisation; rationalisation.
Middle disc Consultative; empirical; unstructured; implicit; perceptual; psycho-linguistic; co-educational; reactionary; motivational; academic; conceptual; experimental; socio-economic; hypothetical; ideological; theoretical; developmental; compensatory; diagnostic;

meaningful; procedural; significant; democratic; sociometric.

Inner disc Disadvantaged; on-going; informal; ultra; inter-disciplinary; cognitive; relevant; correlated; extra; innovatory; viable; supportive; élitist; micro; creative; advanced; basic; divergent; programmed; operational; affective; child-centred; multi; emotive.

One could go a long way nowadays with this basic vocabulary, plus a few pronouns and simple verbs.

This is perhaps the point at which one should attempt a definition of *diseased English*. It is 'English which, either deliberately or unconsciously, is used with so serious a lack of precision that it ceases to be an effective means of communication and serves only to confuse or mislead'. The disease may manifest itself in single words or phrases, or in passages of any length.

One must emphasise that diseased English is not the same as misused English. The BBC sub-editor who, in the course of writing a news-item, said 'She was taken to Poole General Hospital, where she was said to be satisfactory', was merely careless or semi-literate, since it was the lady's condition, one hopes, not the lady herself, which was satisfactory. Nobody, however, was confused or misled by the mistake. Similarly, the use of 'the promoter is wide-open' instead of 'the choice of promoter is wide-open' may be inelegant and unfortunate, but it is not diseased, at least in the present *Dictionary's* use of the term. 'Superb gourmet dining', on the other hand, in an advertisement for an expensive and fashionable restaurant, serving notably undistinguished food, is diseased. Such a description is aimed at causing the customer to believe that he is getting food close to the world's best, when in fact what he is being sold is an assembly of expensive edible clichés. The fact that most of the restaurant's customers are willing partners in the swindle is an indication of how deep-rooted the disease has become.

The present *Dictionary* is the result of an extensive and not always pleasurable search through books, newspapers and periodicals published in the English-speaking world during the past ten years. It is necessarily illustrative, rather than comprehensive. 'This,' it says in effect, 'is what feckless, ignorant and socially irresponsible people are doing to our language.' Every page and every item is meant to be a call to arms. It is not a culturally-neutral volume and some readers will undoubtedly find it prejudiced.

But the situation has become too serious for the suppression or toning-down of one's convictions. If any improvement is to be possible, one has to hit out. As George Orwell so wisely said thirty years ago, 'one ought to recognise that the present political chaos is connected with the decay of language, and that one can probably bring about some improvement by starting at the verbal end'.* The process of decay, Orwell pointed out, feeds on itself. 'A man may take to drink because he feels himself to be a failure, and then fails all the more completely because he drinks. It is rather the same thing that is happening to the English language. It becomes ugly and inaccurate because our thoughts are foolish, but the slovenliness of our language makes it easier for us to have foolish thoughts.' Modern writing at its worst, he went on to say, 'does not consist in picking out words for the sake of their meaning and inventing images in order to make the meaning clearer. It consists in gumming together long strips of words which have already been set in order by someone else, and making the results presentable by sheer humbug.'

The cumulative effect, the gumming together, is what matters most, nonsensical and twisted in themselves as the individual words and phrases may be. A dictionary can only indicate the bricks; the walls from which they are made are material for an anthology. *An Anthology of Diseased English* would be a natural companion to the present volume, and one hopes that its appearance will not be long delayed.† Meanwhile, one can do no more than indicate the kind of extracts it will contain. Publishers' advertising, for instance, would be well represented:–

'The world's greatest writers of fiction have all created stories that are immortal masterpieces. Works of such imaginative power that they have the force of actual experience. Works of such wit and wisdom that they illuminate the nature and meaning of life. Works of such rich variety, that they penetrate every aspect of human existence and have become part of the literary heritage of all mankind.

* 'Politics and the English Language'. Originally published in 1946 and quoted here from *The Collected Essays, Journalism and Letters of George Orwell*, ed. Sonia Orwell and Ian Angus, Vol. IV, 1968.

† For some time the *Washington Star* has given its readers an opportunity to build up at least part of such an anthology with very little effort. It runs a regular feature called 'Gobbledygook', which is devoted to examples of officialese. $10 is paid for each entry printed. A typical item (19.10.76) was: 'When previously processed prior pay period adjustments were made for multiple pay periods, the overtime hours and/or premium pay was computed in the same manner as each of the other pay periods, using the overtime hours and/or premium pay from the period with the highest amount of overtime hours or premium pay (except for the Christmas period) to provide employees with the maximum possible benefit.' This was part of a notice to U.S. Postal employees.

Now, for the first time, these masterpieces of fiction are to be published in a truly luxurious collection – forming a library of great literature unlike any other ever published before. A private library devoted *exclusively* to the greatest stories of the world's greatest writers of fiction.

Each of the one hundred guest authors represented in this collection is a giant of world literature. A towering figure who brought the art of fiction to a peak of perfection. And each volume in this unique series will contain the finest stories of one of these great authors. In one hundred sumptuous volumes, each bound in genuine leather – this magnificent edition will include . . .'*

The dividing line between 'diseased' and 'exaggerated' is thin and elusive, but the exaggerations so liberally scattered over the passage just quoted are the symptoms of disease and are certainly capable of bemusing and confusing the more innocent reader and, with luck, hypnotising him into buying books which he may or may not eventually enjoy.

The art writers would certainly be present in our anthology in force with such flashes of insight as: –

'It seems wholly illogical that although most of Barbara Hepworth's drawings are representational, most of her sculptural oeuvre is organic. It would therefore be impossible to simplify down to the inner arresting movement if confined to chiselling a synthesis of human figuration. When art has to be fundamental no distracting detail is possible. There must only be a totality concentrated in Oneness.'†

and

'What attests to Boogaert's increased self-assurance as an artist is that he realises that he does not need a blatantly obvious pattern or configuration to get across the idea of an imposed mental structure; it is inherent in the fact that he has broken a continuous unmarked temporality into discrete units. That the differences between the individual frames of a given contact sheet frequently lie beneath the

---

* Supplement to the *Boston Sunday Globe*, advertising the Franklin Library, 3rd October 1976.

† *Connoisseur*, Vol. 163, Sept./Dec. 1966. A high proportion of the art critics writing in English are of Continental, especially German, origin. This is certainly one reason for their strange jargon. They use it primarily as a kind of lingua franca, for communication with other art critics, not with the public.

threshold of perception does not disturb him. He is after all only reporting the results of applying a particular schema upon a natural phenomenon.'*

The psychologists and psychiatrists would have a generous contribution to make:—

'Other group modalities often used with children and play, behavior modification, and the verbal approach . . . Play materials are selected to evoke group members' expression and resolution of personal conflicts. Therapeutic ingredients are the therapist–child relationship and therapist clarification-interpretation of feelings expressed through the child's play. Member-to-member interaction is seen as less important in play than in activity-group treatment. In behavior techniques, the armentarium of behavioral techniques is applied. Treatment goals are limited to the modification of specific behaviour patterns. The verbal group therapies include client-centred counseling and insight-oriented psychotherapy. Definitive features of these modalities and discussion of the patients' problems and mobilisation of member-to-member and member-to-therapist interaction to improve psycho-behavioral functioning.'†

The sociologists would be queueing up for inclusion, with such passages as:—

'A factor of considerable importance in naturalistic socialization contexts is the timing of punishment. In home situations, punishment is often delayed beyond the completion of the deviant behavior. Does the timing of the administration of a punishment affect its effectiveness as a means of inhibiting undesirable behavior? Mowrer (1960) has provided a theoretical framework for predicting the effects of the timing of punishment. According to Mowrer, each component of a response sequence provides sensory feedback in the form of response-produced kinesthetic and proprioceptive cues. Punishment may be administered at any point during the sequence of responses and result in a relatively direct association of a fear-motivated avoidance response with the response-produced cues occurring at the temporal locus of punishment. If the punishment is administered at the initiation of

---

* *Arts Canada* July/August 1976. Article on Pierre Boogaerts by Walter Klepac.
† *Archives of General Psychiatry* Chicago, March 1976.

the deviant response sequence, the maximal degree of fear is attached to the cues produced by the instrumental acts involved in initiating the sequence. In this case, subsequent initiation of the sequence will arouse anxiety that activates incompatible avoidance responses, which are reinforced by anxiety reduction if they are sufficiently strong to forestall the deviant behavior.'*

And so on through the management writers, the educationists, the politicians, the wine and food writers, the lawyers, the theologians, the ballet, music and literary critics, and the rest of our contemporary wordmongers for whom simplicity and directness are apparently so difficult and unnatural. One uses the term 'wordmonger' deliberately, because, nagging away in the back of one's mind there is always the suspicion that these people may really have nothing to say, and that mere words are all they have to offer, that the medium is in fact the message. It is a matter of experience and observation that someone with a genuine piece of information can usually manage to communicate it in a reasonably straightforward and intelligible way. The verbal nonsense tends to come from people with nothing to say, but with a powerful vested interest in saying it impressively. Sorting out the sheep from the goats is a skilled business, which demands great ruthlessness and objectivity and is certain to make enemies, many of them in high places.

The reader may feel that the present work deals somewhat harshly at times with certain categories of writer, more especially perhaps those who earn their living, or part of their living, from giving their opinions on music, ballet, painting, food and wine. This is certainly from no spirit of malevolence. On the contrary, it is fully recognised that the task of expressing sensual pleasures in words is extraordinarily difficult and that it is right and natural to strain language to the utmost in an effort to communicate what one has seen, heard and tasted. Such striving and wrestling with words is the poet's everyday problem and duty. There is nothing new or unreasonable about it. What has to be remembered, however, is that the critic, unlike the poet, is paid to communicate. If the wine critic of *The Times* or the ballet critic of *The Guardian* writes and publishes something that makes no sense to the majority of the people who read these articles, then the critics must be considered to have failed. A critic is a communicator, and if his attempts to communicate meet with little success, he should either try another approach or look for another job.

* Ronald A. Hoppe et al. *Early Experiences and the Process of Socialisation* New York, 1970.

An editor or a publisher can be put in a very difficult position by such specialists. On the one hand he must trust them and, up to a point, give them their head, but on the other he has a responsibility to his readers to restrain the most extreme excesses. He must have the power to say, 'This makes no sense'; 'Do something about it.' This, however, can be dangerous, because today's apparent nonsense can be tomorrow's crystal-clear good sense. The first-class critic, like the first-class artist, is always to some extent ahead of his times. The editor of an internationally famous art magazine confessed to the present author that quite frequently he found himsef unable to understand the articles written by one particular expert on contemporary art. 'But,' he went on to say, 'I think he's an honest man, so I print what he sends me'. It is a point of view which is bound to command one's respect, however baffling the articles in question may seem.

It will be evident from the following pages that a special effort has been made to track down and struggle to interpret the often very strange language employed by an interesting and influential body of experts, the wine-writers. This is partly because the problem is important in itself—a great deal is written and read about wine in the course of a year—and partly because wine-writing is a microcosm of at least part of our culture. By analysing it and trying to understand what is in the writer's mind, one is brought on close terms with what is admirable and absurd, rewarding and futile, in our society. Discussion about wine with wine-professionals is usually as fruitless and infuriating as conversations between a devoutly religious person and someone who has never experienced the power of religion. At some point the expert is likely to have to say, 'I can't put it any more plainly. There are no words to express what I feel. You'll simply have to believe me and take it all on trust.'

But, as we have said before, there are great dangers in accepting this point of view. It makes life too easy for the phonies, for those who see advantages in disguising themselves as the real people. If one tries as hard as one can to understand what another person is saying, and no sense comes out of it, it is always safer to assume that one is in contact with a fraud, rather than a genius. One may be wrong at times, but less often than by assuming the opposite. Any good communicator understands very well when something is likely to be difficult to explain or express, and at such times he will use all his skill to meet his listeners or readers half-way. The poor communicator either fails to understand the problem or dismisses the doubters and questioners as morons.

Wine-critics do, in all fairness, occasionally try to reveal what lies behind their strange language. They rarely succeed. Their explanations are often as perplexing as the words that occasioned them. The wine-critic of *The Times*, for instance, a lady highly and rightly respected in her profession, recently made a big effort to instruct the readers of a popular women's magazine* in the significance of wine-words. The term 'finesse', she said, 'has been neatly summed up as the sort of thing that makes you order the second bottle so as to find out more about what the wine really is like'. It is hardly a definition, and she has little better luck with two other favourites, 'breed' and 'elegance'. These, one is told, 'are terms that it's easy to interpret as regards wine because they mean virtually the same sort of thing as when you are describing people – a wine can obviously have 'breed' (sic), even if you don't really like it, and it may be 'elegant' on some occasions when you couldn't have expected it to be more than adequately turned out.' We are, alas, not a great deal further forward.

It should be emphasised with all possible vigour that the *Dictionary* has absolutely no prejudice against innovation and change in English or any other language. Nor can there be any objection to necessary technical terms. It is essential that every generation should make its own contribution to the strength and flexibility of the mother-tongue. Ideas and circumstances are always in movement and language, if it is to remain in a state of health, has to adjust itself to new patterns of living. It cannot remain static. What the following pages try to dissect and expose is bogus innovation, language which has a shiny and saleable veneer and nothing but rotten wood underneath. Four classes of people are particularly guilty of this crime against their fellow-men:–

1. *The padders and puffers*, those who have a given amount of space to fill and whose living depends on filling it at all costs.
2. *The inflators*, those who have something very simple or banal to say, but who feel driven, for reasons of prestige, to make it sound much grander than it really is.
3. *The whitewashers*, those who are hired to put a pretty face on ugly things.
4. *The confidence tricksters*, those who have nothing to say at all, but whose livelihood and power demand that the public shall be hypnotised into thinking that they are giants and geniuses.

Diseased English is spread by these people. They are carriers of infection and need to be identified, isolated and, wherever possible, cured, before their kind of English becomes accepted as normal.

Correspondence on these subjects is often far from easy. A firm, a Government department or an individual is likely to react badly to the slightest suggestion that it, he or she has been responsible for prose which is anything less than crystal clear and impeccably stylish. Threats of prosecution are not uncommon. During 1976, for instance, one of the foremost management recruitment companies in Britain had a large newspaper advertisement, which included two seriously ungrammatical items, the first, 'our client are continuing', and the second 'the companies service'. The firm was asked if what actually appeared in print, 'is an exact reproduction of the copy you sent in, since newspapers do occasionally make a mistake', and it was suggested that advertisements phrased in this way might do the reputation of the company no good. The reply was 'that the advertisement in question appeared in the form it did as a result of factors beyond the control of this company', and that the company 'would reserve the right to take such legal action as might be deemed appropriate if your comments in a published work were in any way similar to those expressed in your letter'. Words, however, do not select themselves. If the blunders referred to did not come from the recruitment company, either the client or the newspaper must have been responsible. Illiteracy was clearly in the air and contaminating this particular job to such an extent that fully educated candidates might well have decided not to apply. No threats of legal action could blow that fact away.

The major villains in the language play change somewhat from decade to decade. In the 1930s the principal culprits, at least in English, were probably advertising people, with the lawyers and the civil servants hard on their heels. During the 1940s, the politicians, the bureaucrats and the armed forces overtook and passed the front runners of the previous decade, the war years having added greatly to the power and influence of all three. The Fifties and Sixties, however, gave immensely increased opportunities to social scientists and to the Booming Economy and Good Life people, who developed their own kinds of nonsense language at an alarming speed and almost without the linguistic doctors realising that the disease was changing its symptoms. The entries in this *Dictionary*, covering the years 1966–76, consequently have a different flavour from what one would have found if the pond to be dragged had been, say, 1936–46. 1976–86 will almost certainly produce its own peculiar crop. This is a dictionary which, in the public interest, needs to be re-made every ten years.

To some extent, the proportion of entries from different fields of human activity reflects the number of words which each of these has hurled at the ear and the eye during the decade. The sociologists, the psychologists, the management experts, the new-style bureaucrats, the industrialists with the bit between their teeth, the people with holidays, hotels and restaurants to sell, the entertainment impresarios—all these have had a prodigious amount to say for themselves during a period in which they, at least, have never had it so good. Forecasts are always dangerous, but there is no harm in chancing the opinion that the top producers of linguistic rubbish between 1976 and 1986 will be the trade unions, religious bodies, the medical profession and extremist political groups—all people who flourish when times are bad.

Some things, none the less, are timeless, and in reading the entries which follow, one should never lose sight of the fact that communication is quite as much a matter of the emotions as of the intellect. One can write or speak absolute rubbish, but, if it is the right kind of rubbish, it can bring one an abundance of friends and allies among people who habitually use the same variety of nonsense language. There are no stronger links than those between sufferers from the same illness, even when that illness is madness. To the irreverent layman, 'each component of a response-sequence provides sensory feedback in the form of response-produced kinesthetic and proproceptive cues' sounds like pompous piffle, which indeed it is, but to a fellow psychologist or sociologist it indicates a friend, someone with his head and heart in the right place, someone worth knowing. For the initiates it is rank-closing, masonic language, with no power to stimulate those who live outside the group. The magical quality of linguistic rubbish can be underestimated, but one is still entitled to say that such language rots both society and the individual, and this *Dictionary* takes pride in making its point of view clear, no matter how much it may annoy and unsettle those who believe that group loyalty is the supreme virtue.

There is, however, one encouraging feature to be noticed, and it would be a pity not to end this Introduction on a note of optimism. The wretchedly corrupt English of the groups which happen to enjoy great power at any particular time always, in a democratic society, produces a reaction against it. This sometimes comes in the form of ridicule, sometimes of direct attack. The advertisers, the doctors, the lawyers and the sociologists, for example, have all been pilloried for the follies and crimes of their language, and the world is a sweeter place as a result. A comparison between some of the professional journals now and twenty or thirty years ago will reveal a very great improvement. It would be rather tedious to list here the professions and publications which have done themselves great benefit in this way,* but an illustration can do no harm. The *British Medical Journal* is quite remarkably free from jargon these days. This seemed to call for a letter of congratulation to the Editor, whose answer deserves the widest possible publicity.

'We do have a strong feeling about the English language,' he wrote, 'Our copy is fairly heavily subedited—particularly in the teaching sections (that is, leading articles and Medical Practice) and we also routinely change wrong phrases (mitigate against) wherever they occur. I am particularly interested in trying to eliminate gobbledygook. I think many articles remain unread because subliminally the effect of bad English prevents the reader from glancing through more than the first paragraph, and I have run a number of courses in medical writing in Britain, Europe and the Middle East to try and get this across.'

It can be done.

---

* The task has been carried out with some thoroughness in the author's forthcoming book, *The Jargon of the Professions*, due for publication by Macmillan in 1977.

A

Able

Much favoured by writers on education. Nowadays it is impossible for a child to be stupid, unintelligent or idle on the one hand, or clever, intelligent or hardworking on the other. More able and less able are the preferred equivalents. 'In mixed ability groups, which is what we aim at, the least able and the most able are equally mixed'. (Hunter Davis: *The Creighton Report*, 1976) Cf Less able.

Above-the-line

A costing or budgeting item, often used in a very vague sense. Strictly speaking, an above-the-line cost is one that is to be charged to a particular budget, whereas anything below-the-line is ordinary expenditure, covered by the general financial provisions of the organisation. In the case of a television producer, for instance, heating and lighting his office and giving him a telephone service would be below-the-line, but a camera crew and fees paid to actors would be above-the-line. This distinction is by no means always observed by industrial and commercial concerns. 'His experience will include both above and below-the-line marketing activities' (*D Tel*, 27.11.75), for example, is a far from precise sentence, which is probably intended to convey no more than that the applicant for the post should have had wide experience of modern marketing methods. But 'below-the-line marketing' can also mean expenditure on giveaways, gimmicks and competitions, by contrast with advertising, which is reckoned to be 'above-the-line'. There is, however, confusion with the meaning given to the words in bridge, where there is a line drawn across the score-card. 'Above-the-line' points are scored for game, honours, overtricks or rubber, or for the failure of one's opponents to fulfil their contract, and 'below-the-line' points are for tricks bid and won. The linguistic muddle surrounding 'above-the-line' and 'below-the-line' is, in fact, so considerable that it seems prudent to avoid the terms wherever possible, however adventurous they may sound.

Abrasive

A very with-it word, with a spectrum of meaning that ranges from 'sharp and creative' at the one end to 'irritating, negative and destructive' at the other. How, for instance, should one interpret, 'The underclass has its most abrasive contacts with the ruling élites less at the point of production than outside it' (Teodori, 1969)? 'Violent'? 'Exhausting'? 'Hostile'? 'Head-on'? 'Unpleasant'?

Absolute

Usually no more than a meaningless intensive. 'Built only two years ago on an absolute deep waterfrontage block' (*National Times*, 1.3.76). Water which was absolutely deep would presumably have no discoverable bottom, a terrifying prospect for mariners. Each room 'designed to give you absolute comfort' (Wentworth Hotel, Sydney, 1975 brochure) shows a similar degree of exaggeration. Absolute zero is a reality; absolute comfort is unlikely to be achieved in this world. A hotel which advertised nothing better than great or considerable comfort, however, would presumably be left standing by its competitors.

Accent

Both the noun and the verb have been in high fashion for some time among American advertisers and have, unfortunately but inevitably, now crossed the Atlantic. An 'accent' is an outstanding feature, a characteristic which hits the eye immediately. So, '. . . natural brick accent walls' (*Axiom*, Oct 1976), and 'We've even carpeted, draped and professionally accented five of these houses' (*Boston Sunday Globe*, 10.10.76). In the first case, the 'natural brick accent walls' are, on the evidence of a photograph, no more than brick walls, and, in the second, 'professionally accented' appears to mean that someone had been engaged to think about the interior decoration as a whole, instead of the matter being left to the local furniture store and do-it-yourself shop.

Acceptability

In correct usage, one can refuse to accept an argument, a knighthood or a telephone call for reasons one believes to be sound. A dirty knife is unacceptable to a fastidious person sitting down to a meal. The industrial would appears to view the word differently, however. 'The vital task will be to decide on the acceptability of information and its contribution to commercial growth' (*Fin Times*, 18.11.75). It is possible for information to be perfectly accurate, but distasteful, so that the recipient closes his ears and eyes to it. Does the *Financial Times* mean this, or are we to understand that 'acceptability' means 'relevance' or 'significance'? If one of these two words is meant, why not use it?

Accessorised
Used as an accessory, possessing the qualities of an accessory, or provided with accessories? 'A good suit, fashionable and properly accessorised' (*Signature*, Jan/Feb 1976) is clumsy and leaves one in doubt as to the meaning. Is the suit sold complete with accessories? Is being 'properly accessorised' part of the suit's goodness?

Acclimate
A barbarism, which in some circles is reckoned to be more impressive and 'professional' than 'accustom', and more specialised and technical than 'acclimatise'. So: 'The first lesson was a practice lesson, largely to acclimate the trainee to the video-tape equipment' (JER,63/3, Nov 1969).

Accommodating
A pompous piece of businessese for 'meeting', which is felt to be too ordinary to be dignified. 'The key task will be to lead the continued development of the manufacturing operations whilst effectively accommodating the current demands of a volatile market' (*D Tel*, 5.2.76). This is not a muddled, illiterate way of saying 'accommodating oneself to the current demands of a volatile market'. Industrial leaders meet challenges head on, never 'accustom themselves' to them, which would suggest compromise.

Accomplishments
Now often used as a synonym for 'achievement', apparently because modern industry demands something better, even if the result is confusion and nonsense. When one referred to a Victorian lady's accomplishments, one was thinking of her taste, artistic and musical prowess, charm and beautiful manners. Not so the modern business world. 'We are looking for a uniquely talented individual with a proven record of accomplishments' (*S Times*, 30.5.76). It is unlikely that the person required would be expected to produce evidence of his ability to play the piano, sing and do fine needlework, although, since he needed to be 'uniquely talented', one never knows.

Accountability

In these numerate days, a more sought after and more highly remunerated quality than mere 'responsibility'. 'Members of our account management group are given early accountability for providing a comprehensive recruitment service to a number of clients with diverse activities' (*D Tel*, 1.7.76). A surgeon is accountable for the number of swabs he places inside one of his patients and a soldier for the weapons issued to him, but an accountant is hardly accountable for his advice, unless, perhaps, he should happen to leave it lying about, allowing it to be stolen.

Accrual

'Accrue', properly used, conveys the notion of something being added to something else. It is a synonym for 'accumulate', not 'grow' or 'increase'. A plant cannot accrue, nor can a small boy or a balloon. One therefore blinks a little at 'the framework is accrual in scope' (*Business Horizons*, Aug 1975). All that is meant is that the scope of the job will increase as time goes on, but this would be nothing like grand enough to attract the right kind of candidate.

Acculturated

A very nastly barnacle on the American language. No-one but a sociologist would have any difficulty in writing 'rooted', 'absorbed' or 'associated with ', but since sociologists feel a need to prove that they are not as other men, we have: 'the measure of a Jewish student's desire to become more acculturated in the Jewish tradition and culture' (Pride and Holmes, 1972), with no sign of shame at the ugly repetition of 'acculturated' and 'culture'.

Achieve

One is usually safe with 'achieve' when it is used transitively. 'He achieved nothing', or 'she achieved what she'd always wanted, an apology from Henry' make good sense, but 'If you have leadership potential, with the desire to achieve' (*The Citizen*, 8.10.76) is quite another matter. Achieve what? 100,000 dollars a year? A seven-foot wife? A coronary? An invitation to dine with the President? Peace of mind?

Achievement

'. . . when taught in a manner consonant with their achievement orientations' (JEP. 64/2, 1973). Any word with 'orientations' tagged on to it brings problems of interpretation. One is never sure if the person in question is turning round, thinking of something, or navigating by something, but psychologists and businessmen love their 'orientations', so we shall probably have to suffer it for some time yet. Here, we might perhaps translate 'when taught what is likely to help them in their career', or 'what (or in a way that) suits their ambitions' or, even less politely, 'in a way they can understand'.

Action

In the world of business, a capacity for action is the supreme virtue. People are not hired to sit around and think, although thought translated into action is tolerated, as evidenced by: 'The incumbent will be an action-oriented thinker' (*S Times*, 30.5.76). The increasingly common use of 'action' as a verb produces sentences which do not stand up well to close examination. Consider, '. . . for individual training and experience requirements to be identified and actioned' (*D Tel*, 1.7.76). A rendering of this into ordinary English might be: '. . . to make sure that employees get the right training and experience', but that is not nearly impressive enough for the purpose.

Active

Bacilli are active and so apparently are some hospitals, but not all. What is 'a 500-bed fully accredited active treatment hospital' (*Hospital Administration in Canada*, Aug 1976)? It cannot be 'a hospital in which treatment is actually carried out', because that, one has always supposed, is true of all hospitals. Or is there, perhaps, a category of hospital in which people simply lie in bed and wait for nature and the passage of time to put them right? Or do some forms of treatment, 'active treatments', have a higher prestige than others? What, the person who is not a hospital administrator has a right to ask, is 'active treatment'?

Activist

An activist, broadly speaking, is a person who, in the eyes of the authorities, engages in politically disreputable activities. There is no such thing as a good activist. All activists are bad. We therefore find: 'Teachers with an activist orientation risk administrative sanction' (*Educ & Soc Sci*, Vol 1, No 2, July 1969). For anyone who has difficulty in understanding this sentence, the key piece of information is that 'risk' is a verb. The meaning then becomes plain enough;

teachers who take an active part in left-wing politics, and especially in demonstrations, are likely to find themselves in trouble with their employers and may get fired. But how different the flavour of the translation is and how much more veiled the threat of the original.

Actual

A useful word that has taken a sad battering during the past twenty years or so. Nowadays its function is often no more than to indicate that the following word should be emphasised, although it can also serve as a source of confusion and bewilderment. 'The Museum's specimens of actual wooden furniture are mostly fragmentary' (*Con*, Vol 166, Sept/Dec 1967), means nothing more than 'specimens of wooden furniture'.

Actualise

An unnecessary and unhelpful word. What does it mean in, for example, 'The index would show only such contextual subordination as had been actualised' (Perreault, 1969)? The nearest one can get—and this is only an intelligent guess—is: 'The index would show only items mentioned by name in the text'.

Acumen

The word properly means 'sharpness of wit, keenness of perception', and is almost a synonym for 'intelligence'. It is not, however, thought fitting or decent for an advertisement to demand publicly that a senior industrial executive shall be intelligent, and one therefore finds: 'This position calls for a man with high acumen' (*S Times*, 30.11.75). Acumen, however, is measured by the thinness and sharpness of its cutting edge, not by its height. It needs no benefit of adjective, it is sufficient by itself. In the jargon of the industrial/commercial world, however, 'high-acumen' is showing worrying signs of becoming a compound noun.

Additionally

A space-filling reinforcement for 'and', with no extra meaning in itself. '. . . and additionally provide assistance to our customer . . . ' (*D Tel*, 2.1.76)

Adjacent

The prestigious equivalent of 'near,' 'close', or 'on'. '. . . a profitable company adjacent to North West coast' (*D Tel*, 6.2.76) leaves the reader in doubt, possibly deliberately, as to whether the factory is near the coast or on the coast. How close is 'adjacent'?

Advisement
The in-word for 'advisory', designed to dazzle the layman with the scientific basis of the advice being given. 'An academic advisement system for boys may need to be different from one for girls' (*JER*, 63/1, Sept 1969), but whether the clients are boys or girls what is offered is simply advice on the educational courses to which they seem best suited.

Affectable
'Affectability', says the *British Medical Dictionary*, is 'the quality or state of being responsive to a stimulus'. One may, in this sense, be affectable by a sunset, a pretty woman or a restaurant menu. What is less intelligible or useful is to make 'affectable' refer to a thing or a process, instead of a person, as in 'the affectable changes in attitude and involvement by Museum visitors' (*Mus News*, Jan/Feb 1974). This presumably means the changes in attitude brought about by visiting a museum and looking at its exhibits.

Affordability
Anything on the market offers reliability, good looks and value for money in varying degrees. 'Affordability', however, is no kind of a quality at all. Whether or not one can afford to buy a Rolls Royce depends on the state of one's bank balance, not on any intrinsic merit of the Rolls Royce itself. To suggest that a commodity contains built-in affordability is a majestic swindle. 'A car that satisfies one's pragmatic sense by its surprising affordability' (*New Yorker*, 11.10.76).

Age-group
We have reached the stage, it appears, at which one's age-group is more important and more easily understandable than one's age. Employers are consequently fond of referring to 'the successful applicant who is expected to be in the age group 35 to 55' (*D Tel*, 28.1.76). The old way of putting this, 'between the ages of 35 and 55', is too personal, too emotive, too precise, whereas to belong to an age-group is merely to indicate a figure to be fed into the computer. To ask a woman her age is not polite, but to enquire her age-group is as neutral and inoffensive as enquiring about her height or blood group.

Age-peers
Contemporaries. Although one may not have realised it at the time, the people in one's form at school were one's age-peers, but 'Why don't you hit someone your own age?' somehow sounds different from 'Why don't you hit one of your age-peers?, which one assumes to be the usual form of speech in the home of a social scientist, who finds it natural to investigate 'the extent to which the old interact with age-peers' (*B J Soc*, Mar 1968).

Aggressive
Modern business is always trying to recruit 'aggressive' people, by which it seems to mean men with the urge to get ahead fast, knocking over and treading on anybody else who happens to be in the way. Usually the man himself is expected to be aggressive, but sometimes the adjective gets transferred to his aims and we have that very remarkable phenomenon, the aggressive goal. Examples of both usages are: 'We seek an ambitious, aggressive graduate as National Sales Manager' (*The Age*, 1976) '. . . ambitious technical contributors who have aggressive career goals' (*Boston Sunday Globe*, 10.10.76). For some reason, the word is applied only to men. No example has so far come to hand for a company looking for aggressive female staff. Some firms, indeed, make it clear that aggressive women are not acceptable as candidates. An anonymous 'professional money management organisation located in San Francisco, California', for instance, is on record as saying that the woman it requires as an administrative assistant/social secretary must be 'non-aggressive, supportive' (*Times*, 22.7.76)

Aid
A crossword synonym for 'help', rarely used by anyone but journalists, but very important to them, as proof that one is a true professional, at least on the *Mirror* and *Sun* level. The occasions when it is and is not used are interesting. 'It may be days before aid gets through' (B.B.C. News, 8.2.76), on the low-brow Radio 2, but two minutes later on the same day, the B.B.C.'s Radio 3 News, which is aimed at an educated audience, said 'It may take days to get help to them'. Recently, both as a noun and a verb, 'aid' has shown signs of spreading outwards from journalism into writing of a more serious and permanent kind, e.g. 'The survey's potential for aiding architects and planners' (Michelson, 1975). This can hardly be because 'aid' is

felt to be punchier and more arresting than 'help' (Christian Aid; Aid for Shipwrecked Mariners). A more likely explanation is that, at least in some contexts, 'aid' is coming to be thought of as the cold, scientific, impersonal word, by contrast with 'help', which is warmer. A drowning person does not, as yet, shout 'Aid!'. There may be some justification for using 'aid' rather than 'help' or 'support' when one country is providing money or resources for another, for example, 'British aid for victims of the Romanian earthquake'. 'Aid' would then be the equivalent of public or governmental help.

Alcohol

In these mealy-mouthed days one has to be very careful about saying that a person is drunk. It is more socially acceptable to say, if he was driving at the time, that the alcohol content of his blood was above the legal limit or, if he was on foot, that he had an alcohol problem. The results of this euphemistic approach can be misleading. Nothing could be more objective and clinical than 'He was asked to attend hospital for treatment of an alcohol problem'(*SMJ*, 15.4.76), but in this particular case the man concerned had been convicted of being drunk and disorderly and assaulting a policeman. It might almost be true to say that he had a policeman problem, as well as an alcohol problem.

Alignment

Agreement, commitment. The non-aligned countries are those which have refused to identify themselves with the quarrels and rivalries of the Soviet Union, China and the United States – the good, honest old word was 'neutral'. Politicians are expected to 'reveal their alignment', i.e. to make clear how they intend to vote, or whose interests they propose to support, and what used to be called 'consensus of opinion' or, even more straightforward and old-fashioned, 'general agreement', has now become 'alignment of intelligence'. 'There is a strong alignment of intelligence demanding a reppraisal of Australia's position' (*Queensland*, 1974).

Alternative

The political left has fostered the curious myth of two societies existing side by side within each of the 'capitalist' countries. One society is 'established' or 'official' the other has no connexion with the corrupt, evil world of government, taxation and careers—although the closest and most fruitful links with the system of unemployment pay and welfare arrangements of all kinds—and is quaintly known as 'alternative'. We therefore have references to '. . . the development of alternative and community newspapers' (*New Statesman*, 20.8.76). The bourgeois and individualistic word 'independent', it should be noted, is never used by the Left, although 'alternative newspapers' are, in plain, non-socialist terms, 'independent newspapers'. But, because they are capitalist, 'independent schools' cannot be 'alternative schools', a term which is reserved for a type of school which, although outside the State system, is run at a subsistence level for the children of difficult parents and for dissident teachers, and always has a left-wing atmosphere.

Ambassadorial

A word much loved by estate agents and meaning 'large, pre-1914, and expensive', as in: 'The extensive accommodation is of ambassadorial standard' (*S Times*, 23.11.75)

Ambience

Environment, surroundings, atmosphere. Correctly used, it implies no judgement as to the quality of the 'ambience'. A steel-works and the premises of a Paris couturier both have 'ambience'. In the English-speaking world, however, this potentially useful word gets out of control, as in: 'The ambience of the painting is involved with people who are all going towards a similar thing' (Russell and Gablik, 1969). More serious, however, is the apparently irresistible tendency for it to acquire snobbish overtones, so that it now has the connotation, more often than not, of 'an atmosphere suggesting money, taste and good breeding'. The best people can visit at least one Toronto hotel with complete confidence, 'knowing they can count on the ambience, the service' (Toronto *Globe and Mail*, 7.10.76).

Amiable, Amiability

A favourite piece of nonsense among wine-writers, although in trying to decide what it means one person's guess is as good as another's. We are told, for example, that 'Asti styles vary from the ultra-amiable to the austere' (*Times*, 2.2.76), That 'some shippers feel that in time they (i.e. certain wines, not the shippers) may develop, more amiability' (*Times*, 31.7.76), and that a particular variety 'gives the amiability and appeal when used in certain blends of grapes for many classic Italian wines' (*Times*, 12.6.76). But, however many examples he accumulates, the lay observer is likely to be no closer to understanding what this mysterious quality of amiability is. If he is told instead that the wine in question is 'friendly' or 'likeable', he is no further forward, but in cases like this it is probably wiser to admit defeat.

Ample

Another word much bandied about in wine literature, e.g. '. . . a wine that is ample, but never too much so' (*Times*, 6.3.76), and ' . . . the 1971 Montagny is a bright, definite gold colour, with a scented warm bouquet and slightly ample taste' (*Times*, 21.2.76). This appears to mean 'containing a satisfying amount of body' or, less reverently, 'not too watery', but a connoisseur would undoubtedly regard this as a far from satisfactory translation, although unable to do any better himself. 'Ample', he is all too likely to say, means 'ample', no more and no less.

Analogous

Comparable, similar. 'In-depth experience in an analogous environment' (*D Tel*, 22.1.76) means 'good experience in a similar job'. 'Analogous', however, suggests, to those who know no better, computers and modern management techniques and is often preferred for that reason.

Analysis

A scientific-sounding and often flattering word for 'examination'. One can do no more with facts than collect and examine them carefully, whatever the 'analysis' may pretend. A chemist analyses, in the strict sense of the word, and all other uses are figurative at best and a swindle at worst. What, for instance, is one to make of 'Competitor activity analysis' (*D Tel*, 28.1.76)? Does it, can it mean anything more profound or valuable than 'an examination of what one's competitors are doing'?

Anecdotal

Backed up by example. A piece of social-science pomposity. If we 'provide anecdotal support for the idea that a parent's imitation of a child is pleasurable for the child' (Hoppe, 1970), we mean, believe it or not, that someone has noticed that a small child who has just said 'wabbit' is happy when his mother or father says 'wabbit' back to him.

Antiqued
Made to look old, given a nice 18th century colour and patina, an activity which might be thought to deserve criminal proceedings, rather than publicity and pride. No British example has yet been observed, but the word is common enough in America and can hardly fail to cross the Atlantic in time. Meanwhile, here is a typical example, relating to leather upholstery which is 'hand-padded, antiqued and polished in a wide assortment of pieces' (*House Beautiful*, Oct 1976).

Antisocial
An increasingly widely used euphemism, concealing the fact that an individual or a group are behaving like savages. Going on the rampage after a football match is 'antisocial', and so is setting fire to one's school or ripping up the seat covers in a train. Considerable demands are made on the reader's imagination by such sentences as: 'Some Pacific Island immigrants respond to alcohol in a more apparent antisocial manner than citizens from other ethnic backgrounds' (*BB/NZ*, 1975). One must not, for some reason, do more than hint that the nature of the Pacific Islanders' antisocial behaviour is that they get disgustingly, violently and destructively drunk. To be drunk is, so to speak, one's own responsibility; to be guilty of antisocial behaviour conveys the idea that it is at least partly society's fault, which is, of course, in accordance with the spirit of the age.

Antithetical
Opposed to, against. Why not use these simple terms, instead of indulging in such pedantries as 'This position is not really antithetical to Piaget's basic ideas' (*JEP*, 64/1, 1973)? 'Quite antithetical to the proper functioning of the school' (*Educ & Soc Sci*, Vol 1, No 4, Feb 1970) is a worthy Australian contribution.

Apparel
A shopkeeper's up-grading of 'clothing'. A firm can consequently be described, to someone in the trade, as 'producing curtaining, furnishing fabrics and apparel' (D Tel, 22.1.76). It is not clear why this faintly ridiculous word is found necessary. 'Apparel' is no more comprehensive than 'clothes' or 'clothing', and even the most exalted people are not ashamed to admit that they buy and wear clothes.

Appreciate
One of the most notorious cover-up words of modern times. In correct usage, to appreciate something is to understand and enjoy it. Politicians and diplomats think differently, however. To them, 'appreciate' means 'unfortunately have to listen to', and they use the word in this sense, the normal connotation of 'enjoy' being used as a fraudulent veneer. Cyrus Vance does not really 'appreciate' something that General Amin has just said. He is baffled and infuriated and despises the man who is responsible for it. When a politician uses 'appreciate', he should certainly never be believed and not infrequently goes on to hang himself with his own rope. So, for example, 'Obviously we all appreciate the frankest possible speaking at the United Nations and elsewhere, but it is not necessarily my view that that kind of speaking is good for either the Western Alliances or the United Nations' (*H. of C. Oral Answers*, 5.2.76).

Appropriate
A perfect word for the administrator. It should normally be translated, 'If you're lucky', 'If we think it's politic or safe', or 'If it can't be avoided'. If something is deemed 'inappropriate', one should understand the official to mean that, for reasons he does not feel inclined to explain, he has no intention whatever of following that particular course of action. There is no shortage of examples. Here are two. 'Housing may be available in appropriate circumstances' (*Times*, 28.11.75); 'It was recognised that in view of Papua New Guinea's advance towards independence it might no longer be appropriate that a major socio-economic research organisation should be a unit of a university of a foreign country' (*ANU*, 1973).

Aristocratic
Expensive, of high quality. A particularly potent word in the United States, which has always, except in 1776, had a soft spot in its heart for British aristocrats. So, 'aristocratic linens, a versatile contemporary design from the hunt country to your home' (*Washington Star*, 17.10.76). Knowing too much about their own variety, the British seem to find French aristocrats more romantic: '. . . the deliciously aristocratic Giscours'—a wine (*Times*, 17.7.76). And for American males, who apparently cherish a deep longing to smell like European dukes, there is, to oblige them, 'an aristocratic new fragrance for men' (*New Yorker*, 13.9.76).

Armamentarium
Body, group. A business school word, easier to write than to say.
'. . . to equip the managers with a definitive armamentarium of
skills' (Rapoport, 1970).

Articulate
The with-it word for express, expressive, expressed. '. . . simply a
way of articulating her dissatisfaction' (Perreault, 1969); 'Articulate
apparel for men' (*Panorama*, Boston, Oct 1976); 'Its design is
articulate through darker streaking within a densely grained area'
(*Con*, Vol 161, Jan/Apr 1966). This strange and regrettable usage is so
far confined to America. The English way of abusing a good word is
seen in the demand that a prospective employee shall be 'highly
articulate, with the ability to communicate well' (*D Tel*, 27.11.75).
Things have reached a pretty pass when a firm finds it necessary to
insist that its executives shall be able to talk. 'Jeremy Barlow gave a
brisk and articulate account of the E minor flute sonata' (*Classical
Music*, 20.10.76). This probably means 'expressive', but 'with the
notes well-defined', or 'easy to hear and follow' are also possibilities.
On the other hand, it may signify no more than that the critic liked it,
but was frightened of letting his profession down by using an old-
fashioned word like 'pleasant'.

Artifact
Properly, 'a product of human labour' but, as used by the business
world, it is not a word to spend time over. It means 'consequence' or
'product', when it means anything. 'The apparent inconsistencies
may be an artifact of our trade-off approach' (Michelson, 1975).

Aspect
Image. Usually found in association with 'company', as in: 'This is a
major appointment, finalising a senior management team which is
responsible for the development of the company aspect' (*The Age*,
28.2.76). We translate the last part of the quotation as 'which is
responsible for improving the company's public image'.

Assertive
Makes its presence felt; not shy and retiring; with a forceful
personality. This can be used either of people—'The successful
candidate must be assertive and highly motivated' (*Times*,

28.11.75)—or of wine—'The Côte Chalounais reds can accompany the sharper matured cheeses of the British Isles, on account of their assertive and definite character' (*Times*, 21.2.76). An age not bothered by sex discrimination acts would probably say 'masculine'. Among wine-writers, however, 'assertive character' has almost become a compound noun, as 'luxury flat' did years ago. 'Chilsdown is very well made. With the assertive character of the Reichensteinen grape, it makes an agreeable mouthful' (*Times*, 29.5.76). The noun 'assertiveness' is also used, with equal vagueness. 'Torres de Casta Rosado has far more assertiveness than many rosés' (*Times*, 20.3.76). The rule with these prose-poem wine adjectives has to be, never use them, unless one can complete the sentence, 'Waiter, is this wine . . . ?', without mirth or embarrassment. Few people, even wine writers, could imagine themselves asking, 'Waiter, is this wine assertive?'

Astringent
Properly, 'having power to draw together or contract the soft organic tissues', like surgical spirit on the skin, or a slice of lemon or a sloe in the mouth. It is difficult to think of music which has quite the same effect, although music critics appear to find no problem and write, for example, of 'the astringent lyricism that is unique to early Prokofiev' (*Times*, 4.3.76). A singing lemon is indeed worthy of note, and so is a wine which touches the palate in the way a lemon does. Yet there is wine, we learn, 'with excellent bouquet and flavour and a clean, delicate astringency' (*National Times*, 1.3.76). What does it all mean?

Attack
Management English for look at, deal with, improve, review. These verbs are too gentle, too static for the modern manager, who is always, sword in hand, leading his troops into battle. Even to attack is not enough. Something even more vigorous and determined is required in the never-ending search for efficiency and profit, and so now we have what must be very close to the ultimate, the 'aggressive attack'. 'The manager will be responsible for an aggressive attack on production methods' (*D Tel*, 1.7.76)

Attenuate
Weaken, but coldly and scientifically, without allowing the emotions to be involved. 'These studies were introduced mainly to dem-

onstrate one more factor attenuating parental influence' (Hyman, 1969).

Attitudinal
Always used absolutely and therefore with little meaning. 'His current research interests focus on attitudinal changes in college students and group counseling with college underachievers' (*JER*, 61/10, July/Aug 1968). Changes in the attitude of students to what? Their work at college? Girls? Boys? Their careers? The weather?

Attractive
To journalists, the most gallant of men, all women below the age of 40 are attractive when they win a competition, appear in public, are in any kind of trouble or have dark hair. 'Vicki is an attractive 21 year old brunette' (*Voice*, 1975). Blondes do not need to be attractive; to be blonde is enough.

Attrition
Wastage, drop-out. 'Reducing the total educational attrition to 54.2 percent'(*JER*, 63/3, Nov 1969) sounds better than 'reducing the total educational drop-out to 54.2 percent', but means exactly the same.

Audience
To the business world it means 'body of clients'; 'field of recruitment.' 'The job is unquestionably the first of this kind in Britain, in a facet of business which our limited audience would not even have considered as a career' (*D Tel*, 17.12.76). 'Our limited audience' means, as one discovers after several minutes' hard thinking and study of the context, 'our very conservative clients', a fact which the advertisers themselves could never reveal in all its brutal nakedness.

Augment
The word for those who look down on 'increase' and 'enlarge'. Nowadays a company 'wishes to augment its electrical maintenance team' (*D Tel*, 17.12.76). It does not take on more electricians, which would be altogether too plebeian.

Austere
Dry, in the sense of 'causing the mouth to pucker', dry as a judge's wit is dry. A wine-writer's word, apparently used as an alternative to

'astringent' (q.v.) '. . . the Saar, where the wines can sometimes seem austere' (*Times*, 3.4.76).

Author

When used as a verb, seems to mean 'to write'. It is interesting to wonder if there is any difference between 'Dr. Kluppel has authored several articles' (*JER*, 61/9, May/June 1968), and 'Dr. Kluppel has written several articles'. 'Authored' may possibly imply that the articles are on a higher plane from those which are merely 'written', or that Dr. Kluppel masterminded them, leaving his inferiors to carry out the menial task of writing. A comparison might be, 'Dr. Kluppel has sired several children', and 'Dr. Kluppel has fathered several children', 'sired', sounding as if it has thoroughbred implications.

Avant

Advanced, a shortened form of 'avant-garde'. 'W. M. Fraser's avant concept in forged flatware' (*New Yorker*, 29.9.75), a combination of words which could have come from the brain of a copy-writer with either a highly sophisticated sense of humour or no sense of humour whatever.

Award-winning

One of the biggest of all verbal swindles. The technique is to avoid mentioning what award it was. One can therefore, without falling foul of the law in any way, eat award-winning jam, sleep on an award-winning bed, ride in an award-winning train and pat an award-winning dog on the head, without being given the slightest clue as to the name or source of the award. Every issue of every magazine contains examples. Here is a random selection. 'Beautifully reproduced prints by award-winning American-Indian artists' (*New Yorker*, 20.9.76); '. . . an award-winning artist in her own right' (*Panorama*, Boston, Oct 1976); 'Stephen Burrows — America's most exciting award-winning fashion designer' (*Harpers and Queen*, July 1976); 'Award-winning homes from only £6,990' (*Times*, 3.12.76); 'This resort hotel, located on its $11\frac{1}{2}$ acre award-winning site' (Brochure of Boston Marriott Hotel, 1977).

Aware

Aware of what? By those who use the word, this is felt to be a ridiculous, irrelevant question. One is either 'aware', or one is not, one possesses 'awareness', or one does not. Humanity is, in fact, divided into the aware and the unaware, and an up-to-date firm looking for staff naturally wishes to recruit only the aware, often taking pains to emphasise its own awareness. 'Young aware company covering London and Southern England' (*S Tel*, 25.4.76); 'The person will be dynamic, recreationally aware . . . ' (*D Tel* 26.11.76). The same quality is evidently reckoned to be an advantage in the want-a-bride columns of the weeklies: 'Aware provincial, intelligent, tall Englishman . . .' (*New Statesman*, 20.8.76) The sociologists and critics have also found the word sufficiently vague to be useful to them, and speak, for example of ' . . . a meaningful creative experience that enlarges our awareness' (Mueller, 1967).

B

Background
Experience. 'A background in claims handling' (*D Tel*, 28.1.76). Because the writers of this kind of material are only, as Orwell put it, sticking pieces of gummed tape together, the meaning of the individual components is often ignored in the interests of the total impression, and we therefore find such absurdities as 'Applicants should have a good background of commercial experience' (*D Tel*, 27.11.75), that is, good experience of commercial experience, when all that is meant is that applicants should have had good commercial experience. It is a pity that 'background' should have come to be used in this way since, in assessing candidates one does indeed require to know their background, that is, details of their education, family, interests and travel abroad, as well as their experience directly related to the job. Someone whose 'background', in this sense, was claims-handling would surely be somewhat narrow and hardly worth meeting.

Backlash
Often no more than 'feeling', although it suggests a much greater degree of heat and violence. 'The anti-student backlash which we have seen in the past eighteen months' (Rubinstein & Stoneman, 1970) gives the impression that students are being physically attacked—a lash is not a gentle method of argument—whereas all

that is meant is that a good many people have come to dislike students.

Back-taste
After-taste? No precise definition is available, but the wine writers who use this not particularly elegant word—it has echoes of 'backfire'–may be referring to the taste which remains in the mouth after the wine has been sipped and swallowed. '. . . a profound, long wine, with a beautiful back-taste' (*Times*, 19.6.76).

Back-up
Support. There does not appear, therefore, to be much hard thinking behind the demand for a person who 'will provide back-up support for the General Manager' (*D Tel*, 8.1.76). A personal assistant or deputy general manager can certainly be expected to provide support for their general manager, and to back him up in any way they can, but supporting support might be thought to be pushing the point a little.

Balance
The wine writers again. The 1967 clarets, we are told, 'possess good balance' (1976 catalogue of Ellis Son and Vidler, Hastings and London); 'the La Tour Bicheau has a balanced, close-textured svelte style' (*Times*, 31.7.76), and we cannot fail to enjoy 'the big, velvety Léoville, with its charm, balance, and superb after taste' (*Times*, 17.7.76). But what is this quality called 'balance'? Balance between what and what? A tight-rope walker's balance we understand, but a wine contains nothing but alcohol, tannin and water, together with its flavour and aroma. Should we be thinking of the balance between all these, or any two of them? Or is it something as subtle and indefinable as a woman's smile? Or just a word, put in because it looks and sounds nice, and incidentally helps to fill up the line?

Banditry
Political intervention or activity by people one disapproves of politically, especially by a non-socialist state. A Communist word. '. . . overcoming the effects of imperialist banditry on their country' (*Comment*, 29.11.75).

Bathtime
Children have the noun—'It's your bath time'—adults the adjective,

'Continue the green theme right into your bathroom, with Bradmill's bathtime compatibles' (*Woman's Day and Australian Parent*, 23.2.76). Some skill is needed to interpret this. One has bath*room* co-ordinates, matching fixtures, curtains and decorations, but bath*time* compatibles, the soap and other materials with which one gets to work on the various parts of one's person. These things, it should be noted, are chosen to match one another. It is only their appearance which is compatible. Chemically, their mutual interaction may well be disastrous.

Bearing

Appearance. 'The personal characteristics of the appointee will include professional bearing, strong negotiation (sic), conceptual appreciation . . .' (*The Age*, 28.2.76). This advertisement was for someone with an accountancy training and applicants for the post would presumably understand what the quotation meant. 'Bearing' does, even so, involve the reader in a certain amount of doubt and uncertainty. A 'soldierly bearing' implies a straight back, chest well forward and chin up, but what is a 'professional bearing'? How does one hold oneself like an accountant or, for that matter, behave like an accountant? Something more than a dark suit and tie seem indicated, but precisely what remains obscure.

Beauty care

One is either beautiful or one is not, but one can certainly make the best of what one has. This is what 'beauty care' means, improving a little on Nature and covering up the ravages of time. It does not mean 'caring for a beauty', flattering as it might be to think otherwise. Those who manufacture and sell cosmetics deal in what their customers hope and believe is magic and in no branch of commerce is the sales-language received more willingly and with less critical examination. Sentences like 'She determines your skin-care needs and prescribes your personal beauty routine' (*New Yorker*, 22.3.76) are taken, for the most part, gratefully and at their face value.

Behaviour

In correct usage, 'the way a person or animal behaves'. The social scientists, however, with their talk of 'behaviourism', which many people have heard of, but few understand, and with the weird compound nouns which they have fashioned around the straightforward word 'behaviour', have poisoned the wells. Anybody with a reasonable degree of education is therefore quite likely to feel bothered and inhibited about the risk of using 'behaviour' in what they might fear was an old-fashioned sense. Consider, for example, 'Teachers with an inexpressive classroom behaviour orientation' (*Educ & Soc Sci*, Vol 1, No 2, July 1969). This probably means, 'Teachers who behave in a non-committal way in the classroom', but to anyone who moves in an atmosphere where people think and talk of one another's behaviour orientations such a translation is both inadequate and insulting. To have a behaviour orientation is a mark of the professional; to behave is what might be expected of someone who had not had the benefit of a college education. In a context such as that quoted above, the neighbours of the word 'behaviour' change not so much the basic meaning as its flavour, which is to say its power to communicate. There are many people who accept and understand 'behaviour' without difficulty, but who switch off as soon as they hear or see 'behaviour orientation'.

Bell

'Breast of chicken in a port and brandy sauce, served in a special glass bell' (T.H.F.menu, Coventry, February 1976). The 'bell' turned out to be not unlike a large brandy glass, but the fact that the food was served in such a vessel made absolutely no difference at all to its taste or nutritive value, and to suggest otherwise was an absurd deception. One could just as relevantly have said 'served in a soup plate'. This kind of fraudulent build-up is one of the restaurateur's most significant contributions to linguistic disease.

Below-the-line

Cf. 'above-the-line'. 'The Company's below-the-line marketing activity' (*S Times*, 27.6.76).

Better

The comparative used as an absolute, Cf. 'the oilier oil'. Better than what? Better than those which are not so good, of course. An advertising trick that has been with us for many years and shows no signs of disappearing. 'A leading specialty chain, selling better ladies' fashions' (Toronto *Globe and Mail*, 6.10.76). This has got a little out of hand. More fashionable fashions for ladies? Fashions for more fashionable ladies? More expensive fashions for ladies? Better-value fashions for ladies?

Big

Satisfying? Mouth-filling? The reader must decide for himself, with
the help of examples, what this wine word means. 'A big wine to be
drunk with something to eat' (*Times*, 21.2.76); 'A royal welcome
would await it from the loyal hunters of big reds' (*National Times*,
1.3.76); '. . . a bigger wine than many made in England' (*Times*,
29.5.76).

Biosocial

Man as a social animal. This unnecessary word, which promises more
than it offers, allows old-established theories to be warmed up and
served as freshly cooked. '. . . the biosocial view of the person. In this
perspective, a person is defined as a biological entity, which has
endowed (sic) or has achieved certain social rights and duties'
(Ruddock, 1972).

Black

A most difficult word to use, since it has different connotations in
Africa, England and the United States. In Africa, whole countries are
populated by people who are black, and to speak of, say, Ghanaians as
black is simply a statement of fact. In America, most of the 22 million
people of African origin now prefer to call themselves 'black' instead
of 'negro', as a sign of their changed status in the community and of
their intention to bring about improvements in their social condition.
In Britain, however, a large proportion of the non-white population
is of Asian, not African, stock and resents being considered 'black',
however hard black militants may try to enrol them in their crusade
against 'white domination' and to claim that all non-whites are
blacks. Even within the United States, 'black' is often used in a way
which contains more heat than sense. 'When black students at
Brandeis University took a building to demand a black studies
program' (Miles, 1971). Even among American blacks one will find
little agreement as to what a 'black studies program' is or should be. Is
it to be concerned with the history and culture of all the black
countries, or only of the black people in North America? What is the
material of such a programme to be? And to what extent is it possible
or desirable to keep the historical contribution out of it? Is the tone of
the course to be sober, scholarly and objective, or is it to be primarily
a rallying point for black militancy? What is certain is that in a multi-
racial society any sentence containing the word 'black' will be

interpreted differently by blacks and whites. Different sets of prejudices will be aroused and a different degree of importance given to the particular idea or piece of information linked to the mention of 'black'.

Bland
Properly means soft, smooth, mild, not stimulating, but used as an insulting word in today's art world, in which excitement is prized above everything and the idea that art may sometimes have a reputable soothing function is likely to be met with hostility and incredulity. So, in reference to Nolan's paintings, 'Those indifferent to their charm dismiss them as "bland decoration" ' (Walker, 1975).

Blue-chip
Originally a blue, high-value counter used in poker. From this, a stock considered to be a reliable investment and, as an extension, any reliable enterprise. Its use can, however, cause problems, as in 'an extensive and growing list of blue-chip clients' (*D Tel*, 22.1.76). Does this mean 'clients wishing to buy blue-chip shares', or 'reliable clients'?

Blurring
Moving so fast, so packed with excitement, that the onlooker cannot obtain a clear impression of it. 'The blurring pace of downtown Boston' (Brochure of Boston Marriott Hotel, 1977) does not, however, recall any part of the Boston one knows.

Body-conscious
Flattering to the shape of the body, allowing one to move comfortably. 'Pyjama-inspired jump-suit in body-conscious Lycra spandex' (*New Yorker*, 29.3.76).

Boisterous
Meaning unknown and unknowable when the word is applied to wine. 'Big boisterous burgundies should be abandoned' (*Times*, 2.7.76), is a nice piece of alliteration, but a poor piece of communication between the expert and the enthusiastic amateur.

Boss
The normal anti-establishment term for an employer or senior manager in a non-socialist country. '. . . the largest donors being the

Engineering bosses' (Matthews, 1975).

Bourgeoisification
Apparently 'the acquisition of bourgeois or middle-class habits and characteristics', but probably in a slightly pejorative sense. 'Each age has its own index of bourgeoisification' (*B J Soc*, Mar 1968).

Bracket
Range. Usually applies to salaries and wages, as 'All these jobs are in the £3,000 p.a. bracket'. (*D. Tel*, 7.1.76) 'Bracket' is nowadays considered rather low by the top firms. The better class of candidate would not usually consider a company with brackets, although such concerns clearly feel that the word is a sign of progressive habits.

Brand-awareness
Both people and companies are permitted to show brand-awareness. The term is frequently used, but difficult to define because the precise meaning varies with the context. A customer with brand-awareness knows a good thing when he sees it; a shop with brand-awareness stocks and promotes this rather than that because it can be sure it won't hang around on the shelves; a manufacturer with 'very high brand-awareness' (*D Tel*, 27.11.75) has infinite faith in the virtues of his own product.

Brawny
Just strong, muscles not being required. 'Lee's unequalled brawny twill of 100% texturised Dacron polyester' (*New Yorker*, 22.3.76). Since twill is used nowadays mainly for men's clothing, 'brawny' is considered a specially appropriate adjective to describe it, the implication being that there are to be muscles under the twill, so making twill itself a virility symbol.

Breed
Sort, kind, but with a strong suggestion of good pedigree. 'This is a 3-carat emerald cut diamond. It is a rare breed.' (*Art in America*, Sept/Oct 1976). Diamonds do not, of course, breed, although many people undoubtedly wish they did, but the word has commercially useful associations of thoroughbred racehorses and elegant women with neat heads held high. Compare: 'These wines have great breeding' (Ellis Son & Vidler, Hastings and London, 1976 catalogue).

Brilliantly
Frighteningly, vividly. 'A sad and brilliantly cruel film' (*The Age*, 20.3.76). A film shining with cruelty is not an agreeable thought, but all the author of the review probably had in mind was that the cruelty was sufficiently nasty, vicious and obvious to attract and please big audiences. The brilliance was therefore in the commercial flair of the film's backer and director, not in the artistic quality of the film itself.

Brisk
Making the palate shiver slightly? Making its presence in the mouth felt quickly? A brisk person or a brisk manner one understands—quick, anxious to get the job done, no time to waste—but a brisk wine leaves the reader, if not the drinker, guessing. The word is, however, used in this context, and one makes of it what one can. 'A dry, brisk, rather lemony wine' (*Times*, 2.7.76).

Build
When used of an inanimate object, means 'the building of'. A man can be of heavy build, but a machine cannot be of prototype build. Yet, '. . . from the stages of feasibility study to prototype build' (*D Tel*, 28.1.76). This peculiar phrase is presumbly intended to give the advertisement a more professional feeling, a flavour of scientists hard at work.

Bullets
Manifestations, acts. A piece of Leftist melodrama, as in 'discrimination and other bullets of racism' (Mullard, 1975). To prefer a white man to a black man for a job, no matter what the reason is, is to prove oneself that most dreadful of all monsters, a racist, that is, someone who is old-fashioned enough to like to be surrounded by people of one's own skin-colour. To act on this preference is to fire 'bullets of racism', a phrase which contains a certain degree of exaggeration.

Bureaucratic
a Communist term of abuse for any institution in a non-socialist country. 'The bureaucratic institutions of the E.E.C.' (Matthews, 1975). The word is also used throughout the world for any large organisation which is felt to be inefficient.

Burnished

'. . . his husky, burnished voice filling out the long lines of the apparition scene' (*Classical Music*, 20.10.76). The ordinary meaning of 'bright, shiny, polished', with the suggestion that such an effect has been produced by rubbing, would hardly seem in place here, unless the idea is that the flow of notes has polished the larynx or, alternatively, that a sandpaper-like larynx has polished the notes as they rise up and out. But 'husky', which carries a feeling of roughness, conflicts with 'burnished', which makes one think of smoothness. On the other hand, silver and gold are burnished and so we may have a synonym for 'golden' or 'silvery'. There is still 'husky' to get in the way, however, and one is left with the strong possibility that the author of this sentence had no precise thoughts in his head whatever, and simply brought out 'husky' and 'burnished' as rabbits from his music-critic's hat. 'Burnished' can be used for any musical sound, however produced, but the meaning is clearer when the instrument is the violin than when it is the human voice. We may have a vague idea of what is intended by 'a marvel of smooth legato, and richly burnished tone, beautifully bowed' (*Fin Times*, 7.2.77), although a definition would be difficult.

Businessman

An extremely difficult word to use in any form of transatlantic communication since, like salesman, it does not carry the degree of respect in England that it does in America. In American, it does not mean simply 'someone who makes his living from business'. There is the additional sense, nearly always present, of someone who subscribes to a particular set of values, the private enterprise world of Rotary, hostility to all forms of 'socialism' and 'state interference' and an outspoken belief in the virtues of 'standing on one's own feet'. In Britain, although these associations certainly exist, they are used more by local journalists than by those working at the national level, and a slight, sometimes more than slight, pejorative sense is never far away. For these reasons, one does not know what to make of: 'Successful applicants will also be expected to establish themselves as leading businessmen in their local communities' (*S Times*, 16.11.75) since, although it appears in an English newspaper, it has a non-English feeling about it. The job was for high-level, highly paid technical salesmen. How do such men 'establish themselves as leading businessmen in their local communities'? By their style of life? By setting up a business of their own on the side? By taking some specially active part in community life? By functioning, in thought, word and deed, as beacon-like advertisements for their employers? Would the right men do this instinctively, or would they have to be sent on a course to learn?

Butter-fried
Quite different from 'fried in butter'. The compound adjective is believed, probably correctly, to be much more evocative and sensual, much more likely to tickle the taste buds and get the saliva flowing than the bald, unprofessional statement that some item of food has been merely 'fried in butter'. 'Butter-fried, garnished with soft roe, lemon and tomato' (T.H.F.menu, Coventry, Feb 1976). 'Garnished' (q.v.) intensifies the effect and the difference. The technique, of American origin, is now universal in the restaurants of the English-speaking world.

C

Capability
Potential. A piece of technological/management nonsense. 'A vacancy exists for a person to operate this monitoring system and thus to contribute to the development of Irish offshore capability' (*Irish Times*, 27.8.76). The last three words of this read like a literal translation from some other language, as indeed they may be; what is meant is 'the development of oil reserves off the Irish coast', but something as straightforward as this would never do. Faced with the straight choice of sounding plain and simple but everyday, or pompous and illiterate but impressive and grand, the management consultancy world would go for the second every time.

Capitalise
Properly, to convert into capital, or to compute the capital value of periodical payment. More loosely and often inaccurately, it is used to mean 'draw upon', 'build on'. 'An effort has been made to capitalise upon the student's interest in his own past experiences' (Green, 1968) means only that the student has been persuaded to act as his own guinea-pig, but 'capitalise upon' cleverly adds the idea that the whole

of one's life is a form of investment in oneself.

Capitalist
Anyone who supports the capitalist system and appears to be doing well out of it. Originally and properly, the owner of a business; a person living on the proceeds of capital invested in some form of commercial or industrial enterprise. In left-wing circles, however, it has acquired an abusive connotation—a person who does no work himself and lives by exploiting the labour of others. 'The capitalist class' does not by any means include only people possessing industrial shares. In Communist jargon it is, broadly speaking, synonymous with the upper middle-class, sometimes with a small leavening of the titled, the artistocratic and the landed, although these are not essential. Anyone owning a large house, or expensive car, or racehorse, or with children at independent schools is unquestionably a capitalist, and no further evidence of guilt is required. It is also possible to be a capitalist by association. The salaried managers of non-socialist businesses are capitalists, to those whose world view encompasses only capitalist bosses and exploited workers, and so are members of the boards of directors of any company with shareholders. The latter category is singled out for attack in 'the course of developing activity against the capitalists' (Matthews, 1975).

Career-oriented
Wholly devoted to the idea of getting on and making money. A nice phrase for a rather nasty life-style. 'This position is a unique opportunity for a high achievement, career-oriented individual' (*The Age*, 28.2.76).

Caring
The range of meanings of this greatly overused verbal fashion accessory is so wide as to make it useless as a way of communicating between one mind and another, although as a class to class and prejudice to prejudice link it may possibly have some value. It can roughly mean, 'warmhearted', 'anxious to get every detail right', 'I am my brother's keeper', separately or mixed in varying proportions. 'He's a very caring and funny man' (*Metro Telecaster*, Halifax, 10.10.76); 'As a director I'm very caring and alert' (Paul Sorvino, theatre director, reported in *Washington Star*, 17.10.76); 'A commitment to social responsibility and a caring philosophy would be essential' (*Times*, 6.8.76).

Carriage-trade
Concerned with the social and financial élite. 'Our profession is a
carriage-trade profession' (Advertisement from San Francisco company in *Times*, 22.7.76). The profession in question was that of
investment counsellor, which some might call a skill, trade or
occupation, rather than a profession. But the word 'carriage-trade'
takes the whole operation many miles away from the down-to-earth
and slightly sordid business of dealing with the investments of the
rich.

Carving
Usually means moulding. One of the great American frauds.'You'll
be able to feel the crispness of our carving' (*New Yorker*, 11.10.76).
This referred to a teaspoon, which had, of course, moulded, not cast
decoration. 'Carving', however, gives the feeling of hand-
craftsmanship, which, in these machine-made days, always deserves
and gets a higher price.

Casual
Informal. 'Casual' has gone up in the world enormously during the
past century. In Victorian times it meant 'unmethodical, haphazard',
and carried an unmistakable mark of disapproval. Now, however,
when leisure has a higher prestige than work, and fecklessness and
living like the birds are at the top of the virtues, 'casual' is a high-
prestige word. It can usually be eliminated from a sentence without
the slightest loss of meaning. Consider, for example: 'An outstanding
investment in casual comfort' (a chair, *New Yorker*, 22.3.76); 'Guests
seeking the ultimate in a casual vacation' (*New Yorker*, 21.6.76);
'With the casual elegance and enduring beauty of natural cedar' (*New
Yorker*, 14.6.76). In all these cases, 'casual' tells us nothing about the
furniture or the holiday, but certifies that these things are being
bought and used by the right kind of people, casual people. What is
intended by 'land and homes of casual magnificence' (*New Yorker*,
14.1.76) is more open to doubt. The Vermont property company
responsible for this advertisement might well be asked to explain how
something can be both casual and magnificent at the same time. A
company in Connecticut, called Casual Living, goes half-way back to
the Victorian meaning for 'casual', advertising a clock with the hours
marked 'oneish', 'twoish' and so on, no minute-markings and a note
headed 'The Leisurely Life of Ish', which continues, 'A clock that

29

doesn't push you, but rather guides you casually through the day' (*New Yorker*, 7.1.76).

Cathedral
Unusually high. An estate agent's word, calculated to give potential buyers the feeling that they are being offered something altogether more spacious than a house or flat. A typically palatial place in Toronto had 'skylights, track lighting, cathedral ceilings and more' (*Globe and Mail*, 31.1.76).

Causality
Cause, causes. In nine cases out of ten, 'causality' is used by social scientists merely because 'cause' is felt not to sound sufficiently impressive. 'The science of our field has only recently moved from the concept of single causality to a more comprehensive approach' (Duhl, 1963) is a case in point.

Cellar-style
Presumably, when applied to wine, such as might be found in a well and knowledgeably stocked cellar. 'A distinctive cellar-style red, with complex bouquet' (*National Times*, 1.3.76). The adjective appears to convey no meaning whatever, since the colour of red wine ranges over many shades, none of which has the monopoly of bins in a cellar, and even if the wine, rather than the colour is referred to, both good and bad wines come out of cellars.

Cerebral
Intellectual, often in the sense of over-intellectual, too clever. Used by writers and critics, from D. H. Lawrence onwards, to stigmatise people who use their heads too much and their emotions too little. In recent years, 'cerebral' has become almost a synonym for 'élitist', 'characteristic of someone who despises popular appeal'. All these senses are found mixed up in a 'a welcome contrast to the cerebral research pamphlets published by many of the Conceptual artists' (Walker, 1975). Here the author's objection seems to be to the pamphlets as such, the implication being that an artist should be wholly concerned with understanding and presenting life in terms of the senses, and writing, which must to a great extent be a 'cerebral' activity, is not his province. But the frequent use of 'cerebral' as a disparaging word causes uncertainty as to what, if anything, Walker really does mean.

Challenge
Opportunity. A favorite word among headmistresses and businessmen, both of whom tend rather to overdo the fact that life consists of overcoming difficulties and problems and that this or that job constitutes 'a challenge'. The implication is that for everyone worth his or her salt the key question is, 'Am I good enough?', the only satisfactory answer being to prove that one is indeed good enough. There is nothing whatever wrong with this attitude in principle. Criticism and doubts only begin to arise when one notices that the 'challenge' is in connexion with something that hardly deserves such strong language. The challenge of bringing up a mongol child or rescuing an old lady from a burning house is one thing, but 'the challenge of working with C.T.V.'s News Department' (*Metro Telecaster*, Halifax, 10.10.76) does not seem to be on quite the same plane. The word may well be in danger of exhaustion. So many jobs nowadays promise a challenge that one becomes a trifle suspicious of any that does not. Sometimes 'challenging' is a synonym for 'extremely difficult', 'almost impossibly frustrating', 'enough to try the patience of a saint'. 'Working in any extremely challenging environment' (*Times*, 26.1.76) could probably be translated as 'working in a place that has brought better men than you to a breakdown and early retirement'.

Character
Non-standardised appearance. 'A detached period house of character' (*Country Life*, 26.2.76) is worth a second glance; 'a house of immense character' (*S Times*, 30.11.75) one may actually remember the next day. 'A character house' (*Bristol Evening Post*, 7.5.76) is more of a problem. Is it a house suitable for characters? Or, on the lines of 'monkey house', full of characters? Or so odd in its appearance that 'character house' is the kindest possible description? Pressed to explain himself, the estate agent concerned with this sale would probably say that it was 'different'. A person, one should note, may be of good character or bad character; a house has only 'character'.

Charisma
A special gift of leadership or authority; extraordinary charm. 'Like many of his generation, he succumbs to the Kennedy charisma' (*Spectator*, 3.6.67). The word has been greatly debased, to the point at which it means little more than 'public appeal' or 'magnetic

personality'. This trough has been reached in 'One of the few European artists whose charisma rivals that of leading New York artists, such as Andy Warhol' (Walker, 1975). Mr.Warhol may have reputation and success to show, even charm, but to claim charisma for him is to render the word worthless. 'In each case the charismatic leadership of a college president was an essential ingredient for reform' (Corwin, 1974) is equally exaggerated, although one or two college presidents may just possibly have God-given charisma. Confusion can be caused by the continued use of the words 'charisma' and 'charismatic' in their old, theological sense of 'the gift of God's grace', as in 'He is also one of the six international advisers of the Catholic Charismatic Renewal throughout the world' (*Listener*, Auckland, Vol 80, No 1886, 1976). The non-theological sense of the word appears to date from the 1920s, when the German sociologist, Max Weber, decided ex cathedra to apply it to mean 'a certain quality of an individual personality by virtue of which he is set apart from ordinary men and treated as endowed with supernatural, superhuman, or at least specifically exceptional powers or qualities'. Weber has a great deal to answer for.

Charm
Fascinating quality. It is difficult to see quite how this essentially visual word can be applied to wine, but the attempt is frequently made. 'The two wines from Burgundy are now showing charm and elegance for present drinking' (1976 catalogue of Ellis Son & Vidler, Hastings and London). Both 'charm' and 'elegance' are usually space-filling equivalents of 'good' or 'recommended', and all the sentence means is, 'The two Burgundies are good and recommended for drinking now'. So, too, 'a lightly charming wine' (*Times*, 21.2.76) and 'the 1966 Vicomte d'Almon is extremely charming' (*Times*, 19.6.76).

Checked out
Checked. The English 'checked' is not strong enough for the American taste, at least at the end of a sentence, but on both sides of the Atlantic it is now customary to 'check out' at a hotel, i.e. to leave, having settled one's bill. At the very best hotels, however, one still 'leaves', the assumption being that customers of that class would never leave without paying the bill. Some English users of 'check out' appear to be in a confused mid-Atlantic condition, as evidenced by 'Prince Bernhardt wants the report checked out' (B.B.C. News,

9.2.76). Prince Bernhardt would undoubtedly have wished to see this particular report, that he had accepted bribes, checked out, never to return, but this is probably not what the news editor meant.

Chinese

An intensitive, with no particular meaning when used in this way. 'They must have been out of their little Chinese minds' (Denis Healey, Chancellor of the Exchequer, reported in *Times*, 24.2.76). The use of the word is picturesque, if a trifle undiplomatic, and sufficiently absurd and jingoistic to make an appealing linguistic novelty in England.

Choose

Be given. 'Choose from 372 practically priced rooms' (*New Yorker*, 14.1.76). This hotel advertisement is highly misleading. A visitor to this or any other modern hotel takes the room the reception desk gives him. No choice is involved, but the rooms are usually built and furnished to a standard pattern, and this does not matter very much. Even so, it is worth pointing out that one cannot present oneself at the hotel and say, 'Room 225, please', which is what 'choose' would mean to anyone who decided to take the company at its word.

Church-related

One supposes this to mean, 'Charitable, for the benefit of a church or churches'. 'Our client is an international, church-related, non-profit organisation' (*Fin Times*, 4.11.76). What, one wonders, is the difference between a 'church-related organisation' and a 'religious organisation', and if, as one suspects, there is in fact no difference, why was 'church-related' preferred? The answer can only be that it is felt to be easier to raise funds for a church, which suggests people, than for a religious organisation, which introduces the worrying complications of theology and spirituality.

Class

According to Communist folklore, all non-socialist societies are divided into two sections, the working-class and the bosses, which are perpetually and inevitably at war with one another. The battle between them, the working-class struggling to get what are known as 'their rights' and the bosses holding onto their power and privilege and refusing to give an inch, is called the 'class-war'. A long series of compound nouns drives the point home and shows how the class-struggle affects every aspect of life. 'Class-enemies' are to be found everywhere, 'class-medicine' bars members of the working-class from the treatment they need, 'class-education' gives working-class children wretched schools and wretched teachers, and 'it is class law that put Des Warren in jail' (*Comment*, 29.11.75). Cf. Middle-class.

Classic

Usually, conservative. 'The quiet rooms are furnished in classic style' (Athenaeum Hotel brochure, Jan 1976); 'The classic, expensive, yet casual look is the secret of Rodier's success' (*Panorama*, Boston, Oct 1976). Rodier, it should be noted, makes and sells clothes. One cannot say 'conservative' in these contexts, since, for many people, it has the implication of 'behind the times', 'disliking modern ideas', which is a suggestion nobody in business dare make. 'Classic' meets the situation admirably and allows everyone concerned to hunt with both the hare and the hounds. The wine writers use 'classic' in something of the same way. 'Big, full-bodied classic wines' (Catalogue of Lay and Wheeler, Colchester, 1976); 'St. Estèphe, a wine so invariably well made that those teaching claret use it as an example of classic style' (*Times*, 17.7.76). One cannot be sure about this, but what 'classic' means here is probably 'made and allowed to mature in the old-fashioned way, without gimmicks or new-fangled ideas'. The difficulty with this is that, in today's snobbery-powered world, 'classic' carries inevitable associations of 'class', so that a 'classic wine' is not merely an old-fashioned wine, but a first-class wine, drunk by the best people, as well. And so with the Athenaeum's classic hotel rooms and Rodier's clothes. There is good reason for this. Simple people do not like simplicity, as a study of both men's and women's clothes makes abundantly clear.

Classifactory

Originally an anthropologist's term, applied to a system of terms describing kinship. Its length, rhythm and Latinity have made it popular among social scientists as a whole, however, producing such imcomprehensible masterpieces as, 'In a classifactory situation, the relative index to the schedules can be of great utility' (Perreault, 1969).

Clean-cut

Properly means sharply outlined or defined, applied particularly to faces. But what is a clean-cut wine? A sharp wine? A vinegary wine?

'The non-vintage is a vigorous, clean-cut wine' (*Times*, 19.6.76) suggests a wine to be praised and drunk, rather than avoided, so that the degree of clean-cutness cannot have been too marked.

Client

Customer. The difference between 'client' and 'customer' has always been elusive and a source of great difficulty to foreigners. The broad distinction is that the professions have clients, except when they have patients, and commercial institutions have customers, but this rule has never been exactly observed and the situation is now more fluid than ever before, largely because so many occupations would like to be professions. The position is further confused by the American preference for 'client' over 'customer' in most white-collar relationships. The trend is clearly to try to grade up all business connexions to the client level, except when it is patently ridiculous to do so. A greengrocer still has customers, not clients. 'Client' certainly makes business dealings appear more ethical and less mundane than most of them in fact are. A paint company can persuade itself that it is an architectural practice by 'advising existing and potential clients' (*Obs*, 15.2.76) and an engineering firm can be so unsure of what 'client' means anyway that it advertises for staff with 'the ability to speak French to client personnel' (*D Tel*, 8.1.76). Social workers, it should be noted, have abandoned the word 'cases' for the people they help, 'case' being taken to imply that there is something odd about the person in question, and always refer now to their 'clients', which has a more professional ring to it.

Climax

To culminate. The use of 'climax' as a verb goes back at least to the 1830s, but throughout the nineteenth century it was always considered rather low. The noun appears to have been first used in the sense of 'orgasm' by Marie Stopes in 1918, but the use of the verb meaning 'to achieve orgasm' is much later, being seldom used before the 1950s. In England, 'to climax' is still reckoned to be either a vulgarism or an Americanism, although at the same time prudish. In writing aimed at a popular market, both the nineteenth and twentieth century 'people's' senses of the verb tend to coalesce, so that the sexual meaning is never far away, especially in a musical context, concerts for the masses being much less inhibited than those for the musical élite. 'The concerts climax an extraordinary Miller revival' (*Melody Maker*, 7.2.76) and the 'The tour, which climaxes with a giant show at Wembley' (*Melody Maker*, 7.2.76) illustrate the point.

Close-out
Completion. A crude and unnecessary piece of business jargon. 'A background in contract close-out' (*D Tel*, 28.1.76). The 'completion' or 'signing' of a contract is reckoned to suggest an over-respectable and slow-moving company, whereas 'close-out' is appropriate to the dynamic, shirt-sleeved brigade.

Close-packed
A wine writer's word. '. . . an exquisite, close-packed flavour' (*Times*, 27.11.76). Cf. Close-textured.

Close-textured
Should mean smooth, in the way a fine, tightly-woven fabric is smooth. Wine writers, however, get a little tired of saying 'smooth' and feel, anyway, that it has gone down in the world by being so much used by beer writers and beer advertisers. 'Close-textured' has been selected to fill the gap, which it does reasonably well, as long as people realise what it means. 'The La Tour Bicheau has a balanced, close-textured, svelte style' (*Times*, 31.7.76). Cf. Close-packed.

Closure
A psychologist's jargon word, in the phrase, 'to form closure'. It means, 'to come to terms', 'to settle'. 'His inability to form closure with respect to what he 'wants' or 'can get' . . .' (*JEP*, 61/1, 1970). The superiority of 'to form closure' over 'to come to terms' is not evident.

Coal face
The place where the hard, primary work is done. 'Career opportunities exist for remaining at the coal face while deepening your skills' (*N Soc*, 26.2.76); a Social Services Dept. advertisement. A phrase calculated to make social services workers feel less middle-class.

Coherent
Able to reason clearly, to put forward well thought out arguments. Until very recently, it was possible but rare to use 'coherent' in this sense. The word was usually applied to a noun, not a person—'a coherent argument'—or someone who had suffered a shock or illness—'he was still coherent'. It has now been revised as a valuable

addition to the vocabulary of management. 'Mid-twenties, intelligent, analytical and coherent, this paragon will probably have a degree in Economics' (*D Tel*, 17.12.76). Meaning 'able to handle words with confidence', it makes a pair with the fashionable 'numerate', which could be translated 'able to handle numbers with confidence.'

Collectibles
Things one can and should collect. 'Our products are high quality collectibles, including de luxe limited edition leather bound books, crystal, porcelain . . .' (*The Age*, 2.3.76). The emphasis is on 'should', the implication being 'all the best people are collecting these things now and you don't want to be left behind, do you?'

Colonial
Late eighteenth-early nineteenth century. The word is common enough in America, where it has roughly the same flavour and prestige as 'Georgian' in Britain. In both cases, the bogus is in much greater supply than the genuine, but either is a favoured badge of gentility and breeding. The recent appearance of 'colonial' in Britain, a country where the adjective has never been applied to houses, causes one to think hard about the reasons and implications. The 'superior detached modern house in Colonial style' (*Times*, 26.2.76) is evidently imitation Georgian. The reason for the un-British label can be deduced from the address, Diss, Norfolk. This is American Air Force country and the owners, or their agents, very probably have thoughts of a buyer with dollars in his pocket.

Combinational
Sociologists' jargon. '. . . combinational mediations between the dominant political élite and the political subject (*B J Soc*, Sept 1966). What is apparently meant is 'communication between the dominant political élite and the political subject', which somehow sounds rather ordinary.

Comfort
One is either comfortable or one is not, but the advertisers cannot leave matters there. Comfort must be measurable on a ten-point scale and the aim must always be total comfort, whatever that may be. We are therefore promised, not merely a comfortable room, but 'each room designed to give you absolute comfort' (Wentworth Hotel,

Sydney, 1976 brochure) and something equally good on our way to
Washington by Concorde, 'in just 3 hours 50 minutes, and in
unprecedented comfort' (*High Life*, British Airways magazine, June
1976). The first we can dismiss fairly quickly (C.f. Absolute), but the
second deserves a little dissection. What Concorde offers is speed and
nothing else, and if comfort is in proportion to the shortness of one's
journey, then Concorde passengers do indeed travel in 'unprecedented comfort'. Their discomfort lasts fewer hours than ever
before, which is just as well, since their seats and armrests are
narrower than they would have had on a slower aircraft. But British
Airways clearly have more positive ideas of 'comfort' in mind. When
one takes the trouble to find out what this is, one discovers that
'comfort', in Concorde terms, means specially attentive stewards, an
extra-abundance of rich food and a never-ending supply of 'complimentary' alcohol. Since all this adds up to indigestion and since few
people equate comfort with indigestion, one is left wondering
whether British Airways are really as concerned with the comfort of
their passengers as the advertisement suggests.

Command

Order. A Frenchman commands, an American or an Englishman
orders. In English, 'command' is a much stronger word than 'order'.
It conveys the idea that the order has come from high up, from
Royalty, possibly, or from a general. There is therefore something
suspiciously pretentious about 'You can arrange for a secretary, send a
telex, organise a conference, or just command a quiet dinner en suite'
(*Fin Times*, 4.11.76). This is surely calculated to give businessmen
delusions of princely grandeur and one can only hope the hotel will
not disappoint them.

Commit

Use. '. . . the decision was taken to commit to videotape as a
production medium' (*Mus News*, Jan/Feb 1974). The writer shies
away from the simple word and gets his chosen alternative seriously
wrong. Would the Managing Director have said to his staff, one
wonders, 'We have committed ourselves to videotape', or 'We are
committed to videotape', or 'We shall commit our programmes to
videotape'? 'Use' would have avoided the whole problem.

Committed

A rather tediously fashionable word. (a) Seeing one's art as belong-

ing to 'the people', or serving a political ideal. ' . . . the successes as
well as the failures of the fully committed painter' (*The Bulletin*,
19.10.74). (b) Total. '. . . how the author's own style has been
sparked into rhetoric by a committed involvement with his subject'
(Wörner, 1973). (c) Determined. 'An authoritative and experienced
news team committed to being the best in Canada' (*Metro Telecaster*,
Halifax, 10.10.76).

Commitment

An infuriatingly vague word. (a) Belief, conviction. Used by a wider
range of people than 'committed', but with as little reason. '. . . the
company commitment to a philosophy of profitable sales attainment'
(*D Tel*, 27.11.75), i.e. the company's belief in selling goods at a profit,
a fact which would hardly seem worth stating; '. . . written with
passionate moral commitment' (*THES*, 28.11.75), i.e. written with
conviction. (b) Agreement, acceptance. 'Numeracy and the ability
to gain commitment to your proposals are both important attributes'
(*Obs*, 30.11.75); ' . . . to obtain commitment from all levels of staff '
(*S Times*, 16.11.75). (c) Atmosphere. '. . . to develop their own
abilities in a non-directive, therapeutic and social commitment' (*N
Soc*, 19.2.76). (d) Vocation. 'He or she must have a genuine
commitment to children overseas' (*D Tel*, 17.12.76); or, referring to
the playing of the Smetana Quartet: 'The difference was marked,
revealing, but not encouraging to teams who neither play together,
nor come within leagues of such commitment' (*Fin Times*, 7.2.77).
There is some encouragement in the fact that examples of 'committed' and 'commitment' do not seem quite as frequent now as they
did a year ago. With luck, these woolly words may be on the way
out.

Community

District, area, suburb. 'Situated in one of Toronto's most historic
communities . . .' (*Globe and Mail*, 31.1.76); 'The film is located in
an attractive community' (*D Tel*, 27.11.75). The use of 'community'
in contexts such as these is fraudulent. A community is a group of
people living close to one another and probably, although not
essentially, with some kind of official or voluntary organisation to
give it cohesion and identity. These people live in houses, but the
people, not the houses, are the community. A bank or post office may
serve a community, but it is in a district, not a community.
'Community', however, is a warm word, whereas 'district' and

'suburb' are cold words. An advertiser will go unhesitatingly for the warm word, however inaccurate it may be. One may compare 'houses', which agents in fact sell, and 'homes', which they purport to sell.

Community-closure
The creation of closed communities, not the closure of communities. 'Black Power contains features which can be interpreted as attempts to produce the necessary conditions for community-closure' (*B J Soc*, June 1969). The problem of misinterpretation is ever-present with this habit, so common among social scientists, of using nouns as adjectives.

Community relations
Racial relations. What are so euphemistically called 'community relations' are in fact the relations between white people on the one hand and black or brown people on the other. 'The term "community relations" was a godsend. It successfully hid the true nature of the subject; it implied that the real problems were community ones, which had little to do with race' (Mullard, 1973).

Commuter-convenient
Presumably convenient for commuters, not to commuters, although the compound noun allows both possibilities. 'Commuter-convenient houses' (*S Times*, 23.11.75).

Compact
(a) Small, small by comparison with one's rivals. 'This is a new appointment with a compact company' (*D Tel*, 6.5.76); ' . . . whose legal department is compact but expanding' (*Times*, 18.5.76); 'We have been building a compact team of young engineers' (*D Tel*, 29.4.76); 'Appealing compact air-conditioned building' (*AFR*, Sydney, 4.3.76. A 6-storey office block). In an age of growth and mammoth corporations, it is a crime to be small, so that the business world does everything possible to avoid using the term. In Britain it is still possible to make and sell a small car; in America the only small cars are imported. American manufacturers produce full-size or regular-size cars or, for those with less money to spend, compacts.
(b) A little of it goes a long way. '. . . the slightly earthier, but compact, mouth-filling style of Bourg' (*Times*, 31.7.76). Bourg is a wine.

Company-minded
Willing to devote himself 24 hours a day, 7 days a week to the affairs of the company, or intending to stay with the company for years and years, if not for the whole of his working life. 'We require a company-minded executive' (*S Tel*, 21.3.76) may indicate either of these two possibilities.

Compassionate
Properly, showing sympathy, compassion, but the meaning does not always appear to be well understood. 'Tod Browning's long-banned horror classic. Probably the most compassionate film ever made' (*The Age*, 20.3.76). It is not impossible for a horror film to show compassion for the victims of whoever is perpetrating the horror, but it is very doubtful if this would justify the claim made above. The author may perhaps have been confusing 'compassionate' with 'passionate'.

Compelling
Usually forcing people to look twice, but '. . . to help you to make your home more compelling' (*New Yorker*, 1.10.75) is a puzzler. Does it mean anything more than 'attractive'? Is there perhaps a suggestion of 'making one's friends and neighbours jealous?' The difficulty of interpretation arises only because 'compelling' is used absolutely. If we were told what the refurbished home compelled people to do, there would be no obscurity.

Compensation
In the ordinary sense of the word, compensation is payment for suffering or deprivation of some kind. One can be compensated for loss of earnings due to jury service, for injury arising from an accident or for wrongful arrest and imprisonment. The use of 'compensation' to mean 'salary and fringe benefits' consequently seems a little odd. 'Company offers an excellent compensation package' (*Times*, 6.8.76) cannot surely imply that service with the company causes such misery to its staff that compensation is called for, but, if this is not intended, why use the word at all?

Competence
Operation. 'To direct and cost-effectively organise the total manufac-turing competence of a highly successful and very profitable U.K.

company' (*S Times*, 4.4.76). In British industry today, every attempt is made to draw attention away from the sordid fact that it exists to manufacture things. One way of achieving this is to take over an inoffensive word, such as 'competence', which is completely free from factory associations, and add a note of professional respectability to a job which might otherwise appear less attractive.

Complementarity
Meshing interests. During the 1950s and 1960s, the great period of mergers and take-over bids, the interests of the two firms concerned were almost invariably said to be 'complementary'. In simple language, this meant either that one made different things from the other, so that the sum had a greater range of goods to sell than either of the parts, or that the smaller company had a product, premises and labour force which it suited the larger concern to acquire. The principle involved in all this became known as 'complementarity', which sounds scientific enough to have been invented by Einstein or Sir Isaac Newton, but in fact was no more than a veneer for boardroom lunches and horse-trading. 'They like to talk of complementarity' (*Fin Times*, 14.1.76).

Complex
Indefinable, even by advertisers. '. . . a distinctive cellar-style red, with complex bouquet' (*National Times*, 1.3.76). This means, in cruder terms, that one finds it difficult or impossible to say what the wine smells like.

Complimentary
Free. 'Free' has become an obscene word in commercial circles, where the idea that one can get something without paying for it is certainly not to be encouraged. The allowable alternatives are 'complimentary' and 'courtesy'. In America, and now increasingly in Britain, hotels no longer say that the cost of breakfast is included in the room price. The expression is 'complimentary Continental breakfast served in your room' (*New Yorker*, 21.6.76), which has all the mark of a gracious host and puts breakfast on a par with the equally complimentary matches and notepaper, and the chocolate peppermint cream by the side of your bed.

Componentry
A much grander and more acceptable business world word for

'components'. 'Manager will control the warehousing of componentry' (*D Tel*, 27.2.76). Looking after 'componentry' clearly demands a superior type of person, compared with mere 'components' and justifies a higher salary, which in turn brings the recruiting agent a higher commission on the deal.

Comprise

A pretentious word for 'consist', the preposition 'of', which correctly follows 'consist', being attached to 'comprise', where it has no place whatever. A sure sign of semi-literacy and, for this reason, very common in the commercial world. '. . . the cuisine which is comprised mainly of classic French and traditional English dishes' (Royal Lancaster Hotel brochure, Jan 1976); '. . . a division comprised of four companies' (*D Tel*, 6.1.76).

Comptroller

A strange spelling of 'controller', found until recently only in certain official designations, such as Comptroller of Household. It has recently been adopted by commercial companies with delusions of grandeur . 'A group of companies in the publishing and printing field requires a Financial Comptroller' (*S Tel*, 9.5.76). It is worth noting in passing that, even with its normal spelling, the rank of controller was never found in industry and commerce before 1945, although now titles such as Controller of Public Relations are common enough. The trend is interesting evidence of the sub-conscious longing of large businesses, such as I.C.I. and the Imperial Tobacco Company, to be thought of as branches of the Civil Service. Much of the guilt for this unhelpful process must be laid at the door of that semi-official body, the B.B.C., which had its controllers long before anyone else did.

Conceptual

Properly, means concerned with understanding; as grasped, comprehended or shaped by the mind. It is now, however, used by psychologists in a variety of senses, mostly vague, and has consequently become popular with those people who wish to add an intellectual flavour to their statements, without running the risk of being pinned down to explain what they mean. 'The personal characteristics of the appointee will include . . . conceptual appreciation' (*The Age*, 28.2.76) defies translation.

Congenial

To one's own taste, sympathetic. The use of the word is pointless and meaningless unless one knows who the other party is. One congenial person exists only by reference to another person. X is congenial to Y. He cannot be simply congenial. In some cases, one suspects that 'congenial' has been confused with 'genial', although it is impossible to be sure. What is meant, for instance, by 'applicants who are congenial and self-motivated' (*D Tel*, 2.1.76)? Is it 'likely to be congenial to other members of the staff', or 'a cheerful extrovert'?

Conscious

One supposes this to mean 'Well-informed, sensitive to atmosphere and people', but it is impossible to be sure. 'Active and conscious person required for small independent school in Cornwall' (*Times*, 7.8.76). The post was for a bursar/administrator. Why did the school not advertise for an 'energetic bursar', which is what it evidently wanted? If 'conscious' meant 'interested in education', or 'aware of the problems involved in running an independent school', why not say so? One can surely assume that the bursar would be conscious; the important point is for him to be conscious of the right kind of things.

Conservative

Non-trendy, clean, neat and tidy. 'He will be of conservative appearance, personable' (*Sydney Morning Herald*, 28.2.76), probably means that he can be depended on to come to work wearing a suit, collar and tie, and without hair hanging on the shoulders. It may also mean that applicants with beards have no chance of getting the job, although this is less certain.

Consolidate

Either (a) mark time, or (b) add weight, create order out of chaos. When a company is 'entering a period of consolidation', it is either about to stop growing for a year or two, or to gather all its resources together in an attempt to survive. '. . . a vacancy for a manager to consolidate our existing team' (*D Tel*, 30.3.76) creates more problems, however. The most likely explanation is that the team is, in fact, no team at all, but a collection of brilliant individualists, and that someone is needed to find ways of persuading them to work together. One can hardly say this in an advertisement, however.

Consonant

Suited to. Some examples require major analysis, e.g. '. . . when taught in a manner consonant with their achievement orientations' (*JEP*, 64/2, 1973). 'Achievement orientations' could perhaps be translated 'what they are interested in and best at doing', and the full rendering might then be 'when they are taught in a way that is suited to their interests and abilities.'

Constellation

Patchwork, interaction, grouping: '. . . while the emotional constellations which make for very different student revolts are strangely similar' (Lipset, 1971). To describe the mixed-up thoughts, feelings and motives which agitate a student's head and heart as a constellation is exceedingly flattering. Does it really have this star-like quality?

Construct

This rather ugly noun has four legitimate meanings and a number which, if one could decipher them, would probably turn out to be illegitimate. A construct can be (a) a group of words forming a phrase; (b) a combination of past and present impressions; (c) a concept devised to be part of a theory; (d) a mathematical configuration. Trendiness has made something else of 'construct', however, an amalgam of all the senses listed above with nonsensical results, as one sees in such examples as 'Man is a social construct' (Ruddock, 1972) and 'June Wayne has recreated the quintessential stereotype of the woman artist, clearly intended as an imaginative construct embalmed in the mind of the beholder' (*Art Journal*, Summer 1976).

Contextual

Must mean belonging to the context. How then does one interpret 'The person appointed would be expected to teach in the School's interdisciplinary contextual programme' (*Times*, 24.5.76)? 'Interdisciplinary programme' causes no particular trouble, but in what way does 'contextual' add anything to the meaning? The only possible context of the programme is the policy and activity of the School and the university. If, on the other hand, the programme itself is concerned with contextual problems, what does that mean? All academic work has to do with contextual problems. Why specify this here?

Continental

Vaguely French or Italian. A restaurant word, meaning practically nothing, but allowing the proprietor to get away with murder. 'Ixtapa. Where you can dine on authentic Mexican food, fresh fish or continental cuisine' (*New Yorker*, 27.9.76). In this context, 'continental' can be translated 'the American idea of European', just as in Britain it means 'the British idea of French'.

Continental breakfast

The 100 per cent carbohydrate and fat breakfast; the laughable British idea of what people on the continent eat for breakfast. The phrase, it should be noticed, is purely English and untranslatable. There is no point in providing an example. It can be found on the menu of any international hotel, anywhere in the English-speaking world, but the breakfast that answers to the label will vary enormously in both content and quality. Practically never will it correspond to the crisp rolls, unsalted butter and good café-au-lait that one gets in France and Belgium. More than one American hotel has its own ideas about what goes on within the confines of the European continent and informs its visitors that 'In the morning you'll be served continental breakfast that's truly continental—Florida fruit juice, French brioche, Danish pastries (cheese and fruit), coffee and milk' (*N Y Times*, 12.10.76).

Control

Supervise. 'The Colonial exterior architecturally designed and controlled' (Toronto *Globe and Mail*, 31.1.76). The business of an architect is first to produce an acceptable design and then to make sure that his client's wishes are faithfully carried out by the contractors. Are some Canadian builders so likely to run amok that it is necessary to tell prospective customers that one architect at least knows how to control them?

Contour

Shape of the body. This euphemism is now much used by those in the weight-reducing business. 'Reshape your body contour' (*Vogue*, Jan 1977) means 'Take fat off it'.

Convictions

Standards. 'His (or her) strongest convictions' is a favourite entertainment world and publishers' blurb phrase. For these people one cannot have convictions, only strongest convictions. 'Michael is pressurised into betraying his mother's strongest convictions when he became a member of a street gang that is terrorizing the neighbourhood' (*Metro Telecaster*, Halifax, 10.10.76).

Cool

Relaxed, restrained. 'Cage requires a submergence of personality to produce a cool, dry expressiveness' (*Times*, 15.10.76; a quartet by John Cage). The musicians must, in other words, put nothing of themselves into the performance; the music must be allowed to express itself, with neither the composer nor the performers involved emotionally in any way. This, one presumes, is 'cool, dry expressiveness'. But, the uninitiated are bound to wonder, is it worth the effort? Is it, perhaps, all a confidence trick? Is there any meaning behind 'cool, dry expressiveness'? Is this 'cool' the same as the one in 'Erskine opened with some beautifully cool photographs of the Canadian Arctic' (*Arch J*, 18.2.76)? Are these pictures, too, relaxed? What is the Arctic, if not cool?

Cordon bleu

Now applied only to cooks, in theory to those of outstanding quality, a prince among cooks. There is, however, no official way of acquiring the title. Anybody is free to describe a cook or his work as 'cordon bleu', and to that extent the phrase is meaningless. Cookery schools exist to teach what is described as cordon bleu cooking, in the French style, but anyone can set up such a school and to have attended one may or may not be evidence of distinction. It is, even so, a good thing to get the spelling right: 'Alice Pascoe and Katrina Smith. Cordon bleau (sic), Paris. Cordon Bleau, London.' (*The Age*, 20.3.76).

Corpus

Properly, a body of literary or artistic material, considered as a whole. In these days, however, when hardly anybody in the English-speaking world understands any Latin, the use of the word is somewhat pretentious and unnecessary, and a barrier between generations. One might just as well say 'body', which is all that 'corpus' means. 'There is a great corpus of Lear drawings in the world today' (*Con*, Vol 164, Jan/Apr 1967) means little, if anything, more than 'there are a great many Lear drawings in the world today'.

Cosmetologists
People who make one look more beautiful, students of the art of cosmetology. The once-popular 'beautician' is now outmoded, mainly because it applied only to someone who looked after the appearance of ladies; today's cosmetologists devote their skill equally to men and women. A cosmetologist, one deduces, is responsible for making the complete head look its best: 'All Century Twenty-One stylists are trained cosmetologists' (*Key*, Dallas, May 1973).

Cosmopolitan
Properly, a person who is free from national limitations and at home anywhere. Often used in the sense of 'someone who has been abroad and understands foreign ways', or 'people of foreign extraction'. Sentences such as the following, however, are likely to puzzle the reader, no matter which definition of 'cosmopolitan' he has in mind. 'Teacher satisfaction will be significantly higher for cosmopolitans who perceive a low degree of bureaucratization' (*JER*, 60/2, Oct 1966). A careful reading of the article in which this occurs suggests the following as a possible, but by no means certain translation: 'The teachers who are likely to be most satisfied are those who have been abroad and have very little bureaucratic organisation to annoy and frustrate them'.

Cost
Price. Cost and price are, in most contexts, synonymous. Bills and documents indicating the cost or price of something. The 'cost of a bill', however, is the cost of preparing and issuing it, not the price mentioned on it. The journalist who referred to 'the soaring cost of gas bills' (B.B.C. News, 16.1.76) was not at his best. It is the cost of the gas, not of the bills which soars.

Cost effectively
With the profit constantly in mind, making a particular piece of effort yield the greatest possible profit and the least waste. One sometimes has to wrestle for some time with sentences containing 'cost effectively', e.g. 'the successful candidate will be expected to apply orginal thinking cost effectively' (*D Tel*, 6.2.76). There are two main possibilities here, and one can plump for either. (a) The candidate is expected to produce orginal thinking of his own and to apply it cost effectively; (b) the candidate has to apply other people's orginal

thinking cost effectively. It would have been important for potential candidates to interpret the company's requirement correctly, in order to avoid a flood of applications from orginal thinkers if such a person was not required, and to ensure a plentiful supply of orginal thinkers if that happened to be what the management wanted.

Counterculture
Anti-establishment culture, alternative culture. There is counterculture, not a counterculture. It may take many forms and have many different philosophies but, broadly speaking, it will always be opposed to capitalism, the acquisitive society, and the existing political system. The existence of so many shades of counterculture makes it impossible to use the word with any degree of precision. Nor, by the supporters of counterculture, is one meant to, since one is concerned essentially with a state of mind, rather than a set of beliefs. '. . . counterculture schools with a radical orientation' (Corwin, 1974); 'California is in the front line of the cultural civil war between the counterculture and the faithful of the "American disease"' (Miles, 1971).

Counter-revolution
Any attempt by a non-socialist party to set up a government. 'The danger of counter-revolution in Portugal' (*Comment*, 29.11.75) refers to the possibility of Portugal's electors voting in a way that would prevent the Communists from gaining power.

Country-fresh
Just fresh. 'Two country-fresh eggs or omelette style' (Menu of Merrimack Valley Motor Inn, 1974). Eggs are either fresh or they are not. The inclusion of the word 'country' makes no difference either way.

Courtesy
Free. '. . . a courtesy bus service' (brochure of Copthorne Hotel, Gatwick, 1974). The tone of the Copthorne Hotel would be seriously lowered by the use of 'free', . . . and so would that of the Marriott Motor Hotel, Chicago, with its 'airport courtesy bus' (brochure of Marriott Motor Hotel, Chicago, 1977). Cf. Complimentary.

Co-vary
A mathematical term meaning that two things change at the same

time and in such a way as the interrelation between the two is preserved unchanged. In the social sciences, however, it often appears to be used merely as a more impressive alternative to 'vary'. '. . . could covary according to the peers with whom students have identified' (*JER*, 63/5, Jan 1970).

Crafted

Manufactured. The use of 'crafted' is an attempt to delude the public into believing that something has been made by hand, in a carefully old-fashioned way. So 'Adam Bennet, crafted in Australia' (*DTS*, 2.3.76; clothes); 'Elegant shoes carefully crafted to Lotus quality' (*Vogue*, Nov 1975); 'WILLIKERS crafted in Australia' (*Sun*, 2.3.76; denim clothes). There is no reason, of course, why goods produced on machines should not be well-designed and carefully made, but 'crafted' does not carry simply the meaning 'well-made'. It draws on the associations of the related word, 'craftsman', who is always thought of as someone who produces fine, lasting work with hand-tools, and it is, for this reason, a swindle word.

Creamery

Made from milk; a butter-factory product. ' . . . served with creamery butter' (Menu at Merrimack Valley Motor Inn, 1974). Unless it is made at home in the back kitchen, butter has to come from a creamery, the mouth-watering word for a butter factory. 'Creamery butter' is therefore 'butter-factory butter', a point which seems hardly worth making.

Creative

Bursting with new, orginal ideas. The creative person makes old things seem fresh, throws new light on old problems, causes us to see the world in a way we never have before. A creative environment is one in which creative people can be more creative. A 'creative biscuit technologist' (*S Times*, 16.11.75) is presumably either a person with a talent for thinking up new kinds of biscuit, or someone whose creativity takes the form of discovering new ways of making old biscuits. 'Los Angeles. Creative supercity' (*New Yorker*, 13.9.76) is a kaleidoscope city, where nothing stays the same for two consecutive minutes. 'The Fellow will be a successful creative writer, preferably with experience of journalism' (*N Statesman*, 20.8.76) describes someone who might be a poet or, more probably, a writer of novels, short stories or 'imaginative journalism'. The phrase 'creative writer' is not a happy one and has a strong flavour of literary weekends and of correspondence courses for people with literary ambitions. All writers create something, by the mere act of selecting and assembling words, but a 'creative writer' is someone who provides the raw material from which critics, teachers and reviewers earn a living, a primary producer.

Credibility
The ability or qualifications to make people believe what you say. 'You will have the engineering credibility and the sales experience to sustain these contacts' (*S Times*, 30.5.76). i.e. customers will respect your engineering knowledge. 'Such matters as communicator credibility' (*Soc Review Monograph 13*, 1969) is a little more difficult. It probably means, 'having the power to make people believe that you have something worth saying', but another possibility is 'being able to persuade people that you are an effective speaker or writer'. 'Credibility is also used in the sense of 'chance of getting the job', as in 'Candidates could have still more credibility if they have (sic) some background in the printing and publishing industries' (*D Tel*, 19.1.77).

Credibility gap
This expression first came into common use in 1965 during the Vietnam War. The extent to which people disbelieve you; your liar-rating. One of the most popular and most mischievous euphemisms of our time. A person with 'a serious credibility gap' is someone whom nobody believes, a convicted fraud and liar. 'An even greater credibility gap between the Commission and black communities' (Mullard, 1973) means that black people do not believe a word any representative of the Commission says.

Crescive
Growing, developing; to use 'crescive' instead of either of these two words is to make an unnecessary parade of one's learning and to cause bafflement to those of one's fellow-citizens, the great majority, who are without benefit of Latin. One could be prepared to accept the author of '. . . both crescive, evolutionary forces and deliberate innovation' (Corwin, 1974) as a scientific genius, even without the word 'crescive' to prove the point.

Crisis

'Crisis' is widely used by journalists, working for such employers as the B.B.C., *Daily Express* and *New York Times*, for any kind of difficult situation – 'the oil crisis'; 'the water crisis'; 'the coal crisis'. It is also the normal Communist word for the politcal and economic situation in any non-socialist country. 'The crisis of the capitalist world in its economic aspects' (*Comment*, 29.11.75). The difference between Communist and non-Communist journalists is simply that for the first the capitalist world, everywhere and in all its activities, is in crisis all the time, but for the second only about half the time.

Criteria-cued

A social science phrase, which can be roughly translated, 'following criteria, proceeding from one criterion to the next'. 'Cued' gives the correct electronic, computer flavour to the term, as in 'An awareness of the criteria of solution evaluation beyond criteria-cued instruction would increase solution quality even more' (*JEP*, 61/1, 1970). The whole passage means, once one has taken the enormous trouble required to work it out, that students who understand how to work through problems for themselves produce more worthwhile solutions than those who are spoonfed with the steps of reasoning they should follow. This one might have assumed, without the help of such a preposterous piece of jargon.

Cross-cultural

Probably, involving people of several different cultures, as in '. . . a good knowledge of cross-cultural teaching' (Toronto *Globe and Mail*, 9.10.76). A more satisfactory, but less prestigious way of expressing this might be 'good experience of teaching classes containing children of different nationalities'.

Cuisine

Cooking, a style of cooking. Oddly enough, one never has 'cuisine' in one's own home, however good the cooking there may be; it exists only in restaurants. Some restaurants, however, have refused to subscribe to this nonsense, and make it known that they offer the results of cooking, not of cuisine, and that the person in charge is the head cook, not the chef de cuisine. Anyone anxious to eat good food and to protect his pocket should make a point of patronising the places where cooking, not cuisine, is the rule. If, however, one must have French cooking out of France and is willing to pay for it, 'cuisine' is fair enough. 'The superb Isle de France restaurant offers cuisine par excellence' (*High Life*, Dec/Jan 1975/76); on the other hand, '. . . the cuisine of the restaurant offers the best in food and wine' (brochure of Royal County Hotel, Durham, 1976) – but wine does not come from a kitchen. It is not part of the 'cuisine'. The Thurlestone Hotel does better: 'The Thurlestone Hotel combines the best in cuisine, cellar, service' (Thurlestone Hotel, Devon, brochure 1976).

Culture
A set of values, the results of putting such values into practice. An extremely difficult word to use in English, although other languages seem to take to it easily enough, a fact which is not always to their credit, since the word often amounts to very little. There is no problem when 'culture' is used in an anthropological context in reference to primitive or relatively undeveloped countries. A phrase like 'the culture of the Solomon Islands', or 'the culture of the Pueblo Indians' is well understood, whereas 'German culture' or 'Spanish culture' or 'Viennese culture' mean both a great deal and very little. 'German culture' may mean 'the ingredients which add up to the flavour and texture of life in Germany', or 'the beliefs and behaviour of a small number of highly educated Germans'. A person may have been formed by having been born and brought up within the influence of 'English culture' in the broad sense, without being 'cultured', in the narrow sense. It is precisely because the English or American or Australian masses or traditionally 'uncultured', even though they may share a vigorous group 'culture', that they are so hostile to and suspicious of 'culture' and 'cultured' people. 'Culture' is consequently a most politically dangerous, socially divisive word in English, a fact which most foreigners find great difficulty in appreciating. English writers cannot depend on being understood when they use 'culture' or any of its derivatives. Here are three examples of half-communication in *Family, Class and Education*, ed. Maurice Craft, 1970: 'culturally poor homes'; 'The maintenance of culture at a dispiritingly low level through continued low standards of living'; 'If children are labelled "culturally deprived", then it follows that the parents are inadequate, and that the spontaneous realisations of their culture, its images and symbolic representations, are of reduced value and significance'.

Within this situation, English-speaking intellectuals have worked hard, but with little success, to force 'culture' into the language. The English tradition being what it is, their efforts usually sound either precious or almost incomprehensible, e.g. 'Herein lies a source of conflict within the culture of teacher education' (Rubinstein and Stoneman, 1970), which is likely to be taken to mean 'a source of conflict in the education of teachers', 'culture' being seen as redundant. The head of the B.B.C's Arts Features Department, Humphrey Burton, has referred to 'the normal notion of television culture' (*Fin Times*, 14.1.76), and the *Financial Times'* television critic has commented that Mr. Burton seems to have been 'referring not to the culture constituted by television itself, which is the most significant in our society today, but to 'culture' as defined by TV arts programmes' (*Fin Times*, 14.1.76). But how many even of the readers of the *Financial Times*, an exceptionally well-educated and well-informed section of British society, would have been able to agree as to what was meant by 'the culture constituted by television itself'? Is it 'the world as seen by television and television producers'? Or 'the influence television has on its viewers'? Or the television habit and environment, complete with television snacks, television critics and quarrels over which programme to watch? Does the word 'culture' really make communication easier?

Culture-fair

Making allowance for personal and family background. 'Attempts to develop culture-fair tests as a solution' (*JEP*, 61/3, 1970). Existing tests were perfectly fair to boys and girls coming from middle-class homes, but they may have put children from poor homes at a disadvantage. What is therefore meant is 'test which measure ability independently of cultural background', longer but more explicit than the mumbo-jumbo, 'culture-fair'.

Currently

A post-1945 word for 'now'; 'nowadays'. For some time in Britain it was considered a vulgar Americanism, or at least a vulgarism, and this is still felt to be the case by many people, especially by the better-educated. In all social classes, it is, for some reason, used much more by men than by women, possibly because it is felt to have get-ahead, identified-with-success, up-to-date associations, which are more important to men. 'Those currently earning less than £4,500 per annum' (*D Tel*, 27.11.75); 'Currently reorganising and expanding its activities' (*D Tel*, 27.11.75). It can sensibly be used to mean 'for the moment' indicating that change may occur in the future.

Customer
Two meanings are often confused here. (a) to special order, by association with 'custom', in such combinations as 'custom-built' (an Americanism rapidly gaining ground in Britain); (b) someone who buys what one has to sell. Advertisements by American companies in British newspapers are particularly confusing for this reason, especially if the Americans themselves seem confused. 'Customer training at the plant' (*D Tel*, 6.2.76) would seem to mean, 'training in dealing with customers', rather than 'made to order training', but 'customer engineering manager' (*D Tel*, 6.2.76) is an examination piece. Is it 'a manager for special-order engineering projects', or 'a manager to be responsible for engineering customers'?

D

Dance
In normal usage, 'dancing' is the action, 'dance' the occasion; 'dancing', except in compounds, cannot have 'the' or 'a' in front of it and 'dance' is preceded by 'a' only. During the past twenty-five years, however, 'dance' has been used instead of 'dancing' to mean dancing of a superior, more intellectual or more exotic kind. Those who study 'dance' do not regard those who learn 'dancing' as in any way their equals. Nothing, however, is easier than to grade up some form of dancing by calling it dance. A group of African dancers, performing their traditional dances on a stage in New York or London, are offering an audience 'dance', not 'dancing', because it is assumed that one is watching an art form, not mere pleasure of entertainment. Anything that takes place in a dance hall is 'dancing', not 'dance', because, however skilful the performers may be, they are reckoned to be there in order to enjoy themselves, not produce art. There is absolutely no logic in any of this, and nearly every occasion on which 'dance' is used is something of a confidence trick at worst, precious and snobbish at best. 'This gave me the opportunity to study the problems of dance first-hand' (Meuller, 1967). How much face would he have lost if he had 'studied the problems of dancing'? Cf. Film, Theatre.

Dancing

Applied to wine, one would have thought 'dancing' meant 'bubbl-ing', but no. Margaux d'Augrudet, we are told, is 'a dancing, happy wine' (*Times*, 31.7.76), and this is not a sparkling wine at all. Perhaps it sets the hearts and minds of the lucky, happy drinkers dancing.

Data base

Records, and nothing more, however many computers, pro-grammers, analysts and other highly-paid specialists are involved. 'To improve the health data base in Australia, the Australian Government has endorsed the objectives of the three year Health Services Planning and Research Program . . .' (*Health*, 1975).

Dazzling

A colour intensitive, illustrated by 'a dazzling pink New York premium table wine' (*New Yorker*, 26.1.76). Any wine which was in fact a dazzling pink would be a chemical curiosity of the first order. Who, in any case, would want to see such a monstrosity on their table? It would be charitable to suppose that 'dazzling' means 'pleasant', and that drinkers were deeply impressed, 'dazzled', by the wine's beautiful colour.

Deceiving

Larger than one might think from the outside. 'A deceiving semi-detached house' (*B & WEC.*, 2.12.75). The introduction of words like 'deceiving' into the buying and selling of houses seems rather unwise. If the space is not what it appears, might the same not be true of the other features of the house?

Decrement

Decrease, on the analogy of 'increment'. A truly unnecessary and pretentious word, which does nothing to improve the quality of communication and argument. '. . . about a 25 % decrement at each rate' (*JEP*, 64/1, 1973).

Dedicated

Careful, attentive, logical, single-minded. A word to avoid, because of the debasement caused by over-frequent 'dedication' to trival and unworthy ends, quite unjustified in the majority of cases in which it is employed. The 'high cruise standards, enhanced by a dedicated Italian crew' (*New Yorker*, 13.12.75) is a piece of nonsense from beginning to end. It is hardly surprising that the crew should be Italian, in view of the fact that they are on an Italian ship, and to mention the fact at all is an act of cunning irrelevance. The standards of the cruise are not 'enhanced' by the crew, which implies they are present as ornaments, but created by them. And the crew, assuming that such praise is justified, are not 'dedicated', but professional, hard-working and efficient. 'A most unusual hotel, with an exceptionally dedicated following' (*New Yorker*, 14.6.76) merely has people who stay there repeatedly, and the 'small team of dedicated craftsmen who have been working with leather fashions most of their lives' (*New Yorker*, 25.10.76) are no more or less than skilled craftsmen, the word 'dedicated' adding no extra meaning whatever. It is a little more difficult to know what to make of 'the soprano, Vivien Townley, an obviously dedicated musician' (*Classical Music*, 20.10.76). Top-line musicians are no doubt 'dedicated to their art', as the jargon phrase has it, but just what are we supposed to understand by 'dedicated'? That they would be miserable doing anything else? That they practise hard? That their life is wholly concerned with their music? All this one could surely take for granted. 'Dedicated' can also mean the same as the less glamorous and spiritual words 'regular' and 'assiduous'. 'Softer, smoother skin, that's the skin you can have with dedicated use of Skin Life with GAM' (*Good Housekeeping*, Feb 1977).

Dedication
The act or fact of devoting oneself or one's belongings or creations to some noble purpose. To speak of the 'dedication' of people working for an engineering company or an alcohol manufacturer is to throw away a valuable and potentially powerful word. So, for the engineering company, 'membership will demand a high standard of personal performance and dedication' (*Times*, 22.1.76) and, for the alcohol, 'There's a simple virtue that separates the extraordinary from the ordinary. Dedication. The kind of dedication that produces the identifiable excellence of Beefeater gin' (*New Yorker*, 31.5.76). Gin, it might be mentioned, is produced by stills and chemists, not by dedication.

De-emphasis
Taking the emphasis off. To speak of 'deemphasis on ROTC', i.e. officer training corps in universitites (Corwin, 1974) is pompous, when all that is meant is that the same degree of emphasis is no longer

given to these organisations. It is rather as if one abandoned the ordinary word 'eating' and referred to 'dehungrification'. Given the will and the necessary perversity, everything can be defined in terms of the opposite.

De-emphasise

To remove the emphasis from. 'It is reasonable to deemphasise this outcome' (*JEP*, 61/1, 1970), i.e. not to attach much importance to it.

Definite

Strong, unmistakeable, not to be confused with anything else. 'The Côte Chalounaise reds can accompany the sharper matured cheeses of the British Isles, on account of their assertive and definite character' (*Times*, 21.2.76).

Definite article

'Cinema star Ronald Coleman' (B.B.C. News, 12.12.75). The omission of the definite article before someone's occupational label is a matter of the greatest liguistic importance and has been quite unreasonably neglected by observers of the social scene. The traditional English usage is with a definite article before the occupation and a comma after it, 'The cinema star, Ronald Coleman'. 'Cinema star Ronald Coleman' is a straight translation from the German and has entered first American and then English via German immigrants to the United States. This, in itself, is harmless enough, although it represents a threat to the traditional Anglo-Saxon pleasure of smiling at the Germans for such mirth-making pomposities as 'Orchestral conductor Schmidt' and 'Handler of colonial foodstuffs Winkelmann'. The reason for objecting to the habit here is twofold; it identifies a person indissolubly with his occupation and turns him into that cumbersome creature, a compound noun, and it gives journalists far more power than is good either for them or for society. Journalists, especially radio and television journalists, would have us believe that all right-minded people are as punchy, grammar-scorning and democratic as themselves, and that anyone who prefers 'The Prime Minister, Mr Callaghan', to 'Prime Minister Callaghan' is an enemy of the people. Thus 'Director Mike Leigh' (*Radio Times*, 10/16.1.76); 'Pianist George Shearing' (*Melody Maker*, 7.2.76).

Degree
Deal. 'The oral time budget takes a great degree of interviewer time' (Michelson, 1975). Translated, this means something like, 'The interviewer has to spend a lot of time persuading people to tell him exactly what they did during a particular period'. 'Degree', instead of 'deal' is simply illiterate, however much the writer may feel drawn towards it.

Delivery
Supply of information, delivery of supplies. The person who is required 'to make recommendations concerning health care delivery systems' (*Health*, 1975) may be about to earn his living either by planning the supply of information to hospitals and doctors or by organising a flow of supplies to such people. With nothing in the context to help him, the outside observer has nothing better than guesswork to lead him to the correct interpretation.

Demanding
Very difficult, exhausting. Employers find themselves unable to say that the work they are offering is exhausting, and we therefore have the advertisement which begins, 'If you are interested in a demanding job' (*D Tel*, 9.12.75) and the company which requires 'a representative to take over a demanding area' (*D Tel*, 12.3.76).

Demonstrated
The new managerial word for 'proven'. 'We are seeking demonstrated managerial ability at a senior level' (*Obs*, 15.2.76). This is a clumsy way of saying, 'The person we are looking for must have demonstrated managerial ability at a senior level', or, better still, 'must have had successful management experience at a senior level'. 'Demonstrated ability' is, in fact, 'successful experience'.

Depicted
In psychological jargon, a 'depicted object' is that familiar feature of our lives, a picture. 'The test consisted of eight depicted objects' (*JEP*, 60/2, 1969).

Deprived
Without a reasonable share of possessions or opportunities. Often used as a synonym of 'underprivileged', i.e. poor. A 'deprived child' is

one from a poor home, but what is the meaning of 'deprived' in 'More and more of the really deprived working-class population have been applying for entry to the Open University' (*Times*, 14.1.77)? Are these people 'deprived' of education, or opportunities to discover and develop their talents, or does the word refer to their income and living conditions?

Depth

A wine writer's word. Nobody can explain what it means. A wine either has it, apparently, or does not have it, whatever it is. 'These are classic wines, with tremendous depth, elegance and fine bouquet' (Catalogue of Lay and Wheeler, Colchester, 1976).

Designation

Qualification. There is an Atlantic problem here. In North America it is just possible, although not well thought of on the upper educational levels, to speak of 'a well-organised hardworking person with an accounting designation' (Toronto *Globe and Mail*, 6.10.76), when what is meant is 'an accounting qualification'. In Britain, 'designation' is not easily understood in this sense. A person's 'designation' is what goes in front of his name, not what goes after it. 'Dr.', 'Professor', 'Lord' are all 'designations'.

Desk

'From the desk of' simply means, 'from', as in 'From the desk of John F. Mee' (*Business Horizons*, Aug 1975). This is a curious, affected usage, almost on a level with 'From the office of . . .'. There are a number of possible implications, all of which may be wrong. 'From the desk of' may mean that the great man himself approved and signed the letter, but did not dictate or write it. It may mean that he wrote it and signed it, or that he wrote it but was not there to sign it. And it may also mean, using 'desk' as a synonym for 'office', that the letter was drawn up and sent on his behalf by someone else in his office. 'From' avoids these chances of misunderstanding, but there are cases in which the confusion is intentional, and in these 'From the desk of' is the perfect phrase.

Determiners

Factors which determine. The single word fits better into the social science style, however, and acts as an additional barrier between the layman and the professional. A good example is 'Further study is needed to uncover the determiners of sole perceptions of high school principals' (*JER*, 63/1, Sept 1969), i.e. 'to find out why high school principals see their role the way they do'.

Devalue
Lessen, weaken. The word is often used without much attention to the sense, producing such nonsense as Harold Wilson's 'The fact devalues the tone of his criticism' (*Hansard*, 5.2.76. Parliamentary statement). 'Devalues his criticism' is just possible, but 'lessens the value of' is better. One devalues the currency, not criticism. 'Devalues the tone of his criticism' means nothing at all. Tone can be lowered, but not devalued.

Dimension
Feature, factor. A very widespread piece of linguistic pollution. The traditional dimensions are those of length, breadth and height, to which has been added in more recent times the fourth dimension, that of time. There are no other dimensions and it is absurd and misleading to suggest the contrary. So 'a significant new dimension in ground force defence' (*Fin Times*, 16.2.76), a guided weapon, is 'a significant new factor'. 'The Ocean House residences add a new dimension to life at John's Island' (*New Yorker*, 5.4.76) is probably intended to mean, 'are the best seen so far', but it is just possible that the new dimension consists of having houses on land which had no houses before. 'Floor coverings from all over the world offer endless possibilities for new dimensions in home deco.' (*Panorama*, Boston, Oct 1976) could be rendered, 'for making your floors look different'. A connoisseur's item is 'Artists and laymen have considerably different semantic dimensions in their responses to modern art' (Michelson, 1975), i.e. 'Artists and laymen use different words to describe their responses to modern art'.

Dimensional
Almost meaningless, except as an emotional link between like-minded people, in such sentences as: 'We thus had the direct experience of a lasting meta-personal inspiration, expanses of calm, dimensional plurality, freedom, spaciousness, and of a medial self-renunciation transcending all our previous experiences' (Wörner, 1973). 'Dimensional plurality' sounds like lots of dimensions, but how this fits into context or how the whole sentence is to be translated must remain a mystery.

Direct-response
Australian, and, to a lesser extent, American version of 'telephone selling'. 'The attractive working environment and a small staff allows exposure to all phases of the direct-response business' (*The Age*, 2.3.76), i.e. 'provides experience of all branches of telephone-selling'.

Disadvantaged
Poor. 'Poor', out of favour for many year, is fortunately showing signs of creeping back, as part of the indignation movement against social science language, but we shall probably have to struggle against 'disadvantaged' and 'deprived' for a long time to come. '. . . disadvantaged home environments' (*JEP*, 61/2, 1970); 'the school drop-outs, who are the most educationally and socially disadvantaged group' (Corwin, 1974); 'Teacher expectations for the disadvantaged' (*Scientific American*, Apr 1968). The difference between 'disadvantaged' and 'poor' is fundamental. 'Poor' is merely a description of how a person is and lives; 'disadvantaged' implies that the person's condition is no fault of his own, that something called 'society' is responsible for his misfortunes. Those who use 'disadvantaged' are saying, in effect, 'It's not your fault', whereas those who say 'poor' are making no comment.

Disaggregated
Split up again into its separate components, disentangled. One first aggregates and then disaggregates. 'Information should be sufficiently disaggregated to be responsive to users' needs' (*Business Horizons*, Aug 1975).

Discerning
Knowing a good thing when one sees it. The hotels that pride themselves on their standards are interested only in 'discerning' guests. One in the North of England which aims 'to cater for the discerning needs of businessman and tourist' (Brochure of Royal County Hotel, Durham, 1976) has unfortunately failed to notice that it is the businessman, not his needs, that are discerning. But the word has been used so much in the hotel, restaurant and motor trades in recent years that 'discerning guest', 'discerning motorist' and so on have become almost compound nouns, so that the force of 'discerning' has nearly disappeared.

Disconfirmation
Failure to have confirmed. 'Disconfirmation of critical expectation constitutes an aversive situation' (*JEP*, 65/1, 1973), i.e. 'People find it unpleasant when their hopes come to nothing'.

Disconfirmed
Not confirmed. The use of this barbarous word is misleading, since it implies, on the analogy of 'discontinue', that what was once confirmed has now ceased to be confirmed. What in fact is meant is that it was never confirmed at all. 'The second production is clearly disconfirmed by the results of correlational analyses' (*JEP*, 62/1 Feb 1971).

Discovery-centred
Based on people finding out for themselves. 'When I was teaching eleven-year-old children in an informal discovery-centred atmosphere' (Rubinstein & Stoneman, 1970). This is a piece of educational jargon. The author means that his method of teaching was based on encouraging children to find things out for themselves, which is neither new nor revolutionary. The use of 'discovery-centred' is reckoned to give this approach academic respectability.

Discreetly
Just this side of downright vulgarity. A suite can be advertised as being 'upholstered in discreetly voluptuous velvet' (*Good Housekeeping*, Feb 1977).

Discretion
Judgement. A high-sounding word, which in some contexts means remarkably little. In 'employing substantial technical discretion and judgement' (*Times*, 20.6.76) it means less than nothing, since the writer is saying in effect, 'substantial technical judgement and judgement'. More charitably, 'discretion' may help the rhythm of the sentence.

Disdain
Feeling and looking superior to its company. Of a Copeland chimneypiece: 'It will subtly settle into its new surroundings and hint with only a trace of disdain . . .' (*Con*, Vol 161, Jan/Apr 1966). How many of us would wish one piece of our furniture to look at another

piece, or even worse at us, with even the slightest hint of disdain? How, in any case, does a mantelpiece look disdainful?

Dispensing

Giving. '. . . and be responsible for dispensing written and verbal advice on a wide range of projects' (*D Tel*, 10.2.77).

Distinguished

All prominent musicians are either 'young' or 'distinguished'. It is, for some reason, considered to be in bad taste to say simply, 'the violinist, Johann Schmidt'. One must refer to 'the distinguished violinist . . .', if that is not too great an exaggeration, or 'the young violinist . . .' if he is under 45. Both words can be misleading, because, as a result of this kind of gross overuse, one has no idea of just how distinguished or how young he is. 'The distinguished French baritone's voice . . .' (*Fin Times*, 7.12.76).

Divergent

Original, unconventional. 'The emphasis on creativity and divergent thinking does not, of course, mean that children will not learn to read and write' (Rubinstein & Stoneman, 1970). 'Divergent' is an unsatisfactory and sometimes dangerous word to use in this connexion, since, for most people, it has the slightly pejorative sense of 'having strayed from the straight and right path'. This may or may not be intended, but the use of a different word avoids the risk.

Do-gooder

Someone who tries to help people, unasked and perhaps against their wishes, as in 'a collection of white, liberal do-gooders' (Mullard, 1973). Society has reached a sad pass when it is a crime to want to do good, but one can understand anyone's wish to beat their own path to salvation, or possibly damnation, without interference from anyone else. 'Do-gooding', to those who dislike it, has the flavour of unwanted help or charity, although to those who offer it, the word 'do-gooding' is likely to sound unreasonably offensive. The term is especially in favour with those who incline towards violent or revolutionary solutions to their own and the world's problems and who consequently regard 'do-gooders', a peaceful race, as a barrier to progress.

Dream kitchen
A well-fitted kitchen. For some unexplained reason, 'dream' is not usually prefixed to other rooms in the house. One never speaks, for instance, of 'a dream dining room', or 'a dream bathroom'. This may possibly be because of the amount of time women spend in their kitchens, so that a 'dream kitchen' becomes a kind of Grail, something always better than what one has already and always just out of reach, a place so well equipped that the work almost does itself and so pleasant that one can forget one is in a kitchen at all. 'These luxury units have a dream kitchen with W.O. stove' (*Sydney Morning Herald*, 28.2.76); 'Dining room, dream kitchen, four large bedrooms' (Toronto *Globe and Mail*, 31.1.76).

Dry
Much used by music critics and not always easy to understand. Sometimes it seems to mean 'objective', 'unemotional', sometimes 'stiff', 'hard', 'brittle'. 'Cage requires a submergence of personality to produce a cool, dry expressiveness' (*Times*, 16.10.76); 'The recording is rather dry and wiry and the performance is disappointingly close to routine' (*Classical Music*, 20.10.76). The sense of 'dry' is clearly not the same in these two sentences and the difference is particularly important when, as in these instances, the music is of very different periods, in one of which 'dry' is a term of praise and in the other of inadequacy.

Dumbness
Does it mean, of wine, 'refusal or inability to speak', or does it mean 'stupidity'? Or, on some occasions, both together? The context can help, but not always as much as one would wish, especially when one does not know how Americanised an English writer may be. 'The 1961s never went through a phase of sulkiness or dumbness' (*Times*, 17.7.76) comes from an English newspaper of the highest standing, which makes few concessions to American idioms, and the meaning here is therefore almost certainly 'refusal to express itself to the drinker', which is a wine writer's flight of fancy.

Dynamic
Energetic, vigorous, successful. 'Dynamic' is much liked by certain members of the business community, to whom the idea of employing staff who are human power-stations, constantly turning out mega-

watts of electrical energy, makes a great appeal, flattering as the concept sometimes is. One concern will therefore refer to 'the recent dynamic growth of the company' (*D Tel*, 17.12.75) and another will insist that 'the successful candidates will be dynamic, self-disciplined professionals' (*D Tel*, 7.1.76). In other cases the place of work itself is dynamic and anyone fortunate to be employed there 'must be able to accept responsibility in a dynamic environment' (*D Tel*, 28.11.75), and in others again a person's whole working life is expected to have been characterised by the magic quality: 'The successful applicant will be expected to demonstrate a dynamic sales career to date' (*S Times*, 20.6.76). What appears to be a significantly different shade of meaning is noticeable in America and may cause special problems for British readers, although it is doubtful if all Americans could achieve a successful translation. This is the Marxist notion that one thing interacts creatively with another, to produce a result that is different from either, the Marxist dialectic, in fact. We have then, 'The dynamic rapport of Tony's vocals and the instrumental genius of the Ruby Braff/George Barnes quartet' (*New Yorker*, 14.6.76) and 'All spaces interact dynamically with the indoor garden' (*House Beautiful*, Oct 1976). So something beautiful is born from the sparks which Tony's vocals knock from the Ruby Braff quartet, and from the pulsating love-making of the indoor garden and all the spaces. Not every observer may be completely clear as to what this beautiful creation is, but the energy, the dynamism, is what matters. The word can be in the plural, 'You must be willing to put in the dynamics and effort required for a start-up situation' (Toronto *Globe and Mail*, 6.10.76), and the noun 'dynamism', as in 'dynamism and planned growth' (*D Tel*, 27.11.75) is an equally frequently found and equally woolly cliché.

Dysfunctional

Unhelpful. 'Designers are frequently in a hurry, and new research may be dysfunctional to the total effort, particularly if appropriate findings have been made available from the work of others' (Michelson, 1975). It is, in other words, dysfunctional to my total effort as a cyclist if first I spend years inventing the bicycle, because someone else has done so already. One does sometimes feel that a sentence has been created solely to allow someone to make use of his beautiful new word, 'dysfunctional', and not from any compulsion to communicate at all.

E

Easy-to-drink

Pleasant, not very intoxicating. '...a light, delicate claret with an easy-to-drink character' (*National Times*, 1.3.76). The possible meanings suggested here are little more than guesswork. If a wine is categorised as 'easy to drink', it may be light and therefore slips easily down the throat; the alcohol content may be low, so that it is easy to drink a good deal without any unpleasant effects becoming apparent; it may have a particularly agreeable flavour, so that it is easy to be tempted to add glass to glass.

Economics

Money. 'In his scale of values he places power and economics at the top of the list' (*Business Horizons*, Aug 1975). In this kind of context 'economics' does not mean money as a bank cashier understands it, but rather 'the ability to make money', 'money as a source of power and influence'. 'Economics' is, of course, an altogether more refined and respectable term than the crude word 'money'. It would not look right to include 'money' in anyone's scale of values, but 'economics', a drawing-room word, is perfectly seemly.

Economic storm

A recession, slump, or what used, in a less mealy-mouthed age, to be called hard times. A favoured phrase with City Page writers, who are always looking for suitable euphemisms with which to calm nervous investors. 'When the economic storm blows itself out' (*D Tel*, 23.4.76) is a fair example.

Economisation

Economy. There is absolutely no difference of meaning whatever between 'economy' and 'economisation', but the extra two syllables make the second word much more impressive and therefore more desirable in certain circles. 'Why not achieve the same economisation . . .' (Perreault, 1969).

Edge
Sharpness? From the wine world. 'Sichel's vintage report describes them as "soft and graceful, with no edges" (*Times*, 31.7.76).

Educationalist or **Educationist**
Properly, a person who makes a study of the techniques and aims of education. This is a much misused word and its precise sense is often far from clear. From the context, it sometimes appears to mean 'someone whose job is to study the methods and organisation of education', sometimes 'a person who earns a living from educational administration', and sometimes no more than 'a teacher'. Which of these senses is intended in '. . . to help both educationists and broadcasters to look at their common problems' (*EB* 75)? A 'broadcaster' is essentially a practical person, not a theorist, and the corresponding function in education would be 'teacher'. If 'educationist and broadcaster' is to be regarded as a pair, the translation would therefore be 'teacher'. But is this, in fact, what the writer was trying to express? Or did he mean 'anybody professionally concerned with education'?

Efficiency
Either the ratio of useful work performance to the amount of energy expended, or, in North America, a bed-sitter with some cooking and washing facilities. The plural is perfectly reasonable in the second sense, but an affectation in the first. 'Rooms, efficiencies, 1 and 2 bedrooms, and apartment' (*Key*, Dallas, May 1973); ' . . . the organisation and control of the day to day maintenance operation on a planned basis to achieve improving mechanical efficiencies' (*Times*, 26.1.76). 'Efficiencies' in the second example is an attempt to sound more technical, in the hope that someone will be impressed. 'Mechanical efficiency' conveys the meaning perfectly well.

Efflorescence
The grand word for 'flowering'. 'This efflorescence of artists was not rivalled by any other of the English schools of the time' (*Con*, Vol 164, Jan/Apr 1967). 'Flowering' is a nice word, understandable to everyone. Why then should one go for the up-stage 'efflorescence', except for reasons of snobbery and to prove one's vocabulary extends that far?

Effluent
Waste liquid. This is a word used so normally and naturally by people in the plumbing and sewage businesses that this comic possibilities are not infrequently overlooked. One firm, professionally admirable, no doubt, but with an inadequate sense of humour, found it possible to offer 'a technical service to customers with effluent problems' (*D Tel*, 30.4.76).

Ego-enhancing
Increasing one's self-esteem, making one feel bigger and better ' . . . ego-enhancing modes of causal attribution' (*JEP*, 61/1, 1970). The translation of the whole quotation is far from easy, even for a psychologist. A possible rendering, put forward without any great conviction, might be 'ways of saying why something happened that made a person feel good', but whether this contains a thought of any great significance is difficult to say. Neither version constitutes a notable contribution to the art of communication.

Ego-fulfilment
Employing one's talents to the full, stretching oneself. The word is often used more for its look and sound than for its sense, however, as by the industrial concern which was looking for qualities of 'leadership, ego-fulfilment, communication' (*Times*, 22.12.75) in candidates for a management post. This seems a little over-condensed. What was probably meant was that the applicant should be able to show evidence of his capacity for leadership and for communicating well with his colleagues, and that the job would offer him an opportunity to feel fully occupied. A candidate might well inform his prospective employers that he was an excellent leader and communicator, but he could hardly say that he was strong on ego-fulfilment.

Ego-protective
Safeguarding one's feeling of identity as an individual or person. 'The occurrence of ego-protective attributional modes' (*JEP*, 61/, 1970) had better be left to bask in its own scientific glory, with the passing reflexion that so few people in the past seem to have been bothered about absence of identity or insufficiently developed ego, while so many in the present, encouraged by psychologists, are.

Ego-transcending

Not bound to a particular person. One of the many compounds beginning with 'ego' which, as literal translations from the German, fit so clumsily and incomprehensibly into English. 'What can be more world-wide, more ego-transcending, more all-embracing, more universal and more momentaneous than the broadcasts, which in *Kurzwellen* take on the guise of musical material?' (Wörner, 1973).

Either

Very frequently misplaced in the sentence, so that one waits panting for words that never come, with all the frustration and exhaustion such a process involves. 'Candidates will either have a background in commercial electronics or university research' (*D Tel*, 28.1.76) is a good example. The semi-literate author meant to say 'a background in either commercial electronics or university research'. As it stands, however, the unfortunate reader is left hanging in the air after 'or', expecting something like 'successful experience in', which is not forthcoming.

Elegant

Beautifully presented to the public, possessing an appearance which suggests that great care has been taken with it? These are unfortunately pure guesses, although they may be somewhere near the mark. The wine trade understandably loves to describe its goods as 'elegant', reckoning that few people are likely to confess their ignorance by asking what the word means. So one firm advertises its 'well-balanced, elegant clarets' (1976 catalogue of Lay and Wheeler, Colchester), and in another place we are assured that 'the slightly flowery, elegant charm of the best reds should appeal to many British drinkers (*Times*, 21.2.76). The same considerations apply to the noun 'elegance'. From the abundant examples we may select, 'The house champagnes of Balls Brothers, Vicomte d'Almon, come from Vertus, with the implication of elegance of the region' (*Times*, 19.6.76).

Elevated

(a) Not on dead flat ground. An estate agent's word, which does not necessarily imply that the house in question is on a hillside, or with far-reaching views. 'Modern detached bungalow in an elevated position' (*SMJ*, 18.12.75); 'Outstanding residential property in

superb elevated position' (*Times*, 20.5.76). It is possible that a 'superb elevated position' is slightly higher than an 'elevated position'.
(b) In hotel jargon, an 'elevated room' is simply a room on one of the upper floors; an upper room, in fact. There is nothing otherwise superior about its quality, although in choosing the word the establishment is likely to be fully aware of this bonus. 'Elevated room offers view of Central Park from all levels' (brochure of Marriot Essex House, New York, 1977) suggests that the room has been specially raised to meet the customers' convenience and wishes.

Elevation
Extension, but whether upwards or sideways is left to the imagination, a term used especially in the field of business management. 'The position is an elevation of the finance and accounting function' (*The Age*, 28.2.76). Since there is nothing superior to the finance and accounting function, this particular elevation is presumably sideways.

Elusive
Extremely subtle. When something is almost impossible to define, there is bound to be a strong possibility that it does not exist, and in such a case the adjective 'elusive' is ideal. 'Rather than attempt to verbalise the elusive qualities which set the Inter-Continental apart from London's many admirable hotels . . .' (*High Life*, Oct 1976), the author naturally prefers to leave the task to the reader.

Embourgeoisement
Acquisition of middle-class characteristics, habits, values. Sociologists claim that 'bourgeois' is a more objective, more scholarly term than the emotionally-loaded 'middle-class', although it is possible to disagree with this view. What is certain is that 'embourgeoisement' is a hideously clumsy word, and far from easy to pronounce. One can do without it. Whatever meaning there may be in 'the embourgeoisement of the working-class' (*B J Soc*, Mar 1968) does not appear to be obscured or weakened if we substitute as a translation, 'the new fondness of the working-class for middle-class habits'.

Empirical
Strictly, guided only by practical experience; making sure that one thing works before proceeding to the next. Sometimes, however, the word seems to be intended to mean more than this, although precisely what is far from clear. How, for example, is one to interpret 'the

entire Engineering Division, which has great empirical strength' (*D Tel*, 2.2.77)? Is 'empirical' a blunder, perhaps, the author's meaning being 'potential'? Or is one intended to understand that the strength of the Engineering Division lies in the fact that it is staffed by empirically-minded men? Should the latter be the case, what is the advantage supposed to be and why does the company think it worth its while to advertise the fact that its engineers have no scientific training and proceed solely on the basis of practical experience? In all probability, the writer of these words had no clear idea in his mind at all, beyond wishing to say that the Company had a strong Engineering Divison. 'Empirical' was put in merely because it sounded impressive.

Encapsulated
Self-contained, fenced-round. A sociologist's word, to be found in such contexts as 'the intense pressures of the encapsulated community' (Lipset, 1971), where several different interpretations are possible. Is the encapsulated community imposing pressures on itself or on other organisations? Is it the fact of encapsulation which gives rise to the pressures? Is the implication that such pressures are a good thing or a bad thing?

Encompass
Deal with, cover. The process is carried out only by things, not people, however. One can correctly say that one's reading has encompassed all the works of Dickens, but not that 'I have encompassed all the works of Dickens'. 'During your training you will encompass a wide range of engineering projects' (*D Tel*, 7.1.76) is a pompous and inaccurate way of saying that 'you will deal with a wide range of engineering projects'.

Encompassing
Providing the opportunity for. 'The company is based in pleasant rural surroundings encompassing numerous activities' (*S Times*, 30.1.77), some of which cannot, one imagines, be specified.

Encounter
Visit, discovery. 'And the caves of Diros, a truly fabulous encounter with their stunningly lit interior' (*Vogue*, 1.3.76) makes sense only if the interior is moving towards one, which in this instance it clearly is not. One has an encounter with something living, a bull, a policeman,

a drunk, but only humorously with an inanimate object, as, for example, 'His car had an unfortunate encounter with a lamp-post'. To have an encounter with the interior of a cave would be to risk severe bruising or worse.

Encumbent
Holder of a post. This strange and quite unjustified spelling of 'incumbent', now common in the business world, especially in Australia, may be due to an unfortunate confusion with 'encumber'. The spelling apart, the use of the word for a person employed in a run-of-the-mill job is an absurd and pretentious attempt to give the job and its occupant a prestige they do not deserve. One can be the 'incumbent' of an ecclesiastical or government office, but hardly of a programmer's desk in a computer establishment. 'The encumbent will also be responsible for the production of sales data' (*The Age*, 20.3.76); 'thus allowing the encumbent to contribute towards corporate goals' (*Sydney Morning Herald*, 28.2.76).

Endless
Long. 'But this is just one of the many exciting opportunities that exist at CRL. Others offering a similar high technical challenge and interest include music and records, speech research, pattern re-cognition, underwater technology–the list's endless' (*D Tel*, 27.2.76). It is not.

End-state
Ends, aims. A social scientist can refer to 'activity directed towards the attainment of certain valued end-states' (*Educ & Soc Sci*, Vol 1, No 4, Feb 1970), but all he means is 'the attainment of certain valued goals'. 'End-states' may be better for his salary, but it benefits the sense not at all.

End-user
Can mean either the manufacturer or the user of a finished product. The 'end-user' of a knife and fork is not, to the business world, a man who sits down to eat his dinner, but the cutlery firm in Sheffield which turns steel into knives and forks and is the 'end-user' from the steel maker's point of view. In 'property with specific end-users in mind' (*Times*, 27.1.76) we have a serious communication problem. What is presumably meant is 'buildings with specific occupants or a specific kind of occupant in mind', but, if this is the correct

interpretation, the reason for insulting a tenant by calling him an end-user is not clear. Even more baffling is the demand by an Australian firm for 'a senior representative to promote sales to existing and potential customers and end-users' (*The Age*, 28.2.76). An end-user is a customer; he buys what the firm has to sell. What, then, is the point of saying, in effect, 'sales to existing and potential customers and customers'?

Enhancement

Extension, improvement. A new favourite in the business world, when anything that suggests bigger and better is now an 'enhancement'. A typical user of the word is 'a company committed to a major enhancement of its already substantial systems based on a number of large on-line data base files' (*D Tel*, 17.12.76).

Enormous

Big (q.v.), but bigger. A wine word. 'From the feel of this enormous red, it has some pressings in it' (*National Times*, 1.3.76). No reliable information is available, but can an 'enormous' wine just possibly be a very heavy wine? To call a wine 'heavy' nowadays is not felt to be polite or good for sales, suggesting as it does that it might make a drinker fat or bring on a heart attack. 'Enormous' might be a way of avoiding these objections.

En suite

Noun, a bathroom; adjective, attached. A house-agent's absurd term. The English and American usages differ, however. An English reader now understands '80 top-class bedrooms with bathroom en suite' (*S Times*, 23.11.75), but might well be puzzled by 'four large bedrooms, master huge, with ensuite' (Toronto *Globe and Mail*, 31.1.76). Why the use of the French phrase 'en suite' should be reckoned to grade up the accommodation is not at all obvious. A bathroom is a bathroom, and experience suggests that French bathrooms are not of any excitingly high standard.

Entelechy

There are two possible meanings: (a) the stage at which what has previously been potential has become actual; (b) the spirit or essence which gives perfection to anything. The social scientists, who are fond of the word, do not always employ it with the precision one might have hoped for. What, for instance, is meant by 'the dominant new generation entelechy' (*BJ Soc*, Sept 1966)? Is it to be translated, 'the main quality which has only come into full bloom with the new generation'? To use 'entelechy' at all is somewhat dangerous and gratuitous, but to make it one of the elements in a compound, such as 'new generation entelechy' is seriously to reduce the chances of communication.

Enviable

Fashionable, much-wanted. For generations, one of the estate-agent's favourite tricks has been to suggest that the house they have on offer is in an area where everyone wants to be. Words like 'sought-after', 'favoured' and 'desirable' have been used at different times in an attempt to bring clients to the boil. 'Enviable' is the latest and nastiest of them. Far from being a sin, envy, to an estate-agent, is evidently one of the prime virtues. 'Detached house in an enviable situation' (*S MJ*, 27.11.75).

Environment

Any place of work, especially a factory. In the world of industrial management 'factory' has for a long time been an obscene word, at least in any contacts with the outside world. So we have, 'a Senior Planning Engineer, who has a background in a light or heavy engineering environment' (*D Tel*, 29.4.76). Often the word is entirely redundant and inserted only in order to keep up with the industrial Jones's, as one sees, for example, in 'Experience in a manufacturing environment' (*D Tel*, 27.11.75), which means 'Experience in manufacturing' or, more brutally, 'experience in a factory', and 'Ideally you should have worked in an overseas environment' (*D Tel*, 28.9.76), where the candidate is merely expected to have worked overseas. The person required to have had 'at least 4 or 5 years' experience in a large-scale retailing environment' (*S Times*, 16.11.75) would have been able to show evidence of 4 to 5 years' large-scale retailing experience. 'Environment' can be a with-it synonym for 'company', as illustrated by 'in a unionised environment' (*D Tel*, 5.12.75) and 'the environment is fast-moving and structured' (*Times*, 30.5.76), or for 'department', as in 'able to demonstrate an understanding of techniques used in an information environment' (*D Tel*, 29.4.76). Sometimes, and very frighteningly, the environment refuses to stay still, as we see in the mention of 'retailing in a fast-moving environment' (*D Tel*, 17.12.75).

Environmental

Present in what surrounds you. 'Eating in SoHo will add to your total environmental experience' (*Sky*, Delta Airlines, Oct 1976). What this particular environment may be is deliberately left vague. Is it SoHo itself, the experience of the SoHo area? Or one's experience of restaurants? Is eating in a restaurant an environmental experience or an eating experience? One suspects, thinking about most of the food offered, that it is probably wise to emphasise the environment. But the 'total environmental experience' would include one's fellow eaters, and that is by no means always pleasurable.

Envision

For those with so much money and so elevated a position in society that the humble 'imagine' is an insult. People of vision can only be invited to 'envision' what they have not yet seen. 'Envision a 1600 year old city carved of stone rising from the lush jungle floor' (*New Yorker*, 8.10.75).

Epicurean

Expensive, and confined to the stereotyped food eaten by the rich and fashionable world. 'Epicurean meals' at Palm Beach Spa, Florida (*Montreal Star*, 16.10.76) would no doubt recall similarly advertised meals at any comparable hotel in the five continents.

Epitomise

Concentrate on; sell nothing but. A manufacturing company can announce that it is 'operating nationwide in markets which epitomise fast-moving consumer goods' (*D Tel*, 6.5.76), completely ignoring the fact that the correct meaning of 'epitomise' is 'summarise, put in a nutshell'. A market might 'epitomise' prosperity; it cannot 'epitomise' goods of any sort.

Equilibration

Balance, balancing. In the following example, 'equilibration' is totally unnecessary and can be dropped without any loss of meaning. 'Whatever modest gains they have been able to make on their level of authority, they have created serious imbalances in the equilibration of the total system' (Corwin, 1974). This means, for those analytically inclined, 'serious imbalances in the balance of the total system', which contains an element of the obvious. But 'equilibration' is no doubt felt to add tone to the sentence.

Equivalent
Equal to. Some things are not as equivalent as their authors would have us believe. What, for example, are we to think of 'the Australian National University's 3203 equivalent full-time students' (*ANU*, 1973)? This is presumably, from a statistician's point of view, the same as 6406 half-time or 12812 quarter-time students, but to use such a mode of expression is to pay little attention to the way human beings actually behave. Someone attending the University half-time very often puts in more work on his own than a student who is on the premises all day. Man is not a mere mathematical unit, whatever the statisticians and administrators may choose to believe.

Escalating
Increasing. A dangerous and misleading word to use, because of the pejorative sense given to it by the military, especially during the Vietnam War. Nowadays terrorism, war and inflation 'escalate', that is, increase by geometrical proportion in severity and unpleasantness, feed on themselves. It is consequently unwise to speak of 'an annually escalating bonus' (*D Tel*, 27.11.75) which, in today's context, is bound to have a menacing tone about it. What is wrong with an 'annually increasing bonus'? Is it reckoned to sound less than an 'escalating bonus'? And if so, why?

Escapism
Escape or relief from something unpleasant. But is this what is really meant by 'more and more are seeking escapism through football, foreign holidays, gambling' (*Times*, 4.2.76)? At one time one used to 'escape' from drudgery by making a fortune, by getting a better job or by taking a holiday, and it still seems more honest and convincing to say that 'more and more people are seeking (or finding) an escape from boredom through football, foreign holidays, gambling', which is, in fact, what they are doing. Are they concerned more with the activity, 'escape', or with the state of mind, 'escapism'? We do not know, because the preference for the fashionable word, 'escapism' has taken away the power of choice.

Essence
The vital centre, what is left when less precious elements have been

distilled off. The metaphor frequently gets out of hand, however, as in 'bringing him into communion with the very essence of the mechanism of creation' (*Con*, Vol 165, May/Aug 1967). Can a mechanism have an essence? Does the quotation mean any more than 'bringing him into spiritual contact with the mechanism of creation'? The use of 'essence' is of course flattering to the writer, because it implies that he has the ability to identify this central quality.

Establishmentarian

Faithful to the established order. This dreadful, almost unpronounceable word, is much favoured by sociologists of the Left, usually in a derogatory sense. 'Hierarchal (sic), élitist, establishmentarian, static, closed, anti-democratic – this was our society until recently' (Rubinstein & Stoneman, 1970).

Ethical

Not on open sale to the public. A soothing word, which in many cases means precisely the opposite of what it suggests to the innocent reader. It is highly thought of by manufacturers of pharmaceutical products, by whom it is used as a synonym for 'sold only to the medical profession', or 'obtainable only by a doctor's prescription'. Such goods can be and often are scandalously over-priced and their marketing may well be the reverse of ethical. The word is invaluable for covering up a host of anti-social practices. It makes a firm sound totally honest and dependable, as in 'a rapidly growing Company, specialising in ethical dermatological products' (*D Tel*, 12.2.76). Sometimes it appears to be intended as a synonym for 'honest', which is, of course, too old-fashioned and straightforward for contemporary commercial use, at least on the higher levels. An example of this is 'ethical purchasing practice' (*D Tel*, 12.2.76).

Ethnic

Strictly, showing common racial or cultural characteristics. Some difficulty of interpretation is often caused by the habit, popular in the United States, of using ethnic as a synonym for 'foreign' or 'exotic'. 'Ethnic prints go sophisticated with this little dress in fine Courtelle jersey knit' (*S Tel*, 7.11.76) is worth an effort to translate. It could mean 'folk prints', that is, prints having the traditional designs on folk costumes, or it could mean something very different, new designs from foreign countries, which might or might not reflect tradition. 'In the vast majority of cases Negroes have not shared a sense of ethnic honour' (*B J Soc*, June 1969) presents an awkward problem. Are we to understand that in the past there has been a special kind of black honour, to which in our own times many negroes have not been faithful? Or, much worse, have black people, in general, never understood what honour is? Or is 'a sense of ethnic honour' pride in belonging to the black community?

Ethnocentrism
The present century has spawned a huge number of compound nouns beginning with 'ethno'. This one means something like 'the philosophy arising from a belief that the habits and thinking of one's own racial group are supreme'. The old word 'jingoism' came close to it, and 'jingoism' would certainly make a very fair substitute for 'ethnocentrism' in: '...found no significant correlation between age and ethnocentrism, a major factor in authoritarianism' (*JER*, 63/1, Sept 1969).

Ethos
Correctly, the characteristic feeling of a people or group. It is, however, often used in the sense of 'scale of values, set of guiding principles'. The understandable wish of the business community to keep its public face shining white must, unfortunately, cause us to regard its fondness for 'ethos' with a certain degree of suspicion or even cynicism, and particularly when we see a reference to 'one of the country's most successful international organisations operating within the ethos of decentralisation and profit responsibility' (*Fin Times*, 1.4.76). 'Ethos' here is a confidence trick. What is meant, and all that is meant, in the last part of the quotation is 'follow a policy of decentralisation and of making each unit of the group responsible for working to a profit'.

Eventuate
A social science synonym for 'result', the extra two syllables adding immensely to the potency of the word. So, 'what eventuated was a complex pedagogical mystique' (Cronin, 1961) and 'Competition for economic interests, power and social esteem can eventuate in community formation only if...' (*B J Soc*, June 1969).

Excellence
The state of being exceptionally good or of insisting on high standards. Often, however, it implies nothing more than 'good', as in

'Excellence in teaching means a successful series of relationships' (Rubinstein & Stoneman, 1970). This can be translated without distortion as 'Really good teaching means . . .' Universities are much given, for financial reasons, to telling the world that they are 'dedicated to the pursuit of excellence', which sounds much more refined and less worldly than 'doing our best to keep standards as high as we can in today's circumstances'.

Excess
'In excess of' means, exactly, 'more than', but for some reason it has come to be thought of as the more suitable phrase for the numerate people in science and industry to use. We therefore have, almost inevitably, 'the Data Centre, which processes in excess of 1200 jobs per week' (*D Tel*, 5.8.76).

Exclusive
Expensive. 'Elegant and exclusive ladies' fashions' (*High Life*, Oct 1976). The house which is 'situated in this exclusive cul-de-sac' (*Sun Times*, 30.11.75) reassures one about one's neighbours, and so does 'Premier 2-storey residence. Exclusive position' (*AFR*, 2.3.76). One Australian estate agent has gone the whole way with 'old-world charm recreated into uniquely exclusive landscaped units' (*Sydney Morning Herald*, 28.2.76).

Executive
An executive is a person who earns a living from administration of some kind. The aim of everyone in the business world is to become an executive, and the title is freely and generously distributed, often without a great deal of justification. One example of this usage, now common everywhere in the English-speaking world, will suffice. The city within which a hotel is situated is advertised as 'a busy commercial centre, with many business executives, from both home and abroad, passing through regularly' (Brochure of Royal County Hotel, Durham, 1976). The noun 'executive' is commonplace. The use of the word as an adjective, meaning 'high-class', is more interesting and more unpredictable. One can, for instance, buy 'Two pairs of executive slacks for only $19.55' (*Boston Sunday Globe*, 10.10.76), stay at 'this truly unique executive resort' (*The Age*, 28.2.76), live in a 'large detached executive style house' (*Times*, 1.5.76) and, more enigmatically, invest in an 'Executive fix-it. A 5″ high hammer, for making small on-the-spot repairs, plus a knife,

screw-driver, ruler and pick. All to make you the hero of the office'
(*Delta Flightline Catalogue*, 1976). Sometimes the use of 'executive' as
a mask, to cover up the fact that the job is not really as executive as
you think, is all too obvious. 'Sales Executive based at
Southampton . . . British Transport Advertising . . . are looking for
a keen salesman or saleswoman to cover territory in the Southampton
area' (*D Tel*, 18.6.76). A sales manager or sales director is a sales
executive; a salesman, alas, is not.

Exemplum
Correctly, an illustrative example, parable, symbol. Usually, however, it is interchangeable with 'example' or 'symbol', and merely
shows someone busily parading his knowledge. 'Even allowing the
importance of Teddy Roosevelt as a virility exemplum, the artists of
the Henri circle pressed their case rather hard' (*Art Journal*, Summer
1976).

Exercise
A grander word for 'use', particularly grand in the passive. 'On the
broad front of industrial activities, initiatives were exercised throughout the year' (*OTC*, 1974). This is mere word-making; the sentence is
hardly worth saying. One could surely take it for granted that an
industrial concern would use its initiative. The absurdity of saying so
is to some extent softened and hidden by putting 'initiatives were
exercised', instead of 'we used our initiative'.

Existent
The noun 'existent' is a being, creature. Few of us are likely to feel
flattered when a psychologist decides to call us an 'existent'. But it
happens all the same, 'Man is an uncharacterised and unintelligible
existent' (Ruddock, 1972). To use 'being' might bring accusations of
being unprofessional, of having strayed into the philosophical or
theological camp.

Exotic
Out-of-the-ordinary. 'Ordinary' and 'out-of-the-ordinary' are supposed to be difficult to use in the commercial field, on the grounds
that nobody wants to buy the ordinary. 'Regular' is often used for
'ordinary' nowadays—most people are happy to be thought
regular—and 'exotic' for 'out-of-the-ordinary'. So: 'Today a really
exotic holiday costs so little extra—but gives so much more' (*S Tel*,

7.11.76, referring to holidays in the Far East.)

Expect
Get. A favourite device of advertisers today is to avoid specifying the merits of one's product, but to say that they are what the purchaser would expect. 'All the quality features you would expect' (*Good Housekeeping*, Feb 1977) is typical. Since the public has no precise idea of what quality features to expect, the firm is on very safe ground. The sentence therefore means, 'All the quality features you're going to get'.

Expenses
Costs involved in doing one's work away from base. 'Expenses' is not a precise term and the understanding of what are legitimate expenses varies from company to company, with the Revenue authority quite likely to hold different views again. The term is sometimes used very loosely by those in the business world who appear to think little about the beauty and precision of English at its best. An example which does the company no credit is 'Company car is supplied with expenses' (*D Tel*, 5.12.75). The expenses, no doubt, will be found neatly packaged in the boot.

Experience
Pleasure, visit, anything that happens. 'An integrated museum experience' (*Mus News*, Jan/Feb 1974) is an example of the fashion for total living. One passes not, as before, from one hour or thought to the next, but from one experience to another. One feels one's way through life. The 'integrated museum experience' is presumably something more than a visit, a combination, perhaps, of seeing, feeling, and thinking, sparked off by a particular museum display. A house 'designed and built to enhance the experience of living' (*New Yorker*, 19.1.76) is, one feels, simply more comfortable, more convenient and more pleasant. There is nothing else a house can be, and any talk of 'enhancing the experience of living' is, to put the point bluntly, nonsense. Restaurants no longer provide food and drink; they offer, indeed guarantee, experience. One is therefore happy to pay for 'a candlelit dining experience, featuring sizzling steaks and seafood' (Brochure of Boston Marriott Hotel, 1977).

Experiential deprivation
Preventing living creatures from following their instincts and from

doing what is natural to them, as part of any experiment. One of the cleverest and most immoral of modern scientific euphemisms, guaranteed to lull most people into feeling that all is well. ' . . . the differences between beagles and wire-haired terriers in response to experiential deprivation' (Hoppe, 1970).

Experiential referent
Something of which one has experience. The educational researcher, bent on making much out of very little, may think it advisable 'to focus pupil attention on some commonly known experiential referent' (*JER*, 61/8, Apr 1968).

Experimentations
Experiments. 'A television production laboratory for experimentations in video techniques' (*Mus News*, Jan/Feb 1974). Nothing more elaborate or profound than 'experiments in video techniques'.

Explication
Unfolding, setting out. Until the 1960s, this word and the corresponding verb, 'explicate', were virtually obsolete. The social scientists and the business writers brought them back, presumably because of their imposing Latinity, causing unnecessary mystification to those outside the select circle. We are consequently in a position to be told now that 'the scenario is an explication of possibilities in the manner of exploratory forecasting' (*Business Horizons*, Aug 1975).

Exposed
In today's management jargon, to have been exposed to something is to have had experience of it. 'The position will appeal to a person who preferably but not necessarily has been exposed to the Ford range of parts and accessories' (*Sun*, Australia, 2.3.76).

Exposure
Experience. 'Candidates who have had exposure to North American and European markets' (*D Tel*, 28.1.76) is a straightforward example, and so is 'successful performance in the Brand or Product Management fields, ideally with 3 or 4 years exposure' (*Sydney Morning Herald*, 28.2.76) and 'An outstanding opportunity for experienced creative programmer (analyst with exposure to mini or large computer systems)' (*Boston Sunday Globe*, 10.10.76). But what is one to make of the opportunity for 'an MBA with prior operating

experience to enter a high exposure, Senior Financial Analyst position' (*Boston Sunday Globe*, 10.10.76)? High exposure to what? 'Exposure to presentation of financial modules' (*D Tel*, 25.2.76) is, one assumes, 'experience of presenting financial statements', but how does one extract the right meaning from 'the proper background will have been gained from insurance company exposure in a public accounting firm' (*Boston Sunday Globe*, 10.10.76)? One can only hazard a guess: 'experience of insurance company accounts, gained while working for a public accounting firm'. To confuse matters further, a completely different meaning is to be found in the estate agents' world. These people are happy to drop the tried and tested 'with sea view' or 'facing the sea', and to substitute 'complete ocean exposure' (*New Yorker*, 5.4.76).

Exquisite

Of the highest possible excellence. One doubts if this very strong adjective is always fully deserved, certainly not by 'Delta posters, exquisite additions to any room' (*Delta Flightline Catalogue*, 1976). 'Delicious meals, exquisitely prepared' (Copthorne Hotel, Gatwick, 1976 brochure) may also be something of an exaggeration.

F

Fabulous

Properly, means existing only in fairy stories, legends or dreams. 'Holidays in the fabulous Far East' (*S Tel*, 7.11.76) are all too likely to reveal to tourists that the Far East contains plenty of unpleasant features to anchor the fairy stories to reality. The travel agent's Far East, in fact, exists only in fable, so that, in this sense, the adjective 'fabulous' may be appropriate. One fears that the house in Sydney, with 'two luxury bedrooms, two bathrooms and fabulous features' (*Sydney Morning Herald*, 28.2.76) may also cause disappointment, as one attempts to track down the 'fabulous features'.

Facility

Often nowadays a synonym for 'premises'. 'Our own production facility at Barnstaple' (*D Tel*, 23.4.76) is a factory, and so is the building referred to by the company 'which has recently relocated to a new facility at Livingdon, Scotland' (*D Tel*, 17.9.76). A 'theatre facility', however, is clearly a theatre, and so 'The Museum's new theatre facility will accommodate an audience of 225' (*Mus News*, Jan/Feb 1974) does not need its 'facility' at all. 'Excellent benefits include a subsidised mortgage facility' (S *Times*, 20.6.76) uses the word correctly and sensibly. One can have a mortgage or not, as one pleases. This is what a 'facility' is, something that is available if one chooses to use it.

Facilitative
Making something easier. A drop of oil would have a facilitative effect on the opening of a door with a rusty hinge, but one might just as well say that it would make it easier and quieter to open the door. 'Facilitative' is an unnecessary word, serving only to overload a sentence. It fits well, however, into the generally foggy style and word-ballets of the pseudo-scientists, when they refer, for instance, to certain facts as having 'important facilitative effects on conceptual problems involving those dimensions' (*JEP*, 61/1, 1970).

Familiar
Commonly shown, typical. This curious use of the word takes a little getting used to. Before one makes the attempt, it is worth allowing for the possibility that the writer is floundering. 'The telephone service on King Island has been characterised by the informality familiar to such services' (Hooper, 1973) may mean 'familiar to people who use such services', or 'typical of such services'. The services themselves cannot be familiar with anything; that privilege is reserved for living creatures.

Family background
A thoroughly misleading term, to be avoided wherever possible. 'Social scientists often use the terms 'family background', 'social class', and 'economic background' almost interchangeably. We think this is a mistake, and will distinguish the concepts. By 'family background' we mean all the environmental factors that make brothers and sisters more alike than random individuals' (Jencks, 1972).

Family house
A large house. Most families are condemned to live in houses much smaller than they really need, and a very few have houses which are far too large for them. There is no British Standard for a family house,

but estate agents have their own ideas. For them, a 'family house' is always much larger than the average. The 'spacious stone family house . . . 7 bedrooms, 3 bathrooms . . . about 5 acres' (*Times*, 27.5.76) would seem a bad joke to most families.

Fantastic

Remarkable, unusual. 'Fantastic' orginally meant 'which existed only in fantasy', but during the past twenty years it has degenerated into the position of a mere superlative. Anything one likes or admires is now 'fantastic'. No particular significance is to be attached to the word in most modern contexts, such as the statement that 'this modern, up-to-date factory has seen fantastic growth since its formulation (sic) four years ago' (*D Tel*, 18.6.76). The truth, that it has expanded considerably, would seem much too tame.

Farewell

To say goodbye to. There is something not altogether friendly about the statement, 'on 11th March the Shah and Shabanon farewelled the Governor-General' (*AFAR*, 1975), almost as if they pushed the unfortunate man into his aeroplane and dared him to come back.

Far-reaching

Extensive. 'Cottage-style bungalow with far-reaching views' (*Obs*, 30.11.75). This would indeed be remarkable, if it were possible. One has always wanted to hear the views of a bungalow.

Fastidious

When applied to wine, does it mean meticulously selected; carefully made? Only living creatures can be fastidious. A wine certainly cannot, yet we find an American claim that 'our Estate and Vintage-bottled wines are perhaps the most fastidious in the world' (*New Yorker*, 5.4.76). For fastidious people, yes, but fastidious themselves, surely no.

Fast-moving

Fast-selling. In these difficult times, when the main aim of many retailers is to hold stock for as short a time as possible and to stop ordering anything that fails to sell within a few hours of being put on the shelves, 'fast-moving' is the greatest tribute that can be paid to any commodity. 'Fast-selling' is regarded as an old-fashioned term, at least in the supermarket world, one company imitating another in its use of 'fast-moving', often with other words attached, to make a standard, predictable phrase. Firm A, for instance, 'manufactures and markets a range of fast-moving convenience foods' (*D Tel*, 6.2.76), and so does Firm B, with its 'range of fast-moving convenience foods' (*S Times*, 8.2.76), which unintentionally suggests an aperient.

Fat
Possessing more of the mysterious quality, so beloved of wine merchants, known as 'body'? Of German wines: 'Those of Palatinate (sic) are fuller, fatter and darker in colour' (1976 catalogue of Lay and Wheeler, Colchester). The difficulty here is both 'fuller' and 'fatter' appear to mean much the same thing, and nobody from the trade has so far been able to suggest a definition for either of them.

Fayre
Fare. Spellings like this, 'tea shoppe' and 'ye olde' are an important part of an attempt to persuade customers that they are getting good, old-fashioned service and goods, when in fact what is being provided for them is the usual standard product. From innumerable examples, one might select: 'At this peaceful hotel, traditional fayre and comfortable accommodation will make your stay a relaxing one' (1976 brochure of Swallow Hotels group).

Featuring
With. Prepositions are too tame for the entertainment world and have to be replaced by a verb wherever possible. So we have, for example, 'a lively night club featuring excellent entertainment' (*New Yorker*, 14.1.76). Since entertainment is a central feature of a night club, the use of 'featuring' adds nothing but a scream to the advertisement. In general, 'featuring' a person—'featuring Greta Garbo'—is tolerable, 'featuring' a thing—'St. Paul's, featuring its famous dome'—is absurd.

Fertilised
Brought to fruition, developed. An art and music critics' word, which aims at bringing a feeling of biological creativity into one's comments on a work. 'These pictorial associations of Chabrier were, however, never fertilised in his music' (*Apollo*, Jan 1966). The superficial vigour of the word is bogus in this kind of context.

Fibre

Strength? A music critics' word, of doubtful value and sense, but likely to impress those within the fold who are comforted by the style. 'A performance of Mozart's K 482 Piano Concerto that was among the finest I have ever heard, beautifully pellucid yet with plenty of fibre when required' (*Classical Music*, 20.10.76).

Fiddle

Theft, swindle, usually involving one's employer's property. There is great unwillingness nowadays to use the straightforward words 'theft' and 'thief'. This unfortunate habit seems to have grown up during the 1939–45 war, when members of the Allied armed forces 'fiddled' everything in short supply, from blankets to cheese, and it has remained to poison life ever since. A lorry-driver who removes a case of whisky from a consignment and a shop assistant who transfers a tin of salmon from his employer to himself have carried out a 'fiddle', not a theft, at least as far as their personal code is concerned. The law, of course, continues to use the old-fashioned terminology. Journalists, on the whole, tend to fall in with the thieves' language and write of 'a refreshments fiddle discovered on trains operating between St. Pancras and Derby' (*Times*, 18.5.76). The three stewards convicted brought in their own inferior quality refreshments, instead of using British Rail's, and profited greatly from the transactions. They were fined heavily for 'fraud', not as the newspaper had it, for 'fiddling'.

Fight

Try hard, do one's best. In journalists' language, doctors are always 'fighting' to save the lives of patients, just as ambulances always 'rush' to the scene of an accident, and important people 'fly' to places, instead of just going there. The feeling of excitement and drama has to be built up at all costs, and the public likes the idea of devoted doctors and nurses 'fighting' fate and disaster. 'Surgeons are fighting to save the sight of an English nurse' (B.B.C. News, 22.12.75).

Fill out

Provide. The Americans and the British use the word 'fill' differently. In America one 'fills out' a form, but in Britain one 'fills it in'. The national difference is of no importance as such, but confusion can arise in international dealings, owing to the British feeling that 'filling out' conveys the sense of giving not just information but extra information. Consider, for instance, a letter written to the Secretary of the American Association of Museums, from a museum whose trustees 'have advised us that we should not fill out financial details on the operation of the museum' (*AAM Financial & Salary Survey*, 1971). This referred to a questionnaire sent out by the AAM. To an American the reply probably meant that the museum would not be giving any financial information at all, but a British reader might well feel that what was being refused was detailed information. In international correspondence it is wise, for this reason, to go for another word, such as 'provide' or 'supply'.

Film
The art of film-making. 'Film', to the cognoscenti, is made up of 'films'. The situation is somewhat complex. One has always had 'music' as the abstract and the collective meaning 'music as a whole, the art of composing and writing music', with 'literature' performing the same service for writing, and 'drama' for plays and the theatre. It is natural, therefore, that the newer art of film-making should crave an abstraction of its own. To begin with it was always 'the film', but during the 1940s 'film' took its place, at about the same time as 'dance' was replacing 'dancing', and for much the same reasons. Used in this way, 'film' is socially divisive, at least in England, and many people find the word affected, puzzling and ridiculous, adjectives which those professionally engaged in the art tend not to understand. 'I was going to teach film' (Rubinstein & Stoneman, 1970) might mean 'how to make films' or 'the appreciation of films'. Cf. Dance, Theatre.

Finalise
Brought to a conclusion, finished. There is no particular objection to its use in relation to abstractions. Arrangements, for instance, have been 'finalised' for many years and we have become more or less accustomed to the idea, although we may ourselves continue to prefer 'completed'. But sentences such as 'The theatre has still to be finalised' (*Melody Maker*, 7.2.76) are worth a fight even now. If the building is what is being referred to, 'finished' is the word, but if, as is just possible, the theatre is still in the planning stage, it could be 'plans for the theatre still have to be finalised'.

Financial
To do with money. There is a certain coyness is some circles about

using the word 'money' in public. A professor of economics once asked the present editor for a small loan in order to buy him a drink in a public house, on the grounds that he was 'temporarily short of liquidity'. 'Financial questions' in business are usually only 'money questions', although there are those who argue that 'finance' is the organisation of money, rather than money itself. A firm which is in financial trouble, however, is undoubtedly suffering from a shortage of money, and more than a semantic quibble will be needed to put its affairs in order. What does one conclude about a new industrial post which is 'oriented to the pursuit of financial improvements' (Mann, 1973)? Will the person concerned be expected to devote most of his time to raising more capital, or to changing its system of borrowing, or to reducing the need for borrowing, or what? 'Financial improvements' is an infuriating phrase, which suggests everything and says nothing.

Financial Services
Money-lending. 'Bowmaker, one of Britain's leading finance houses, specialising in financial services for industry' (*D Tel*, 22.1.76). See also previous item.

Fine
Good, expensive, comfortable. Americans, and by imitation, Australians, find it far from easy to use the word 'good' in many contexts where the British appear to have no trouble. The distinction seems to be that in Britain anything can be good, from small boys to restaurants, whereas in America 'good' tends to be reserved for occasions where some question of morality or behaviour is involved. Within the past ten years, the American practice has begun to spread in Britain, to the delight of some and the annoyance of many. 'For the name of the fine store in your city, please write . . .' (*New Yorker*, 25.8.75); '. . . in fine men's stores throughout the country' (*D Tel*, 30.4.76); 'Barclay is fine living' (*Sydney Morning Herald*, 28.2.76. Barclay is an apartment block.); 'We have been building fine houses for more than 20 years' (*The Age*, 28.2.76).

Finesse
Delicacy, refinement, purity. In recent years the word has acquired the further sense of 'perfection, top quality' and this, added to the existing meanings, sometimes causes difficulties of interpretation. There is no great problem about 'six clarets of real quality and finesse'

(1976 catalogue of Ellis Son & Vidler Ltd., Hastings and London), or 'The finesse of the fruit acid balance is indicative of the wine's superior quality' (*The Bulletin*, 19.10.74), but this taxes one's imagination and ingenuity a little more: 'K.L.M. offers first-class passengers something special. Royal Class. All the first-class facilities you expect and more. Finesse.' (Toronto *Globe and Mail*, 6.10.76). 'Finesse' in this context is probably just an impressively French-sounding assembly of letters. One is not supposed to ask what it means. After being told that Royal Class is even better than first-class, one is expected simply to pay up and be grateful.

Finish
The final taste left in the mouth? Another inexplicable and tantalising wine trade word. 'A sweetish, fruity bouquet with a very full flavour and charming finish' (*Times*, 29.5.76).

Finished
Covered with. Used, for example, to describe the very superior paintwork of very superior motor-cars. A Rolls-Royce or Bentley is never painted grey; it is finished in grey or another distinguished colour. '1922 Bentley Corniche 2-door saloon. Finished in Seychelles blue with beige hide upholstery' (*D Tel*, 2.2.77).Far from superior restaurants have caught onto the trick and advertise such dishes as 'fillet of beef, cut in strips, cooked in butter and finished in a sherry cream sauce' (T.H.F. menu, Coventry, Feb 1976). In both cases, 'finished' has the implication of 'the last final touch of perfection to something which is already of the highest imaginable quality'. One can only hope that the reality matches up to the idea.

Firm
(a) not inclined to melt in the mouth, not very sweet? An untranslatable wine merchant's word. 'The Duquesa is firm and nutty' (1976 catalogue of Ellis Son and Vidler Ltd., Hastings and London). (b) Strong. Much used in business in combination with 'motivation', as, for example, 'engineers with a firm motivation to an industrial career' (*S Times*, 30.5.76). All this means is the old-fashioned, but still perfectly serviceable, 'engineers who have decided on an industrial career'.

Firmness
See (a) in the previous item. 'Firmness' is even more frequently

found than 'firm' in wine language, but a comparison of many examples of its usage has brought us no closer to the meaning. We include two quotations for their poetry alone. 'One that combines an inner sinewy firmness with a beautiful bouquet is a Coteaux du Layon moelleux' (*Times*, 3.7.76), and 'The 1973 Domaine de la Folie, Clos de Bellecroix, has appeal and firmness' (*Times*, 21.2.76).

Flow

An estate agent's word, meaning that one room leads into another, with or without the intervention of doors. Usually unnecessary, as in 'Five inter-communicating reception rooms provide a flow of space to satisfy any individual needs' (*Times*, 27.5.76).

Fluency

Ability to handle easily. The movement from fluency in a foreign language to fluency in figures is not difficult to follow, but the parallel is far from exact and gives anyone who worries about words a considerable jolt. When a person is fluent in a language, the words flow from his tongue, but it is unlikely that figures flow from even the most skilled statistician in the same way, either from the mouth or on paper. What is intended here is not 'fluency with', but 'the application of', or 'the use of'. 'Fluency' is a bright idea gone wrong. But the affectation is common enough, both with the noun and the adjective. One firm, for instance, required 'an experienced senior sales executive, who is fluent in the use of media research' (*S Times*, 20.6.76). The use of media research, one regrets to have to inform them, is not a language.

Forefront to

Outstanding in? 'Forefront to' is a barbarism by any standard. There are two possible, but conflicting meanings to a sentence such as, 'Our Engineering Division is forefront to the development of structures, equipment and techniques for the North Sea' (*D Tel*, 1.7.76). It must be either ' . . .in the forefront of the development of . . .' or 'face to face with the development of . . .'. The first is more probable, but the second, given such a mishandled sentence, is quite possible.

Forever

Meant to last for ever. There are, however, two shades of meaning which are easily confused. Diamonds, we are repeatedly told by jewellers and diamond merchants, are 'for ever'. This means 'I will think of you for ever, since you gave me the ring containing this diamond', and 'Diamonds never wear out. They are everlasting.' If we are concerned with diamonds, the inter-mingling of the two meanings does no harm at all, but with other commodities, such as clothes, it is less fortunate. 'The basic suit shape is forever' (*Signature*, Jan/Feb, 1976) is all very well, provided 'forever' is not too long. Cf. Classic.

Formulation
(a) Possibility, theory. An unwanted social science word. 'While positive, the moderate magnitude of the correlations, however, leads to the formulation that parents are only one of the many agents of such socialisation' (Hyman, 1969). (b) Establishment. The attempt to make 'formulation' a more impressive alternative to 'formation' is more widespread than it should be in the business world, which is already enamoured of 'formulas'. 'This modern, up-to-date factory has seen fantastic growth since its formulation four years ago' (*D Tel*, 18.6.76), i.e. 'since it was set up'. A factory is not 'formed' or 'formulated'.

Forward
Coming forward to meet one's ear, one's eye or one's nose? A critics' word. 'Yet full and forward as was the sound' (*Times*, 12.7.76. Alfred Brendel playing Beethoven); 'The Branaire (a wine) is very forward and fragrant' (Times, 17.7.76).

Four-square
Honest? With an absence of showiness? A music-critic's word. Of three pieces performed at a concert given by a pianist, we are told that they 'were all of them a shade careful, four-square, dramatically unfocussed' (*Fin Times*, 7.2.77).

Fraction
Less. When advertisers claim, as they often do, that their goods or services are obtainable at 'a fraction of the cost' of what other people offer, they are indulging in an old-established confidence trick, because a fraction is anything less than a whole number. It may be a fiftieth, it may be 99/100. The implication is always, however, that the fraction is very small. A firm of furniture manufacturers, for example, can tempt buyers with 'the prime upholstered look, but at only a fraction of the cost' (*D Tel*, 16.1.77).

Fragrance

The up-to-date word for 'Perfume' With the attempts to sell perfume
to men, in the guise of after-shave lotions and other aliases which
deceive nobody but are, in more senses than one, face-saving, a new
word was essential. 'Fragrance' appeared at just the right moment.
'Lentheric Morny Limited, famous for Tweed and Onyx fragrances'
(*D Tel*, 6.2.76).

Fraternity

People one dislikes or despises, one's political enemies. Much used by
Communists and other members of the extreme Left. ' . . . the
advertising fraternity, ever sensitive to public moods' (Matthews,
1975).

Free speech

What the group to which one belongs wants and intends to say. What
anyone else wants to say is dangerous reactionary nonsense and it is
the duty of all good citizens to shout the speaker down immediately.
'Free speech is used as a shorthand term for the range of student
demands of freedom of political activity and social action, as well as
free speech in the narrow sense' (Teodori, 1969).

Free World

The non-socialist countries. A term very well understood, although
often challenged, in the Free World itself, but difficult to translate
into any of the languages of the socialist countries, except by the term
'the capitalist world', which captures the economics, but not the
freedom. 'The Free World' has suffered from serious overuse, often in
contexts where it is not appropriate, such as 'the finest jewelry stores
of the Free World' (*New Yorker*, 22.3.76).

Fresh fruit

Canned fruit, 'fresh' meaning that the fruit was fresh when it was put
into the tin, or that the tin has been freshly opened. 'A snow-white
mountain of cottage cheese, with center filled with fresh fruit
sections' (Menu of Merrimack Valley Motor Inn, Mass., 1974).
Although often on the menu, fresh fruit, in the European sense, is, in
fact, almost unobtainable in American restaurants, being shunned as
unprofitable, wasteful and unhygienic.

Friendly
Welcoming, smiling. American business, and by gradual imitation, that of other countries, sets great store by superficial, welcome-stranger friendliness. Hotels stress their friendly atmosphere and friendly staff, companies assure prospective recruits that they are friendly places to work in, politicians go to enormous trouble to prove how friendly they are. It all means very little and after half a century of it we need to redefine 'friendly' as 'smiling'. The prize for the most nonsensical piece of friendliness must undoubtedly go to United Airlines for the brilliant arrogance of 'Fly the friendly skies of United' (*Washington Star*, 19.10.76, and many thousands of other occasions.)

Fulfil
Meet, use to the full, gain satisfaction from. These senses are often confused, with a similar effect on the reader or listener. People nowadays expect a fulfilling job in which they can fulfil themselves and something of this may have been in the mind of the company which wanted someone who 'must be capable of fulfilling a senior co-ordinating or managerial role' (*S Tel*, 4.1.76). On the other hand all the person may have been required to do was to fill the role.

Full stop
The brooding point. The gap which the reader fills with his own thoughts and fantasies, so benefitting both himself and the advertiser, or so the theory goes. Continous prose offers no such opportunities. 'You chat with your neighbour. Discover he's an Artist. Author. Diplomat. Banker.' (*Qantas* brochure, 1976), or 'So select those that you like best . . . Are most comfortable. Require the least care' (also *Qantas* brochure, 1976). This approach does not always have the desired effect. Some people switch off before the fantasy magic has a chance to work, but industry and the advertising agencies never lose heart. 'Bovis will soon be building nine completely different house designs. Several of them available in two different styles.' (*D Tel*, 28.1.76).

Fun
It is extremely difficult to define 'fun'. 'Amusement' is not quite right, nor is 'pleasure', 'enjoyment' or 'frolicking'. To qualify as 100 per cent fun, the mind must not be operating at all −fun cannot have

an intellectual content—inhibition must be at a minimum, and there should ideally be a fair amount of noise, proved by the existence of a special kind of fun, known as 'quiet fun'. The ideal total fun animals are small children and adults in the earlier stages of intoxication. What one person sees as fun may be utter hell to another, so that the word is a poor communication-tool. 'Revelling in the fun life of a glamorous capital' (*Qantas* brochure, 1976) will be an enticing invitation to some and a dreadful threat to others, especially when the precise ingredients of the fun life are spelt out, as they very rarely are.

Function

Job, department, service. One of the three most loved words of today's industrial world. A brief anthology will indicate its clown-like versatility. ' . . . the successful applicant should have had experience in the accounting function' (*D Tel*, 5.2.76), i.e. 'accounting experience'; '. . . will be responsible for developing an effective training function' (*N Soc*, 4.12.75), i.e. 'an effective training department'; 'a professional approach to the buying function' (*S Times*, 16.11.75), i.e. 'to buying'; 'The job is located at the Group's centralised accounting function at Burnley, Lancashire' (*D Tel*, 18.3.76), i.e. 'centralised accounting department'; 'The successful candidate will initially provide a total personnel function to the Sales, Marketing, Finance and Administration areas' (*D Tel*, 16.9.76), i.e. 'a total personnel service'. A function can have breadth as well as length and depth, as one sees from 'Virtually no limitations will be placed on the scope of the function' (*S Times*, 27.6.76). A ten-year ban on 'function' would be of great value.

Funding

Finding capital. A useful word, often spoilt by a foolish context, and especially by making it the second half of a compound noun, e.g. 'If you have a proven record of getting customer funding for major projects' (*S Times*, 30.5.76). Who is providing the funding for whom is this case? Is the money coming from the customer, or going to the customer?

Futuristic

Belonging to the future, rather than to the present. The main difficulty from the reader's point of view is to decide whether the author is using the word disparagingly or approvingly. There are many shades of attitude between these two extremes. What is baldly labelled 'futuristic' may be thought of as ludicrous, unintelligible, fashionable or threatening. Anything one does not understand can very conveniently be described as 'futuristic'. The following examples illustrate the possibilities. 'The main hall is elegantly lit by some futuristic use of glazed and scaffolded ceilings' (*High Life*, June 1976). (The sentence refers to the new Tegel Airport, Berlin.); 'It unlocks the secrets of such chillingly futuristic word as 'cryonics' (*New Yorker*, 14.6.76. The reference is to a new dictionary.)

G

Game-indulged
Allowed by fond parents to have too many games? ' . . . the game-like quality of the task was more apparent to these game-indulged children' (*JEP*, 60/2, 1969). The difficulty here is to decide whether the children are considered to have had an excessive amount of play, or simply a great deal of play. And is there any difference between 'games' and 'play'? What is a game?

Gang
A group of people hostile to one's own creed '. . . trailing behind the Trotskyite anti-Communist gangs of thugs' (Lipset, 1971). The association is with a gang of criminals or hooligans, rather than with a gang of hardworking, law-abiding dockers or railwaymen.

Garden
A meaningless word, beloved of the restaurant industry. At the middling, pretentious level peas are always 'garden peas', to be served with 'roast Surrey chicken' and 'baby carrots'. So, 'followed by a garden salad' (*Globe and Mail*, Toronto, 7.10.76) the ingredients of which, one can be perfectly sure came from a distant field, not a nearby garden. The essence of the swindle is the attempt to persuade urban people that they are eating something picked that very morning, with the dew fresh on it, from a garden at the back of the restaurant. The sad and curious aspect of it all is the way in which the innocent customers, ripe for cheating, play the restaurant's game and repeat these phrases word for words as they give their order, 'garden peas', and 'baby carrots', as if there were some magic in the name. Ask

for 'peas' and 'carrots' and the spell would be broken, or maybe one would get no food at all.

Garnished

With. 'Butter-fried, garnished with soft roe, lemon and tomato' (T.H.F. menu, Coventry, Feb 1976). The whole idea is to make the gastric juices flow copiously before the food comes, in the hope that they may not dry up completely once the meal has arrived. Nothing could better illustrate the difference between the French and the American attitude to food. In a French restaurant one eats the food, and the menu, which contains hardly any adjectives, is a mere index to what is on offer. In an American restaurant, where the food may nourish but seldom gives much pleasure, except to the starving, one eats the menu and wallows in its prose-poetry.

Generalist-integrator

A non-specialist, high in the power-structure of the corporation, with ears everywhere and with a finger in every pie, a general, in fact. 'The largely humanist-oriented intellectual dissenter is being rapidly displaced by the generalist-integrators, who become in effect house ideologues for those in power' (*Encounter*, Jan 1968).

Generalivity

The opposite, presumably, of 'specialism'; breadth of knowledge and outlook. '. . . what factors may be assigned weight in the social environment for harnessing the forces of generalivity and wisdom so important for the senior manager's role' (Rapoport, 1970). The whole sentence is worth careful study as a piece of ridiculous verbiage.

Generalisability

General relevance, ability to fit into a general theory. '. . . increases the generalizability of this finding' (*JER*, 63/6, Feb 1970), i.e. 'makes it more likely that this discovery will lead towards some general conclusions'.

Generic

All belonging to the same broad category. A term much used by social scientists and those employed in the welfare services. 'To carry a generic case-load' (*N Soc*, 4.12.75) means that all a case-worker's clients have roughly the same kind of problem.

Generous
(a) Slightly above average. 'Generous holiday entitlement' (*D Tel*, 27.11.75); 'Generous relocation expenses' (*S Times*, 30.11.75). 'Generous relocation expenses' is almost a compound noun. It is rare to find the offer made in any other form. It is a clever word to use, because nobody knows what to measure it against, in order to decide whether it is generous or not. It is neither large nor small, but some satisfactory measure in between. The American restaurateur's 'generous scoop of ice-cream' relies on the same technique. (b) Full-bodied, on the heavy side. A wine-word which yields nothing to careful examination. Rhône wines, for example, are described as 'soft, generous wines with great depth of flavour' (1976 catalogue of Lay and Wheeler, Colchester).

Gentle
Not so sharp on the palate? With fewer bubbles to the cubic inch? A pleasant-sounding, meaningless wine-word. 'It is gentler and more delicately enticing, a wine to please those who really do know about champagne' (*Times*, 19.6.76).

Gentleman
Person with substantial income and the tastes to go with it. 'An eye-catching gentleman's weekend trouser' (*New Yorker*, 27.9.76). This is, of course, a snob advertisement, indicating partly by the use of the word 'gentleman' and partly by 'trouser', in the singular, which is very curious, not to say affected. The advertisement is not quite right, however. One has always understood that 'eye-catching' clothes were for the vulgar and plebeian. A gentleman's wardrobe impresses by its reticence and understatement; of course, it could be the gentleman and not the trouser that is eye-catching.

Georgian
Either, built during the regins of George I, II, III and IV, or in imitation of such architecture. Only the first is strictly entitled to the name; the rest is neo-Georgian or bogus Georgian. But this style, so popular with estate agents and the middle-classes, is long-suffering. A high proportion of the houses advertised as Georgian bear little relation to the real thing. A photograph of a '5 bed Georgian style residence' (*S Tel*, 22.1.76) shows something remarkably un-Georgian, in its proportions, fenestration or roof. Only the debased modern versions of one or two Georgian details are there – small-

paned windows and flat-topped porch, with white painted pillars. To many people nowadays, there are only three possible architectural styles, Tudor, Georgian and Ultra-Modern. Every house must be one or the other.

Gestural

Normally reflects the belief that speech is simply another form of bodily gesture. In artistic circles, however, something rather different seems intended, although quite what that is it is often difficult to decide. When one reads of 'the gestural tactics of Abstract-Expressionism' (Russell and Gablik, 1969) and learns that Fried found these sculptures 'abstract and gestural' (Walker, 1975), how is one to interpret the word 'gestural'? Is one to understand that the artists concerned made gestures like monkeys or the dumb, but were unable to communicate with anyone? Or that formalised gestures are at the centre of their work and style? Are we eavesdropping on one artist talking to another, or are these writers making any attempt to communicate with a lay public?

Glaring

Startling, crude. The difficulty of trying to explain one art in terms of another is always present. To find words adequate to describe the appeal of music, painting and food to the senses demands not only the full resources of the senses, but also verbal artists capable of handling such resources. Critics are committed to trying to explain what they feel as well as what they think, but, in terms of communication, the results are not often satisfactory, although as pieces of writing they may be competent and occasionally striking. 'A Brahms *Tragic Overture* in glaring primary colours had sounded a shade rigid' (*Classical Music*, 20.10.76) is a good example of a critic trying very hard to find yet another way of saying that the performance was lacking in subtlety and, assuming the message has reached us, we can sympathise.

Goal

Aim. The use of the sporting metaphor 'goal' is universal throughout the English-speaking world. This would do no great harm, if writers would bear in mind that one can do only two things with a goal. One can either score it or attain it. Most of the tasks we are asked to perform in connexion with goals are either curious or impossible, so that in many cases meaning flies out of the window. 'Nation's goals at stake' (*Herald Tribune*, 28.1.76) is an example. In the days of bear-baiting, a bear was at the stake and therefore under challenge from the dogs attacking him, but the idea of a goal in the same position taxes the imagination somewhat. What is presumably meant is that there is some doubt as to whether the country will reach its goals. 'We won't meet the goals we have as a nation'(*Herald Tribune*, 28.1.76) is better, but not quite right. One meets a challenge or a demand, not a goal. The trouble with 'goal' as a metaphor is that it is only half-dead, a dangerous condition for a metaphor to be in. Cf. Target.

God bless
Goodbye. A nauseating, sentimental phrase, with the Almighty not in any way involved, much used as a farewell by not noticeably religious people, especially in the entertainment industry. 'Good night and God bless' (Mike Yarwood, B.B.C. 1, 7.2.76). Since the phrase is also used by parents before their small children go to sleep, it has a distinctly patronising flavour when aimed at adults.

Good
Large enough to accommodate a double bed and to allow people to walk round it. An estate agent's word. '3 good bedrooms' (*B & WEC*, 2.12.75). For some reason the word is only applied to bedrooms. One never speaks of a 'good dining room' or 'good bathroom'.

Gourmet
An adjective used to glorify a large, expensive meal, particularly in North America and Australia. 'That special, old-fashioned lodge life with gourmet meals' (*New Yorker*, 22.12.75); 'Superb gourmet dining' (Toronto *Globe and Mail*, 31.1.76); 'Sunny balconies, gourmet kitchens, beautiful bathrooms' (*Sydney Morning Herald*, 28.2.76). A gourmet might be defined as a person with a sensitive and informed appreciation of the delicacies of the table, and a gourmet meal as a meal suitable to be placed before such connoisseur. It is doubtful, to say the least, if one per cent of the establishments offering such fare have any business to do so.

Graceful
Such as would not offend the delicate sensibilities of a lady? From the secret world of wine writers. 'Sichel's report describes them as "soft and graceful, with no edges"' (*Times*, 31.7.76); 'Graceful yet loaded

with flavour, this is a middle-weight Meursault' (Hedges & Butler's *Wine News*, Aug 1976).

Gracious

Suggesting the pre-1914 world of money and privilege, when only the best was good enough for the rich. Cruise passengers are assured of 'the gracious service of a superbly trained Italian crew' (*New Yorker*, 13.12.75), which means, assuming it to be true, that the crew were well-trained, immaculately turned out, immediately attentive to milord's slightest whim, and unfailingly polite, all of which is possible but unlikely. Prospective purchasers of a house in central London are tempted by the thought of a 'gracious staircase leading to a large landing' (*Times*, 23.3.75), with daydreams of following a gracious Edwardian beauty walking graciously down the stairs. The situation in Australia is slightly different and the successful man in search of a house more suited to his affluence and position in society is offered 'one of the most gracious homes in Sydney' (*Sydney Morning Herald*, 28.2.76), which turns out to be a flat-roofed modern house, with no Edwardian suggestions whatever. A house in Canada is 'designed for gracious entertaining' (*The Citizen*, Ottawa, 8.10.76), a catalogue offers something very special to 'those who prefer a wine to have the rounded, gracious style' (*Times*, 19.6.76) and, most enigmatic of all, is the guarantee of 'all the intrinsic charm of gracious office living' (*Axiom*, Oct 1976). There is, on reflexion, no reason why an office should not be gracious, but 'gracious office living', with all the phrase involves, would not seem to be within the reach of many employees of even the largest concern.

Graciousness

The essential quality of almost any hotel or restaurant catering for the rich. 'The Athenaeum Hotel is designed to reflect the graciousness of comfortable English living' (1976 brochure of this London hotel). The implication is that the hotel provides its visitors with an environment indistinguishable from the one they are used to at home. If this is true, the English upper classes must be living on a rather grander scale than one suspected, with taxation as it is. It could be, however, that it is yesterday's graciousness and comfortable English living that is being suggested, rather than today's.

Grainy

In correct usage means granular, like the surface grain of wood. To suggest that a singer's voice has this quality does not, to the uninitiated, seem very flattering, but the word is used by music critics and must presumably mean something to them. 'Robert Lloyd's firm, slightly grainy bass' (*Classical Music*, 20.10.76) has, one supposes, something crinkled about it, and it is worth spending a little time, but not too much, wondering what that might sound like, and whether it would be in any way painful, either to the singer or to the members of his audience.

Grandeur

Grand, but possibly more so. 'He boldly dreamed of grandeur schemes' (*Con*, Vol 163, Sept/Dec 1966). This clumsy phrase does not mean 'dreamed of grandeur', at least not for himself. The reference is to an architect and landscape designer who saw it to be his business to provide an atmosphere of grandeur for his clients, in which they might have thoughts appropriate to their wealth and position in society. It is a pleasant, and by no means un-modern idea. California and Texas are full of grandeur schemes, just as New York State and Rhode Island were in their day.

Grass-root

At the level of real action, where something is of personal importance, where ideas grow. The trade unions are as fond of talking about 'grass-root opinion' as they are of 'shop-floor feeling' and both mean very much the same, the sentiments and prejudices of rank-and-file members. 'Information supplied to the C.B.I. indicates that there is still firm grass-root support for sandwich courses' (*Sandwich Courses*, 1976) presents a problem. The Confederation of British Industry is a national organisation with its headquarters in London. Are its 'grass-roots' therefore to be found in the provinces, where most of its ordinary members are, and does the 'grass-root' support mentioned here come from firms who sponsor or take sandwich-course students? Or is it possible that these 'grass-roots' people have no direct connexion with the C.B.I. at all, and that the C.B.I. is merely reporting a situation which it finds to exist among potential sandwich-course students and those likely to employ and train them?

Great

Very good. The Americans have nearly, but not quite, worked this poor word to death, in their need to avoid using the word 'good'.

Some of the best-known examples have become nearly proverbial, or at least proverbial jokes, without any widespread effort to discover what they mean. 'Hilton knows great service means great people' (*New Yorker*, 27.10.75, out of hundreds) has hit the eyes, if not the understanding, of newspaper and magazine readers across the world for a long time now. The copy-writer earned his money here. What was required was a word meaning 'first-class' without having the élitist associations of first-class, since Hilton, becomingly modest, do not claim to be in the first rank of hotels and attract a large number of visitors who, as one's personal observation confirms, are not first-class by any standard. 'Great' does the job to perfection, suggesting grins, backslapping and Rotary, as well as a certain degree of competence and reliability. 'Great', above all, gives the impression that everybody at a Hilton hotel, the staff included, are enjoying themselves every minute of the day, which is assuredly an exaggeration. The same considerations apply to 'Montreal Bonaventure. Excellent meeting facilities. Great shopping' (Toronto *Globe and Mail*, 7.10.76). The following example, however, shows commercial over-enthusiasm of a different kind. A sherry is advertised as 'a very fine dry Amontillado, beautifully balanced, with a full, powerful flavour that shows great age' (1976 catalogue of Lay and Wheeler, Colchester). How old, one may ask, is 'great'? 15 years is a great age for a dog, but not for an elephant. No date is given, but it would be surprising if this wine were more than 20 years old, although 30 is possible. Most people would probably expect it to be at least 50, 80 or even more. This particular wine would, in that respect, disappoint them.

Greening
Buds and new green shoots, Spring. Its appropriateness in many commercial contexts is questionable, but the advertisers are game enough for anything. 'Move into this greening new world. The natural world of Alliage' (*Vogue*, Dec 1975. Alliage is a perfume.) If ever anything was not natural, it is perfume in a bottle, but the idea is to give the customer the feeling that she is walking down a country lane in spring, with the first flowers in bloom in the hedgerows, the hawthorn covered in fresh leaves and the birds singing. All this pleasant fancy springs from 'greening', which is clearly a most useful word, if a trifle misleading.

Grip
Assassin-like clutch at the throat? A wine word. 'The Westhofener

Steingrube is rich and more expansive with good finishing grip'
(Hedges & Butler's *Wine News*, Aug 1976). Does it leave the drinker
in a choking condition, squeeze his palate as the last drop goes down
the throat, or simply cause one to say in admiration, 'The people who
made that have certainly got hold of something'?

Grooming
For cutting one's finger and toenails. 'Rounded-tip grooming
scissors' (*Montreal Star*, 16.10.76). Grooming scissors command a
higher price and have more prestige altogether than nail-scissors, to
which no refined person can now bring himself to refer.

Guest
The customer of a hotel or restaurant. The use of the word 'guest'
allows the pleasant fiction that one is in the proprietor's own house,
and that there will be no question of a bill to pay afterwards. The
word has its pitfalls, however, as in the description of the tag of a bill
as a 'guest receipt' (The Magic Pan Crêperie, Boston, 10.10.76)

Guinea-pig
Properly, an animal used for scientific experiments, and by extension,
someone who forms part of an experiment of any kind. The early
owners of a new model of car are 'guinea-pigs', with whose obliging
help the manufacturer finds out what is wrong with the design. So,
too, are the people in a tour-company's first groups at a hotel they
have never used before. But some examples are more graceful than
others. 'She was picked as the guinea-pig for a facelift' (*Fin Times*,
14.1.76) is one of the others.

H

Habit hierarchies
A regular pattern of doing one thing before another. 'The tendency
of individuals to form stimuli-response habit hierarchies . . .' (*Educ &
Soc Sci*, 1/3, Oct 1969). This means, for those not inclined to attempt
a translation for themselves, that anybody is likely to have his own
pattern of doing first this, then that, and then the other, when a
particular set of circumstances causes him to do so. If the stimulus is

having tripe and onions recommended by a waiter, one person's habit hierarchy may be to shudder, say no thank you, and look through the menu for something else, whereas another, differently constituted, might smile broadly and greedily, announce that he liked nothing better, and wait impatiently until the delicacy arrived. All this from four very impersonal looking jargon-nouns.

Hair-sculpture

Hairdressing. Whether the process is described as 'hair sculpture' or 'hairdressing', the process is exactly the same and so are the tools, a comb and scissors, not, as one might think, a mallet and chisel. 'Hair-sculpture for men and women' (*What's on in Ottawa*, Oct 1976). 'Hair-sculpture', carried out by a qualified hair-sculptor, no less, should, of course, cost more than mere 'hairdressing', and does.

Hands-on

Close to the centre of power, in daily contact with the people who make the big occasions? 'This managerial hands-on position' (*Boston Sunday Globe*, 10.10.76). It is only fair to say that three management-school teachers of long experience offered these three different explanations of what 'hands-on' meant: in daily contact with the most important issues; concerned with practical matters not theory; responsible for policy-making. The reader remains baffled.

Happy hour

A social get-together, usually organised in connexion with some religious body. A 'happy-hour' usually lasts for more than an hour, a fact which those invited to one would do well to bear in mind. 'Special Happy Hour, 5 p.m.–8 p.m. All drinks 50 c. ea.' (*Air Travel Journal*, 15.10.76). In a totally non-religious context, however, 'happy hour' is often used to mean the drinking period before real drinking begins, say between 5.00 and 6.00 p.m.

Hard-nosed

Unemotional, insensitive. 'The hard-nosed fields of management or science' (*Social Work Today*, 3/10, 10.8.72). Social work would presumably be a soft-nosed profession, although the term has not so far been discovered. The word was originally applied to a bull, and still is. A hard-nosed bull is one who does not respond when the ring through the cartilage of his nose is twitched by the person leading him on a pole or rope. The implication is that managers and scientists are

similarly insensitive, interested only in facts and indifferent to the
needs and feelings of the people with whom they come into contact.
It is a treasured myth, with no more truth about it than 'the soft-nosed
field of social work'.

Harmonistic

Tending to agree or harmonise with. 'The harmonistic tinge of the
more extreme versions of the "end of ideology" thesis' (Mann, 1973).
This means that all ideologies tend to come to the same conclusion if
one follows them through to the end, which is an interesting thought,
very badly expressed in the slab of jargon quoted above.

Haunting

Which stays in the mind after one has finished listening to it, reading
it, looking at it. A critic's term, used mainly and obligingly for the
benefit of publishers' advertisements, as in 'this haunting story'. The
word has become a major cliché, and little attention is paid to it for
this reason. 'There is a haunting quality about her writing' (*Times*,
7.8.76) comes from a critic who could find nothing better to say and
was temporarily short of adjectives. No novelist is likely to object to
his work being described as 'haunting'. It is a word which saves a lot
of trouble and may win credit for both the novelist and the critic.

Haute cuisine

In France, cooking with the best ingredients, regardless of cost;
outside France, vaguely French and always expensive cooking. There
are very few restaurants where the phrase means more than this.
'Superb haute cuisine menu, designed to meet the demands of the
discerning businessman' (*High Life*, Oct 1976). The fact that the same
restaurant has an 'erotic floor show every half hour' suggests that the
devotion to haute cuisine is not entirely single-minded. The meaning
of 'cuisine' does not always appear to be well understood. 'The à la
carte menu lists a delicious selection of haute cuisine dishes, all served
with a panache that only the finest cuisine can equal' (Swallow Hotels
brochure, 1975).

Headquartered

Has its headquarters. 'His firm is headquartered in New York' (*New
Yorker*, 15.9.75); 'The Cogar Foundation, Inc., headquartered in
Herkimer, New York . . .' (*JER*, 63/6, Feb 1970). There is no doubt
about the meaning in either of these two examples. The point of

interest is the snobbery which forces a company to say that it is 'headquartered' somewhere, instead of that it 'has its headquarters'. The difference nowadays is very great and splits one kind of institution off from another. 'Progressive', 'modern' concerns are 'headquartered', solid, old-established ones 'have their headquarters in'. If one wishes to be thought the other, the recipe is simple.

Head up
To head. The Americanism, with the preposition, is felt to be more vigorous, more 'managerial', than the Anglicism without it. The American form is gaining ground very fast in Britain, and the day cannot be far away when a new intensive will be needed to strengthen and modernise 'head up'. Meanwhile, ' . . . to head up the existing functions' (*D Tel*, 6.2.76); ' . . . a Technical Manager to head-up our Quality Control and Development team' (*D Tel*, 27.11.75).

Health care
Medical, surgical and pharmaceutical. 'Johnson and Johnson is one of the U.K.'s leading health care manufacturers' (*D Tel*, 25.3.76); 'International opportunities in the health care industry' (*Sun Times*, 25.4.76). A high proportion of 'health care', i.e. the work with which doctors are concerned, is related to ill-health care. The manufacturers would all have been bankrupt years ago if they had been forced to earn a living with those in robust health. There is very little money to be made from people who are well.

Heaping
A restaurant keeper's word, usually a poor description of the facts. 'Four heaping scoops of vanilla ice-cream, ladled over with hot fudge' (Howard Johnson menu, Dallas, 1973) were no more than four scoops of vanilla ice-cream, covered with fudge sauce. The 'heaping' and the 'ladled' were poetic licence.

Heavy-duty
Strong. Used particularly of clothing. 'A heavy-duty elastic waist-band' (*Washington Post*, 18.10.76). A particular kind of strength is indicated here, the ability to withstand the fearful tension across the waist of a corpulent man. 'Heavy-duty' is a very polite way of saying this.

Heavyweight
Of exceptional ability and experience. 'The position calls for a
heavyweight engineer' (*D Tel*, 6.5.76). There is a certain suggestion
of masculine strength and determination about the word, which
might well deter women from applying for the job and so constitute
an effective sex barrier, without the need actually to say that women
would not be considered.

Heirloom
Worth keeping. 'Books of heirloom quality. Each of these superb
volumes will be a masterpiece of the bookbinder's art–fully bound in
genuine leather and lavishly ornamented in 22 karat gold' (*Boston
Sunday Globe*, 10.10.76); 'This handsome hierloom to be . . .'
(*Washington Star*, 17.10.76). In a society and age where possessions
are not expected to last a long time and are always likely to be
replaced by something felt to be better and more up-to-date, the
appeal of just one or two 'heirloom' items which do not have to suffer
this fate is bound to be considerable. They give a quality of
permanence and stability to one's life, which might otherwise be
lacking. They may or may not be handed on eventually to one's
descendants–too much attention should not be paid to this aspect of
the word 'heirloom'–but their presence in the house makes the
owner feel good.

Helping
Alleviating the lot of people in difficulties. Usually applied to some
form of social service. A welfare worker and a clergyman would
think of themselves as members of 'the helping professions'. There is
some competition to be thought of under this heading. A member of
its staff said, 'The A.A. (Automobile Association) is a helping
organisation' (Course in Bristol, 10.5.73) and it is difficult to
challenge his assertion. To come to the help of a member whose car
has broken down is indeed a helpful and friendly act, even if one has
paid a subscription to obtain it. One has to be careful of stretching the
definition of 'the helping professions' too far, however, or the police
and the fire service and no doubt many other services and occupations
would find themselves included, so offending the pride of the welfare
workers, nurses and other founder-members of the club. One will not
find the police or fire service mentioned in *Florida Studies in the
Helping Professions* (reviewed in *JER*, 64/2, Sept 1970). Most authors

seem to assume that their readers know which jobs are included in the definition and that there is no need to specify them. 'Not all those in the helping professions lack an empirical basis of some kind' (Ruddock, 1972).

Hide
Leather. The most expensive motor-cars traditionally have their seats covered with hide, not leather, which means the same but sounds more expensive. '1972 Shadow. Regal Red with black hide interior' (*Times*, 21.2.77).

High-achievement
Hard-working, getting good results. 'This position is a unique opportunity for a high-achievement career-oriented individual' (*The Age*, 28.2.76). A 'high-achievement, career-oriented individual' is one who is totally devoted to his work, with no thought in his head except of how to make steadily increasing profits for his employer and a higher salary for himself; a monster, in fact.

High achiever
A person whose productivity is very high, and who aims at making it steadily higher. Firms are much given nowadays to advertising for someone who 'would be considered a high achiever and self-starter' (Toronto *Globe and Mail*, 31.1.76).

High calibre
High quality. The comparison is with guns, but the adjective is wrong. The calibre, the width of the barrel, can be large or small; it cannot be high. 'High' undoubtedly sounds better than 'large', however, and modern industry always uses it. A firm makes it known for instance, that it can offer 'rewarding career opportunities for high calibre people' (*D Tel*, 27.11.75).

High image
With a good reputation. Firms are greatly occupied with their 'image' nowadays. It is not quite the same as 'reputation', although, pressed to explain the difference, most people who use the word would find themselves in difficulties. The 'image' of a firm is the way it strikes the public, investors and financial journalists. An 'image' is sedulously cultivated and regularly checked by public relations and advertising experts. 'Reputation', on the other hand, is the old-

fashioned word. It implies, as 'image' does not, moral worth, fair-dealing, prompt payment, reliable products, and good treatment of staff. It goes deeper than 'image', which is very much a surface, two-dimensional word. When a company says that it is 'test marketing a range of high-image furniture' (*Sydney Morning Herald*, 28.2.76), it is referring to goods above the middle of the price range, which dealers and the public have come to regard as better made and better finished than the average.

High-popular
Very popular. The use of 'high' implies the existence of a scale or rating. Someone who is 'high popular' has had his popularity measured and assessed in accordance with criteria worked out by psychologists, whereas someone who is merely 'very popular' has never had the benefit of scientific attention. A child can be spoken of as possessing qualities 'making him acceptable to other high-popular children' (*JEP*, 59/3, 1968). Cf. Low-popular.

Highly-salaried
Well paid. 'This highly-salaried position' (*D Tel*, 27.11.75). No 'executive' or professional person can be well-paid these days. This term is reserved for manual workers and could never be applied to managers, at least in Britain. In America, everybody receives a 'salary', so that this particular distinction does not arise. It would just be possible, however, for a member of the British managerial class to be 'highly paid', since the important status indicator, 'highly', is included in the phrase.

High-volume
In large quantities. 'High-volume consignments to worldwide de-stinations' (*D Tel*, 9.12.75); 'Direct selling of high volume fast moving consumer packaged goods' (*D Tel*, 27.11.75). A piece of commercial jargon. The first quotation means no more than 'large consignments', which the company cannot bring itself to say. The second might be translated, without the slightest loss of meaning, as 'fast-moving packaged goods which are bought in large quantities', but neither of these equivalents would satisfy the firms concerned. 'High-volume' is reckoned to have overtones of 'bustling', 'well-organised', which are missing from 'large quantities'.

Hogshair

A substance resembling hogshair. 'A compressed fibre tile, using hogshair of manmade fibre' (*Business and Finance*, Dublin, 8.4.76). This use of 'hogshair', ludicrous or dishonest, according to taste, is probably no worse than 'artificial silk' or 'cotton wool'. How far 'hogshair' is still an advantage to people manufacturing and selling this kind of floor-tile is a matter for doubt. On the one hand it suggests strength, quality, the natural product, but on the other, as purchasers of genuine hogshair tiles have discovered to their cost, these tiles have to be watered every day in order to keep them from shrinking and buckling. 'Genuine synthetic hogshair tiles', which has the best of both worlds, may be the next step.

Home

The place where one lives; its attributes. Homes vary, of course, and for this reason it seems a little dangerous for a hotel to advertise 'all the comforts of home, ready and waiting' (1976 brochure of Wentworth Hotel, Sydney). It would be of interest if visitors to this or any other hotel would make a list of what they consider to be the major comforts of their own home and then see how the hotel measures up to it. Warmth would be comparable, and so, in all probability, would be the beds – although never with electric blankets – the bathroom and the floor-covering. The lighting would certainly be inferior – one reads with great difficulty in most hotel bedrooms – and the noise from the corridors and adjacent rooms, especially during the small hours, would certainly not be acceptable in most homes. The décor and style of furniture might turn out not to be pleasing at all, if not downright vulgar, the pictures on the wall might be dreadful, and the absence of flowers and pot-plants could, to some people, give a chilling effect to the room. 'All the comforts of home'?

Homestyle

As made at home. 'A good homestyle stock recipe' (Advertisement on WTOP, Washington DC, 16.10.76). It is, from the manufacturers' point of view, a sad truth that food intelligently and lovingly prepared in domestic quantities at home does not taste the same as what purport to be the same dishes or ingredients concocted on a large scale in the factory. To pretend otherwise is fraudulent. However nourishing, hygienic and palatable the factory article may be, it is a different product.

Honest

Not pretentious. ' . . . the non-vintage, honest and straightforward . . .' (*Times*, 19.6.76). 'Honest' is a somewhat perilous word to apply to wine, especially to non-vintage wine. Much of what is sold as German, for instance, contains wine imported from Hungary and elsewhere, and much of the French has Algerian blended with it. Very little blending, on the other hand, takes place in Italy, where the native producers have a considerable problem in selling everything that comes from their own vineyards. Whether it is 'honest' for a bottle of German hock to contain a marriage of German, Hungarian or Bulgarian wine is a matter of opinion. In the quotation given above, however, 'honest' probably has a different meaning, that the wine pretends to be no better than it is, an interpretation supported by 'straightforward'.

Honey-sweet

Soft-toned, sweet-sounding. 'A long instrumental that relies on the honey-sweet guitar of Richard Betts' (*Vogue*, Dec 1975) raises certain problems. Is his playing merely 'sweet'? Or is it, like honey, sticky, glutinous? Is the critic saying 'It soothes me', or 'it gums up my ears', 'makes me feel surfeited and sick'?

Hopefully

With luck; perhaps. The battle to prevent the German/American 'hopefully' from gaining a foothold in England was lost long ago, and one can now do no more than point out certain dangers in its use. Its chief merit or demerit is that it is impersonal. One does not know who is doing the hoping, and the writer can retreat from any responsibility in the matter. It may or may not be he who is hopeful. The reader has to form his own opinion. So, in referring to 'an overview which hopefully will provide the reader . . .' (*BB/NZ*, 1975), the author keeps himself in the safe position of vacillating, in effect, between 'with luck', 'I or we hope', and 'there are those who hope'. To say 'I hope' is to commit oneself.

Hospitality

The way one is looked after. 'The hospitality is gracious, the environment is luxurious' (*New Yorker*, 22.3.76. A hotel in New York) 'Hospitality' has a real meaning, being fed and accommodated by a kindly person or organisation, certainly without payment. For a commercial concern to use it in respect of a money-making service is an impertinent lie. A hotel is only very rarely hospitable in the true sense of the word. 'The hospitality is gracious' means that the service is good, even excellent, and there is nothing to be ashamed of in that. One is happy to pay for first-class service and one appreciates it. But to imply that one is a guest in a private house, and that the bill and its payment are nothing more than tokens of esteem, parting gifts between friends, is a confidence trick. 'Hospitality' often appears to be used as a synonym for 'friendliness', 'warm-heartedness', as in 'Cretans are proud of their island and keen to share the magic with visitors. Hospitality is world famous.' (*S Times*, 30.1.77).

Human
Warm, friendly. 'Four of the strongest and most human voices in jazz' (*Melody Maker*, 29.1.77).

Humanist
A humanist, in the modern sense, is someone whose faith is in man, a person who does not believe in God. The traditional meaning, of someone who draws his values from a study of Greek and Roman literature, is still possible, although not used or understood by many people. There is also fairly frequent confusion with 'humane' and 'humanitarian'. What we are supposed to understand by the 'humanist warmth' of Michael Tippett's music (*B.B.C. Radio Guide*, 6th–12th March 1976) is not at all clear. Perhaps it is 'a warm-hearted attitude towards the human race' or, just possibly,' the warmth of a civilised man'. Perhaps–and one cannot prevent the awful thought from lurking at the back of one's mind–it is just a phrase.

Hungry
Greedy for money? Hungry for work? Lusting for power? A popular word among members of the New Management. 'For those ambitious, hungry and committed professionals . . .' (*D Tel*, 27.1.76). The picture of wolf-like men who have not eaten for days is not altogether pleasing.

Hygiene
An organisation no longer rents towels; it hires hygiene, which sounds altogether more seemly, and, from the supplier's point of view, more worth the money. 'The British hygiene-hire market' (*D Tel*, 17.12.75) is a comparatively recent creation, although there has

been such a market in America for many years. Hygiene-hire can also include soap-dispensers and hot-air hand-dryers.

Hyperspace

Total range. One of the social scientists' more bizarre and bewildering coinages. 'This mapping of major fields in the hyperspace of students' study strategies is a method for investigating the task structure of those fields' (*JEP*, 65/3, 1973). One would not wish to deprive readers of the pleasure and mental stimulus of working out the full translation of this quotation for themselves, but, as an incentive, 'the hyperspace of students' study strategies' probably means 'the range of projects which are available for students to carry out'.

I

Ideally

When properly used, can have two meanings (a) everything turns out well; (b) perfectly, in an ideal fashion. The meaning differs according to the position of the word. Before the verb, it is meaning (a), after the verb meaning (b). If the writer ignores this rule, communication between him and his readers can break down, as in 'Each pattern will ideally adapt for draperies, bedsteads or upholstery' (*New Yorker*, 15.1.76). Since this forms part of an advertisement, what the author intended to imply was probably that each pattern in the range is 'perfectly suited to draperies, bedsteads or upholstery' but what he has actually said is 'if things turn out the way we hope they will, if God is with us, these patterns will be equally suitable for draperies, bedsteads or upholstery'. One should, perhaps, give him the benefit of the doubt and forgive him for unwittingly confusing us.

Identify

(a) find; (b) recognise; (c) work hard to achieve. These three senses flow into one another in many contexts, with consequent difficulties for the reader. 'We aim to identify graduates . . .' (*D Tel*, 27.11.75) means 'to find and recruit graduates'. The use of 'identify' here suggests the ludicrous picture of a line of candidates, some graduates and some not, out of which the company's sharp-eyed observers will proceed to sift out one kind from the other. 'We have identified possible openings within the Tobacco, Brewery, Food, Printing and Paper and Board Divisions' (*S Times*, 30.5.76) tells us not that the company has discovered openings lurking in disguise, but that it has satisfied itself that such openings exist. Nobody has in fact done any identifying in 'a new era of development for the Albury-Wodonga area, now identified as a growth centre' (*Health*, 1975). The area has always been there and is now seen to be growing in industrial importance, i.e. 'recognised as a growth area'. A different and widely found modern usage is seen in 'The successful candidate will have an ability to identify with the Company's plans for expansion' (*D Tel*, 25.10.76). One is used to the idea of identifying oneself with a character in a novel, a play or a film, that is, believing in the character and seeing something of oneself in him, but it is surely asking a great deal of someone that he should 'identify with the Company's plans for expansion'. It is, admittedly, a jargon word, which is probably not taken seriously by anybody and, in the present example, a fair rendering might be 'agree wholeheartedly', to the extent of saying, 'the Company's aims are my aims'.

Identity

The person I can be sure I really am. Most people seem to be looking for their identity these days, a problem which, in pre-psychologist, individualist days, does not seem to have concerned our ancestors very much. Obsession with one's identity is a disease of mass-man, living in an age which increasingly wants to standardise, file and index him. But chasing one's identity is so fashionable that one has no real idea, in any given case, if the activity is genuine or not. How seriously, in other words, are we supposed to take 'All his heroes and heroines are looking for an identity, for something they can call *me*' (*Mosaic*, Winnipeg, Winter 1976)?

Idiom

An uppish word for 'style'. 'The facade is in a Cotswold idiom, which seems heavily loaded with classical details, window surrounds and quoins' (*Con*, Vol 162, May/Aug 1966). The use of 'idiom', rather than 'style', could be a cause of worry to many readers, who might wonder if the word meant something more profound and more complex than mere 'style'. It doesn't.

Ill

Not well. 'Ill' and 'injured' are not at all the same, and the habit of journalists, especially those employed by the B.B.C., of making 'ill' an all-purpose word is illiterate, irritating and muddling. 'He's seriously ill in hospital' (*B.B.C. News*, 21.12.75) referred to a man who had been shot, and the man was in hospital as a result of his injuries, not because he was 'ill'. 'She is said to be seriously ill in hospital' (*B.B.C. News*, 2.1.77). The woman in question had been blown up by a bomb in Belfast, and she, too, was injured, not ill. The rule is a simple one. If someone is suffering from an illness, he is ill. With only the wretched B.B.C information to go on, one would be entitled to suppose that the unfortunate woman in Belfast was in hospital suffering from pneumonia or glandular fever, and that the bomb did no more than precipitate the illness.

Illusionistic

The illusion of. A piece of art critic's verbal froth. 'He employed a uniform density of colour in order to negate illusionistic spatial recession' (Walker, 1975), is a way of saying 'in order to prevent the illusion of receding space'.

Image

The associations present in the mind of the public. 'Reinforcing brand image' (*D Tel*, 5.12.75). The task of the image-builders, a powerful and respected group in the advertising and public relations field, is, first, to make sure that the public is aware that the product or the company exists, and that there is no confusion with any other product or company and, second, to do everything possible to create a favourable attitude to what the company is trying to sell. Everybody nowadays is concerned about their image—politicians, manufacturers, trade unions, airlines, teachers, lawyers—and they would be more likely to get a useful answer if they were to look down the telescope from the other end and to ask, not 'what is our image?', i.e. what picture do we project, but, 'what do people think about us?', i.e. what do we look and sound like at the receiving end? To cultivate one's image is vanity; to be concerned about the effect one has on other people is humility, a distinction which 'image' tends to obscure.

Imagine

Faint at the thought of. This is the old trick of inviting people to think of a price and then to tell them that the actual price is rather lower than that. Since the first price is complete guesswork, the real price stands a very good chance of being lower. 'Our pine kitchens are much less expensive than you'd imagine' (*Good Housekeeping*, Feb 1977).

Immaculate

Not in immediate need of redecoration. An estate agent's word. An 'immaculate modern detached bungalow' (*SMJ*, 27.11.75) is probably a house belonging to elderly people and has not been knocked about by small children.

Immediate

Making an immediate impact on the senses, by-passing any delaying action from the intellect. To reinforce the word is unnecessary, since nothing can be more immediate than immediate. 'The impact is forceful and aggressively immediate' (*Apollo*, Feb 1966) means that the picture hits you straight away, but the writer chooses a pretentious way of saying so.

Impact

The quality which makes people sit up and take notice. With so much competing for public attention, the need for 'impact', the power to compel attention, appears ever more important. It is no accident that 'impact' is so popular as a symbol of our time. Some of its contexts, however, are a little disturbing and comic, suggesting that the writer had not thought a great deal about the significance and possibilities of the word. 'Yves St. Laurent's Triangles give even more design impact to your bed' (*Washington Star*, 17.10.76) is not the happiest of sentences. 'Make a nice bed look even better' would have been more reassuring. Any mention of an impact on one's bed is apt to suggest a blow on the head from a burglar or the ceiling falling down while one is asleep.

Imperialist

The traditional Communist adjective to describe the foreign policy of any non-Socialist country, even of one which has not possessed an empire for many years, and which shows no signs of wishing to acquire one again. 'The right-wing Labour leadership works to maintain capitalist and imperialist policies' (*Comment*, 29.11.75).

Importance

Confidence, knowing one is important? A word from the strange world of wine. 'It fills the mouth with its indications of importance' (*Times*, 17.7.76). Is one to imagine the wine saying, 'I'm good and I know it', or 'Wine-writers and the wine trade say I'm wonderful and that I'm high up on their list of the world's most beautiful wines'?

Importantly

Important. An American barbarism, which robs the language of the extra flexibility of having both an adjective and an adverb, with separate and distinct uses. 'Importantly, the Mayor entered the hall', or 'Importantly, the Prime Minister rose to speak' give the right flavour of a heavy, pompous man, conscious of his importance. One does not want to throw the adverb away on '. . . and perhaps more importantly to demonstrate to the government' (*Health*, 1975) especially since, in this context, 'importantly' has got the flavour of 'looking and sounding important', 'pompous', which was certainly not intended.

Impressionistic

Giving a clear, detailed impression. 'Impressionistic' is too easily confused with 'impressionist' to be useful. The meanings are, of course, quite different, but readers who are not sufficiently sharp-eyed could easily be misled. 'The talented artist, Jack Laycox, was commissioned to paint Delta's destinations in this beautiful, lively, impressionistic style' (*Delta Flightline Catalogue*, 1976). The posters referred to are photographically realistic. The word is also used in the sense of 'gained from impressions'. 'There was evidence that impressionistic measures of in-basket performance bore some relationship to impressions of on-the-job behaviour' (*JER*, 63/1, Sept 1969), i.e. performance assessed by watching it and relying on one's impressions, in order to reach a judgement on it. This interpretation does not sound sufficiently scientific and professional, apparently, so 'impressionistic measures' it has to be. 'In-basket performance', incidentally and for the benefit of those not familiar with the term, means 'what one has achieved already', as distinct from what one is doing in the course of one's present job.

Improvise

Properly, to produce something not in the score, text or book of

---

Incite

rules; arrange something temporarily to meet an unexpected situation or emergency. The meaning of the word does not always seem to be fully clear, however, even in places of high intellectual distinction. 'The organising group must evaluate early the extent to which it will be necessary to improvise with the truth in the process' (Schlebecker & Petersen, 1972). 'Compromise with the truth' is presumably meant although it might be possible to improvise truth, if none should happen to lie ready to hand.

Incite

Arouse, give rise to, encourage. 'Incite' usually has a pejorative sense, as in 'incite to violence', 'incite to hatred', 'incite to crime'. One does not normally 'incite' anyone to love or admiration. The possible meanings of 'Public access television incites study on the part of the medium' (*Mus News*, Jan/Feb 1974) are therefore interesting. To 'incite' someone to study is an odd concept, but possible, if one thinks of study as an antisocial activity, but who is undertaking this particular study is not clear. Are those responsible for television broadcasting studying the possibilities and implications of public access television, or does public access television cause people to take a harder, sharper look at 'the medium', i.e. television as a whole?

Incredible

Difficult to believe. The word is often used to mean 'wonderful', 'magnificent', with results like 'Delightful stonebuilt cottage with incredible views' (*SMJ*, 27.11.75). There is presumably no reason, when one looks out of the window of the cottage, to think that the views stretching out in front of one do not really exist. They are, one takes it, genuine but amazing, or possibly incredible until one actually sees them.

Incumbent

Person occupying a commercial or industrial post. The spelling with 'e' is now frequently found in this type of context. Cf. Encumbent, and add this example with 'i'. 'The incumbent will be an action-oriented thinker' (*S Times*, 30.5.76).

In-depth

Detailed, based on profound knowledge, deep-rooted. A trendy, but not particularly elegant word, now very widely used, often in circumstances in which it adds little or nothing to the meaning.

Nearly always 'detailed', now outmoded, would do just as well as 'in-depth', if not better. One firm announces that the person it intends to appoint will be concerned with 'the in-depth review of major areas' (*D Tel*, 27.11.75), another insists that 'candidates must have an in-depth knowledge of the history of Scottish architecture' (*Times*, 20.5.76), and a third requires of a new recruit that he shall have 'an in-depth determination to succeed' (*D Tel*, 12.2.76), whatever that may be. What may be needed here is a young man who can place his hand on his heart and say, 'Here, deep down in me, is a determination to succeed', which would be priggish, but, like everything else in the business world, always possible.

Indicator
Guide, estimate, figure. 'The initial salary indicator is £5,500' (*D Tel*, 26.11.76). Does this mean that the salary is £5,500 or about £5,500? Does the indicator point to the exact salary or to the range of salary? The doubt could have been removed by saying either 'the initial salary is £5,500', or 'about £5,500', but this would have seemed too crude and unprofessional. 'Indicator' adds the necessary touch of class.

Indigenous
Native. European firms operating in developing countries are faced with a difficult problem. If they refer to 'native staff', they run the risk of being accused of being patronising or racist, although it is still in order to say that someone is 'a native of Ghana', or, for that matter, 'a native of France'. The solution has been found in 'indigenous', which makes the people concerned sound rather as if they were plants or wild animals, but is politically inoffensive. One international company therefore finds it possible to make known that its policy is 'to plan and lead effectively through indigenous managers' (*D Tel*, 9.12.75).

Indisposed
Ill. No actor, conductor or soloist, of either sex, is ever ill. The word has to be 'indisposed', which has the correct flavour of 'not able to give an audience of his best', 'resting in order to regain his full artistic powers', to which the coarse phrase 'being ill' is almost incidental. A quartet, for instance, may be 'minus the temporarily indisposed Alan Hacker' (*D Tel*, 2.2.77).

Industrial action
A metaphor drawn from factory life, indicating a concerted attempt
by employees in any kind of organisation to disrupt their employers'
business, in order to win some form of concession, usually an increase
in salary or wages. 'The threat of industrial action by B.B.C.
cameramen could rob more than 400 million viewers in Britain and
the Continent of the European Song Contest' (*Sun GB*, 16.3.77).
'Industrial action' need not be taken in what would usually be
considered as industry. Civil servants, for instance, can take such a
step and so can members of an orchestra. 'Industrial action' means
direct action. The use of 'industrial', however, suggests that the hearts
of all Trade Unionists beat as one.

Industry
(a) The organised employers. 'Industry feels that there is scope for
negotiation' (*D Tel*, 2.2.77). (b) The wealth-creating process. 'When
the Chancellor of the Exchequer uses the word "industry" what does
he mean? Does he embrace manufacturing, wholesaling, retailing,
trading and commerce of all kinds?' (*D Tel*, 10.1.77). 'Industry' is
used now in an exceedingly vague and unhelpful manner. It is found
at its worst, perhaps, in the phrase 'both sides of industry', which
means the employers on the one hand and the trade unions on the
other, with the implication that the two are perpetually and
inevitably divided and that 'industry' is a battlefield. In the absence of
any better definition, it can be assumed that any concern considered
eligible for membership of the Confederation of British Industry is a
branch of industry, which begs the question in a shameless way.

Ingest
Swallow, take in. 'We want an accountant who can ingest a plethory
(sic) of information and succinctly report the facts pertinent to
Wimpey operators' (Toronto *Globe and Mail*, 7.10.76). Wimpey
seems to have missed out a stage in the process. Having ingested all
this information, that is, swallowed it, the accountant must digest it.
That accomplished, he is in a position to 'report the facts pertinent to
Wimpey operators'. It is just possible, of course, that Wimpey does
not know the difference between ingesting and digesting, which, in
the case of such a large and important concern, seems regrettable. Or
did the company originally intend to say 'take in', which can, of
course, mean both 'ingest' and 'absorb', and then substitute the more

refined 'ingest', which conveys only half the possible meaning?

Innovative

Anxious to introduce and apply new ideas. There is a great demand, at least on paper, for 'innovative' people in industry, mainly, no doubt, because they are in such short supply, most of our fellow citizens preferring to continue in the old, well-tried ways. So a Canadian firm wants 'a creative and innovative individual' (Toronto *Globe and Mail*, 31.1.76) and an English one is in the market for people who are 'innovative in the development of new manufacturing ideas' (*D Tel*, 22.1.76). The second example appears to get close to saying the same thing twice over, unless the kind of person demanded is one who will think up new ideas as well as develop them. It should be emphasised, however, that the innovators industry has in mind are people who will keep their innovative habits within prescribed limits. The kind of innovative thinking which is concerned with workers taking over control of the factory is not welcome.

Input

Contribution which begins a process. Before 1945 'inputs' were hardly ever seen or talked about, but since then they had their fellow-travellers, 'outputs' have become a common feature of almost every aspect of our lives. At one time—it seems a very long while ago—the things we bought were called purchases and the things we sold were called sales. Now, as everyone registered for V.A.T. in Britain is well aware, purchases are 'inputs' and sales are 'outputs', which sounds too Germanic to be true. Most unfortunately, the arrival of 'input' and 'output' has produced a huge new crop of linguistic cotton-wool, such as 'The members' wish for more didactic inputs' (Rapoport, 1976)—'didactic inputs' means 'formal teaching'—and, even woollier and worse, 'The faculty has great input through committees, faculty senates, and autonomous departments' (Corwin, 1974). 'Input', in the second instance, must, one feels, mean 'opportunity for presenting its views', but it is tempting to translate 'has great input through' as 'pours out a great mass of words at'.

One sometimes feels that 'input' is used only in order to provide an opportunity for adding an impressive-looking adjective to it. This seems extremely probable in the case of 'The need here is for some teacher-like input, but the problem is how much, if the experience is not to be seen as another taught course' (*Sandwich Courses*, 1976), where 'some teacher-like input' means 'a certain amount of in-struction or guidance'.

Insinuating
Correctly, creeping in; worming its way into. It hardly seems a suitable adjective to use of a wine, but it happens. 'The Amarone has an insinuating first flavour' (*Times*, 12.6.76), i.e., one supposes, a flavour which creeps around one's mouth unexpectedly.

Inspiriting
Which raises the spirits, by analogy with its opposite, the more frequently found 'dispiriting'. One asks oneself why the writer of 'It was an inspiriting evening in every way' (*Classical Music*, 20.10.76) chose to use this particular word. Did he see it as meaning something different from 'inspiring' and, if so, what did he imagine the difference to be? Had he got something against 'inspiring', some unpleasant association which made him determined to avoid the word? Or did he simply feel that 'inspiring' had had its day, and that the time had come for a change; or that 'inspiring' had too grand and religious a flavour for what he had in mind?

Instigate
A legal-sounding word. Proceedings are instigated, an enquiry is set on foot at the instigation of this or that person. It is not a synonym for 'set up' or 'set in force', and there are many contexts in which it is not appropriate at all. The company which believes it 'requires a finalist or qualified Accountant to instigate a costing system' (*D Tel*, 28.1.76) is in error. What it wants is someone to introduce or set up a costing system, which would have quite a different flavour to it, not so grand, it is true, but more honest and more readily understood.

Integrity
When applied only to people, it means 'honesty'. A 'person of integrity' is, as the Latin root suggests, a whole person, a person with no pieces missing from his moral make-up, an honest person. The word is still used in this sense in the business world, when a 'person of integrity' means, roughly, someone who would not rob his em-ployers or engage in sharp practices on the side. 'Managerial ability and complete integrity are necessary for this important and demand-ing position' (*S Times*, 30.1.77). But—and this is likely to puzzle many people—it is now possible, at least in manufacturing and

commerce, for an inanimate object, as well as a human being, to possess integrity. This is illustrated by a recent advertisement for 'the position of Product Integrity Manager. This position carries responsibility for ensuring that materials and finished goods from suppliers, contractors and Levi companies meet the approved quality standards' (*D Tel*, 6.2.76). 'Product integrity', an American invention, is our old friend Quality Control. One has become used to complaining about the quality of the goods we buy; we shall now have to learn to speak of integrity shortcomings.

Intellectual
If, as Bernard Levin has proposed, we define an intellectual as a person who is in the habit of carrying out regular objective analyses of problems and events–then the adjective 'intellectual' describes what such a person does. 'Intellectual conversation' would be devoted to the objective analysis of problems. One can, however, use 'intellectual' to flatter people and the advertisement from a San Francisco company which draws attention to their 'work environment which contributes to intellectual interaction' (*Times*, 22.7.76) does seem to be making rather a meal over what is no more than 'a work environment which encourages people to exchange ideas'.

Interact
Meet, talk, get on terms with. Many of us were brought up to accept that one chemical interacts with another, but the idea that one person's body chemistry interacts with that of another is comparatively new. The salesman who 'must interact with customers' (*Boston Sunday Globe*, 10.10.76) should presumably be careful not to go too far. An explosive mixture of salesmen and customers is clearly not required. And the use of 'verbally interact with', for 'have conversations with' is a strange and unnecessary piece of nonsense. 'Teachers in the course of their instruction verbally interact with children for significant amounts of time' (*Boston Sunday Globe*, 10.10.76).

Interdisciplinary
Cutting across the dividing line between two or more academic subjects. An 'interdisciplinary study' might derive material and enlightenment from both economics and sociology, or from art, music and literature. Only academics, however, think of life in terms of 'disciplines'. Most people are either interested or not interested in a

problem, a pleasure or an opportunity. If they are not interested that is the end of the matter. If they are, they are likely to give their full attention, curiosity and knowledge to it, without troubling to be told that they are following the interdisciplinary approach. Academic arrogance in this connexion can be stupendous. 'We think young people should have the opportunity to work in an open situation, devoting themselves to problems of some complexity. This we call interdisciplinary Enquiry (I.D.E.)' (Rubinstein & Stoneman, 1970). Messrs. Rubinstein and Stoneman can call it what they like. What the youngsters are doing, if they receive the right kind of encouragement, is to try to see what the problems looks like from a number of different directions and to get a little closer to the truth that way.

Interface

Connexion, liaison, meeting point. One of the most popular business English terms, which is slowly creeping into the world of social science. Most issues of 'serious' newspapers and periodicals will provide examples. 'A direct interface with design engineering will be required to aid in resolving assembly and design related problems' (*Boston Sunday Globe*, 10.10.76), i.e. liaison with design engineering; 'Our understanding of the interface between schools and higher education' (*THES*, 13.2.76), i.e. liaison overlap; 'There is a strong M.O.D. interface' (*D Tel*, 27.2.76), i.e. close liaison with the Ministry of Defence; 'The holder of the post will have an important interface with the management accounts of the business' (*Fin Times*, 18.11.76), i.e. a close connexion with the management accounts. 'Interface' is also used as a verb, meaning originally to connect one piece of apparatus with another, so that they work in co-operation. A prize-winning Canadian example is: 'You will interface on an international scale' (Toronto *Globe and Mail*, 6.10.76). 'Interface' with whom or what? Does it mean 'meet important and influential people'? Or simply 'meet people around the world'?

Intermediate strata

The working members of the middle-class. The political Left has had to face the difficult problem of admitting that some members of the middle-class actually work for a living. It has achieved this by means of the brilliant invention, 'intermediate strata'. This allows 'middle-class' to be reserved for the drones, the people who suck away the workers' life-blood. 'Support from the intermediate strata' (*The British Road to Socialism*, 1977), claims a recent policy statement from the Communist Party of Great Britain.

Internally oriented

Inside an organisation. 'The post is basically internally oriented' (*D Tel*, 28.11.75), i.e. most of the work will be carried out with one's own colleagues, or possibly inside the company headquarters, with little or no travel involved.

International

As in 'Property Travel International' (*Obs*, 30.11.75). The position of 'international' at the end of a firm's name is calculated to make the enterprise sound even more international. An absurd, but much practised affectation. In restaurants, any mention of 'international' needs to be treated with great caution, and even suspicion. An 'international' menu or cuisine usually means one of two things. It may be a mixture of the national dishes of Cyprus, Turkey or whichever country the proprietor of the restaurant comes from, with some of the traditional food of the host country. Or it may be 'international' in the Hilton or Holiday Inn sense, that is, one is faced with much the same food in Kuwait as in Tokyo or Dallas. In an American-run hotel, it will almost invariably be the second, whatever fancy names the individual dishes may carry. 'International cuisine served in luxurious surroundings' (1976 brochure of Nova Scotian Hotel, Halifax) appeared to mean something acceptable to everybody, no matter where they might come from. 'The main restaurant, with its international menus' (1976 brochure of the Copthorne Hotel, Gatwick) is faced with all the problems of a hotel close to a major airport. It has somehow to please, or at least not annoy, customers who may come from Mexico, Ghana or the Netherlands, an unenviable task which is bound to lead to a fairly standardised and unexciting menu and style of cooking. There appears to be some reticence on the part of inudstrial and commercial concerns to say that they employ foreigners. 'Overseas personnel' or 'international personnel' are now the polite phrases to use, although the latter phrase suggest that one person has several nationalities, which is possible but unlikely. A company says, for example, that its 'total workforce of more than 700 people includes many international personnel (*D Tel*, 19.1.77)

Interpersonal

Face to face. A new word for an activity that is as old as man, meeting people, reacting to them and talking to them. 'Certain students learn better in interpersonal situations, while others learn better alone' (*JEP*, 60/3, 1969). Learning in an interpersonal situation means with a tutor. 'High interpersonal intensity' (*Am J Psych*, 128/2, 1971) is a condition in which two or more people react to one another with a considerable release of electricity. The person who 'must possess well-developed communication and interpersonal skills' (*D Tel*, 9.12.75) has to be able to get on well with his fellow men and be able to bring out the best in them, for his and his employer's benefit. 'Interpersonal skills' has now become practically a compound noun in the business world. The fact that they are so often asked for suggests either that they may be in short supply or that employers have been badly let down in the past by assuming that an intelligent, well-qualified recruit would have them or could be taught them. 'Good interpersonal skills are a must' (*Boston Sunday Globe*, 10.10.76).

Interrole conflict
The state of being pulled in two directions, familiar to most of us. 'Students who worked many hours tended to feel greater interrole conflict, as did students who were married and had children' (*JEP*, 60/1, 1969). In other words, students felt a painful pull between work on the one hand and play on the other, or between their work and their family. So many millions of people in the world are affected in the same way that the point hardly seems worth making, although it certainly sounds more important when it is described as 'interrole conflict'.

Intervention
Coming between two parties. There can be intervention in a civil war, a dog-fight, or two small girls pulling one another's hair. The use of the word by welfare agencies is not always easy to understand, as in 'different techniques of social work intervention' (*N. Soc*, 4.12.75). Between what parties or forces are the social workers coming? In some cases they may be doing precisely this, between a drunken husband and his maltreated wife, for instance, but for the most part their work is concerned with people who cannot cope adequately with poverty, ill-health, wretched housing and other afflictions. The social workers might be said, perhaps, to be intervening between clients and their Fate, but it seems likely that the quotation meant no more than 'different ways of helping one's clients'.

Intimate
Small. An 'intimate room' is a small room, an 'intimate gathering' is a small gathering. 'Your next intimate wine and cheese party' (*Delta Flightline Catalogue*, 1976) is 'your next small wine and cheese party'. For those who want big things, but cannot afford them, and for those who hate big things anyway, 'intimate', with its added suggestions of warmth and cosiness, is the perfect answer, avoiding the embarrassment of being relegated to the small league.

Intrasender conflict
The conflict between the wishes of two or more people within the same organisation. The exact point of 'sender' is not immediately apparent. It may possibly be used in the sense of 'message'. A definition exists of the phrase, in so far as it concerns the academic world: 'Intrasender conflict: the extent of incompatibility between the demands of various professors' (*JEP*, 60/1, 1969).

Intraspecific
Between members of the same species, group or community. An 'intraspecific conflict' would be a civil war. 'We have good reason to consider intraspecific aggression the gratest of all dangers' (Hoppe, 1970). For those with experience of race riots, civil war or mob violence, 'intraspecific aggression', if they knew what it meant, would seem a most attractive euphemism.

Invertebrate
Spineless, lacking in courage. A gentle academic joke. 'The proposal is merely part of general invertebrate thinking' (Lipset, 1971). There may be some suggestion of 'snake-like' or 'worm-like' thinking in this. It is impossible to be sure. 'Spineless' would have removed the doubt.

Investment
Anything likely to increase in value. Stamps, books, paintings are, on their record so far, reckoned to be an 'investment'. So, in some societies, are wives and children, whose working capacity is a valuable addition to one's well-being. It is a pity, however, that one should be constantly driven to look for the 'investment potential' of objects which give one pleasure. If one happens to be fond of one's 'birthstone bee pin', one does not really want or need to be reminded

that 'a birthstone bee pin by Rosenthal is an investment of lasting beauty and value' (*New Yorker*, 26.1.76).

Invitational

A reception at which the guests are genuine guests, paying nothing for the privilege of attending. 'Announcing Hilton Head's First $95,000 invitational' (*New Yorker*, 13.12.75).

Involved

Concerned. Until comparatively recently, to be 'involved' with something or somebody was to be closely, sometimes too closely, wrapped up in it. One could be 'involved' in a book, 'involved' in a problem, and, if a doctor, struck off the register for being 'involved' with a woman patient. It is now much used by companies who believe that they have a right to demand that their employees should think and live the job 24 hours a day. This creed is sometimes stated with completely unconscious humour. 'You also need flair and versatility to become involved in the most complete range of boilers currently on the market' (*D Tel*, 27.1.76). Becoming involved with a boiler could have unpleasant consequences. More normal, however, is 'an excellent opportunity to be involved with a company which . . ' (*D Tel*, 5.2.76). This is not the old-fashioned concept of working for a company. To 'be involved with a Company' is joyfully to hand onself over to it, body and soul, to become something the Victorians, to their good fortune, knew nothing about, a Company Man.

Involvement

Cf. Involved and Dedicated. Being totally concerned with. 'Complete job involvement is required from a self-starter who . . .' (*D Tel*, 9.12.75); 'Must have personality for executive involvement in publicly quoted company' (*D Tel*, 22.1.76); 'Career involvement was assessed by a sixteen item preference inventory' (*JER*, 60/2, Oct 1966); 'This is total Otis involvement – design, manufacture, installation and service' (*BB/NZ*, 1975). The word is, however, fashionable outside business circles. One can observe and praise 'involvement' in a play, a film, a concert, any occasion on which the intellect and emotions are involved. Conversely, not to be involved is reckoned to be a bad thing, evidence that one is in the wrong place. 'A motley collection of adults sitting on uncomfortable chairs in a very cramped situation for two hours without a cough or shuffle or a

mumbled conversation with their neighbour. Total involvement.'
(Rubinstein & Stoneman, 1970).

J

Jeopardy

Predicament. 'In the context of human jeopardy, the stress should not
be on mere equality, but on diversity' (Rubinstein & Stoneman,
1970). The use of the word 'jeopardy' in this context is curious and
misleading. The authors presumably mean 'The human predicament
being what it is', and the human predicament certainly includes
frequent moments of danger of one kind and another. But we are not
always in danger, and the quotation therefore makes little sense.

Job satisfaction

Satisfaction. There is only satisfaction and dissatisfaction, and 'job
satisfaction' means simply the 'satisfaction one gets from one's job',
not a form of satisfaction that is different in kind from, say, the one
that is to be obtained from a hobby or a friendship. 'To get real job
satisfaction from seeing their projects through from start to finish' (*S
Times*, 30.11.75) can be translated only as 'to get real satisfaction from
seeing their projects through from start to finish', which is a
straightforward piece of communication and all that is needed, since
the projects are wholly concerned with the job.

K

Keenly

Closely. A close shave is obtained by means of a keen cutting edge,
but this does not, as some writers appear to think, make 'keenly' and
'closely' synonyms. In 'Above average remuneration keenly linked to
market rates' (*Fin Times*, 5.2.76) there may be some suggestion of
'eager', the other association of 'keen', but this is certainly spurious,
since there is no reason whatever to believe that the employer

concerned is 'eager' to link his above-average remuneration to market rates.

King-size

Extra-large. One can always say that something is 'king-size', but it is impossible to say how much larger than normal it has to be in order to be entitled to the label. For this reason, the word is an advertiser's dream. He cannot be caught out on it. Manufacturers of beds and cigarettes make the most frequent use of it. A quilt is described as 'King-size: to fit a 5 foot bed' (*D Tel*, 16.1.77). A bed 5 feet wide hardly seems to justify the regal adjective, since it is only 6 inches bigger than the normal double-bed size. There is no regulation as to how large a king-sized cigarette has to be. A manufacturer can do as he pleases, secure behind the royal grandeur of the name, as in the John Player advertisements current in Britain throughout the 1970s, such as 'John Player king-size' (*Good Housekeeping*, Feb 1977). Cf. Queen-size.

Knowledge

Relevant facts. 'The small business model, using a sophisticated knowledge base and stressing self-sufficiency and self-help' (*Axiom*, Oct 1976). There is confusion here between the two senses of 'model' (q.v.), so that it is not clear if the writer means 'the ideal small business' or 'what is assumed, for purposes of research and discussion, to be the typical small business', and the fog is not helped to lift by relying on a phrase such as 'a sophisticated knowledge base' which conceals a 'carefully selected and arranged stock of relevant facts'.

L

Landscaped

Not left as it was when the builders moved out, planted out with a few trees and bushes. Most modern references to 'landscaping' are dishonest. 'Landscaping', as the eighteenth and nineteenth century masters of the art understood it, consisted of imposing the knowledgeable and imaginative hand of man on a stretch of countryside, in order to create a more beautiful and agreeable setting for a house than would have existed if nature had been left to her own devices.

Twentieth century members of the same profession have devoted their skill to improving the immediate surroundings of motorways and factories. What these people do is genuine landscaping and, no matter how large or how small it may be, the area to which they have given their attention can be described as 'landscaped', in the true sense of the word. They have looked at the site as a whole, with its buildings, and produced a total plan for it. To take a piece of rough ground, clean it up a little, plant some trees and lay out one or two paths, which is mostly what is meant by 'landscaped' nowadays, is not the same at all. When builders speak of a 'landscaped garden', this usually means that the basis of a garden has been established, so that the prospective purchasers of the house will not feel too depressed when they look out of the windows on their tour of inspection. 'A large landscaped lot' (Toronto *Globe and Mail*, 31.1.76) means that building will start in something more encouraging than a rough field.

Languorous
Inducing a lazy, dreamy mood. Whether a single glass of any wine can have quite this effect is doubtful, yet 'the Amarone has a gentle, languorous fragrance' (*Times*, 12.6.76).

Large
Bigger than one would usually get. 'Large breast of chicken, filled with ham and cheese and cooked in butter' (T.H.F. menu, Coventry, Feb 1976). This is very subtle. A large breast of chicken must come from a large chicken. Small chickens, unlike small women, do not have large breasts. A restaurant could not say 'Breast of large chicken', however, because that could be taken to mean that the chicken was old and tough. Therefore, in order to persuade customers to order the dish, the breast, not the chicken, has to be large. The restaurant keeper is perfectly safe after that, because there is no specified measurement or weight for a large breast of chicken. A customer who says, 'This is not large' can easily be told, 'Yes, it is', and shown something smaller as evidence.

Large-scale
One sip of which appears to fill the mouth? 'The large-scale nature of the wine' (*Times*, 6.3.76); 'The 1971 Mercurey . . . combining a profundity of bouquet, subtlety as well as large-scale style' (*Times*, 21.2.76). Cf. Big.

Lateral

Sideways, from the side. Used in the phrase, 'lateral thinking', a way of solving problems by unorthodox methods. The term was invented by Dr.Edward de Bono in the mid-1960s, 'vertical thinking' being the traditional logical method, in which the stages of reasoning proceeded in a sequence, while 'lateral thinking' occurred when one decided to break a sequence and attack the problem from another angle. The use of the word in this sense is unexceptionable and clear, but corruption begins to occur when it passes into jargon and trendiness. It is nearly at this point in 'Don't trade on the argument that women have special qualities (intuition, perception, lateral thinking, or what have you) which are denied to men' (*Obs*, 5.11.72) and quite there in 'He will be a lateral thinker' (*D Tel*, 28.1.76), an advertisement for an electronic engineer. No one is a lateral thinker, as if this were a special breed of animal, but it is no doubt comforting for a firm to be able to announce 'We have just recruited a lateral thinker', as it might say, 'We have taken on a systems analyst'. There are people who have the temperament or the instinct for lateral thinking when that seems called for and normal logic has failed to produce results. But it is extremely unlikely that such people spend the whole of their waking time deep in lateral thought.

Legalitarianism

Using the law in order to protect oneself, and to solve one's problems. 'We should avoid getting bogged down in legalitarianism. We cannot count on this society's legal apparatus to guarantee our civil liberties' (Teodori, 1969). 'Legalitarianism', an unpleasant coinage, formed no doubt by analogy with 'egalitarianism', implies that one has a low opinion of the law and its workings. 'Getting bogged down in legalitarianism' means, therefore, 'continuing to put one's trust in the courts and the process of law'. There is no end to the number of pejoratives that could be formed in this way—lectorianism (the ridiculous habit of reading); dormitorism (the pathetic custom of sleeping); thermalism (a reactionary fondness for keeping warm) are only a very small selection.

Length

Leaving the taste behind in the mouth for a long time? This has nothing to do with 'short drinks' and 'long drinks', which have a different kind of length. The length which apparently means something to wine experts is illustrated by: 'The 1972 Clos d'Evêque has an elegance and length that are outstanding' (*Times*, 21.2.76).

Leonine
Lion-like. 'The leonine high spirits of the finale were vividly conveyed' (*Times*, 16.10.76. Beethoven's Coriolanus overture). One has to ponder over 'leonine high spirits' and to think of the lions one has known. A lion is a large beast, playful, when it feels like it, in a rather casual, heavy-pawed way, and much given to growling and roaring. To decide when a lion is in high spirits and when he is not is certainly a professional job. What, then, is 'leonine high spirits' supposed to mean to the ordinary, Beethoven-loving reader of *The Times*? One reader at least confesses himself baffled, after a good deal more thought than that paper's music critic has any right to expect. The fact that Beethoven himself had a lion-like head and a lion's bad temper does not explain 'leonine high spirits'.

Less able
Stupid, not gifted, idle. The brutal words do not accord with today's educational theory, by which all pupils are categorised as 'able' and 'less able'. 'Many schools, therefore, abandoned language teaching for less able pupils in favour of European studies' (*Times*, 21.1.77).

Less academic
Poor at school work. One of the group of euphemisms designed to gloss over the fact that some pupils derive very little benefit at all from the attempts of their teachers to instruct them. It is an interesting and possibly significant fact that 'less-academic' is much more frequently used than 'more-academic'. Pupils who work hard at school and get good results are more or less left alone by the euphemism-brigade. The implications of 'custodial courses designed for the less academic, more troublesome students' (Corwin, 1974) are clear, for those who take the trouble to lift the words up and look underneath them. The courses referred to exist purely and simply to keep disruptive boys and girls who are not interested in school and do no work there off the streets and out of trouble. How one justifies the use of 'student' for someone who does not study is another matter.

Less deprived
Better-off, more cultured. It depends on the base from which one starts. If it is the norm to be deprived, then anyone who lives in

comparative comfort becomes 'less deprived', never, it should be noted, 'not deprived', or 'non-deprived'. The implication is that everyone is deprived to some extent, but some more than others, a fiction which allows the maximum degree of face-saving and sloppy thinking. So we have a tedious succession of such non-illuminating sentences as 'Higher-aptitude students came from less-deprived homes' (*JEP*, 59/2, 1968), which might be translated with ruthless and completely unfashionable simplicity as 'Better students came from better homes'.

Less talented

With no talent at all. Everyone, the theory goes, is talented, but some, naturally, have a high talent rating and some a low one. However, such talent as a person may possess can be and often is completely irrelevant to the task in hand. A boy who is talented at football, for instance, may display no talent whatever for French or mathematics, and vice versa. He must still, however, be described as showing 'more talent' for football and 'less talent' for the other subjects. He must always score something, even though his score is a heavily disguised way of saying 'nil'. The old days when a boy was bluntly told that he was 'no good' at maths, and 'useless' at cricket are far in the past. What was once 'facing up to reality' is now 'hurtful' and 'non-constructive', except among the pupils themselves, who, to every progressive educationist's regret, continue to use the same reprehensible words as their fathers and mothers did. No-one has yet heard one small boy tell another that he is 'less talented' at football. But, once away from the educational world, reality has to be thought about occasionally and in some fields of activity. Nobody watching television wants to see and hear people who cannot sing, act or dance, if these are the skills the programme demands. There are therefore auditions, talent-spotters and competitions, which is all as it should be. 'Through the weeding out of the less talented, many of these beginners are selected for further judging on a national basis' (*Aust CTS*, 1969). This refers to 'talent guests' for television.

Liberal

Believing in gradualism, opposed to revolutionary methods. 'Liberal' is used as a term of contempt and abuse by those who believe the changes they want and society needs can be achieved only through violence, single-mindedness and revolution. At one time, to refer to a man's 'liberal views' was to praise him, but among many of the young, especially black Americans, this can no longer be assumed. The decline of 'liberal' into a pejorative is illustrated by 'a collection of white, liberal do-gooders' (Mullard, 1973).

Liberal-minded

Well-intentioned, anxious to help. Black activists have a particular dislike for 'liberal-minded' whites, believing that they get in the way of progress, progress being defined as 'movement towards a multi-racial society in which blacks are no longer regarded as inferior people'. Such a movement, say the activists, can only succeed if it is organised entirely by blacks. 'We realised that the cost of working with liberal-minded white people was too high' (Mullard, 1973).

Liberated

Stolen, removed, looted. Used in this sense since the 1940s as an army euphemism. Only people can be 'liberated'; from prison, from their families, from themselves. To apply the word to inanimate objects is anthropomorphic at best, ridiculous at worst. The reference to 'the liberated documents from Grayson Kirk's files' (Teodori, 1969) is ridiculous. The documents were kept in the Dean's office at Columbia University. They contained confidential material relating to students. Certain of the students objected to the existence of this material, broke into the Dean's office and stole the papers. These then became 'the liberated documents', an extraordinary use of the word, implying that the filing cabinet was a prison, from which the incarcerated records had been crying for their release. The students may, of course, have retained sufficient moral sense to realise that they were thieves, and in this case 'liberated' would have been a convenient, conscience-saving euphemism for stolen. The verb has formed part of the hippy-anarchist vocabulary for a decade. 'Shoplifting—"liberating" to hippies—costs the English retail trade the staggering sum of £75 million a year' (*D Tel*, 1.5.70).

Life-actor

In the management world, an 'involved' person; one who 'lives' his work, and feels closely bound to those who work with him. 'The management should all be life-actors' (Teodori, 1969).

Life-adjustment

Coming to terms with the realities of life. This is normally achieved by growing older, increasing. the range of one's experiences and having to get on with more people. There are those, however, who believe the process can be accelerated and that boys and girls can gain at least some of this essential experience synthetically. 'Secondary education was failing to provide adequately and properly for the life adjustment of perhaps a major fraction of the persons of secondary school age' (Cronin, 1961). The idea behind this is familiar, that school-children are in a sheltered environment, with no brutal bosses and foremen to shout at them, exploit them, corrupt them and bully them; life's apprentices with no idea of the disappointments and torments that lie ahead of them. An adjustment course with the school life-adjustment specialist would tone them up and fit them for the reefs and breakers ahead. Would that it were so.

Life-denying
Stultifying, inhuman. 'The life-denying aspects of corporate capitalism' (Teodori, 1969). 'Life' in this sense probably means something like 'the freedom to live one's own life, to be an individual, to take a pride and pleasure in one's work', but it is bound up with noble savage echoes from Rousseau and pulsating life-force ideas from D. H. Lawrence. Those who use the phrase 'life-denying', would almost certainly refuse to accept 'inhuman' or 'stultifying' as alternatives, on the grounds that they were too intellectual and insufficiently visceral and 'involved'.

Life-endangering
Likely to bruise or destroy the human spirit. The life referred to in 'life-endangering' is not the life with which a doctor or a fireman is concerned, biological life, but spiritual life. It is therefore possible for an enthusiast to say that 'the summer project presented itself to us as a potentially life-endangering situation' (Teodori, 1969).

Life-style
Way of living, how a person chooses or is forced to live. A way of living can contain no style at all, and yet be called a 'life-style'. The difference is indicated by the adjective. A person or object with style is 'stylish', but there is no adjective to correspond to 'life-style'. A 'life-style' simply exists, although one can evidently improve it. An item of furniture is 'in the spirit of today's life-style' (*New Yorker*, 13.12.75). A person moving up the ladder needs 'a cost-efficient house oriented to today's life-style' (*New Yorker*, 15.9.75). People in Sydney are issued with an invitation to 'see for yourself how a brand

new 2-storey townhouse will improve your lifestyle' (*Sydney Morning Herald*, 28.2.76). From these and many other examples it is evident that a desirable 'life-style' today is rooted in possessions, in what one has, rather than in what one does. One's 'life-style', to a large extent, is the stage which one creates for oneself and one's family to sit, stand and lie on. The better the stage, the better the person.

Lighthearted

Calculated to make people lighthearted, cheerful, not too serious. One is cheerful because one has fought back against adversity, but lighthearted because one has decided to ignore, at least temporarily, the more unpleasant aspects of life, to pretend they do not exist. Cheerfulness is therefore a deeper, more solid quality than light-heartedness. The B.B.C. is fond of taking, in special programmes, 'a lighthearted look at the news', which means that the journalists concerned have decided to remain only on the bright side of the moon. 'Not to be taken seriously' is also the message in 'pretty, lighthearted wines, immediately pleasing' (*Times*, 31.7.76).

Limitation

Lessening, reduction. A polite, soothing word, used in professional circles to describe a state of affairs which may be dangerous and frightening. An elderly judge may suffer from a 'limitation of hearing', and an alcoholic minister from an 'occasional limitation of memory'. A committee appointed to investigate the possibility that all doctors might not be as competent as they should be, spoke of 'a need to recognise a limitation of skill as some doctors age' (*Competence*, 1976), which makes the point as nicely and tactfully as anyone possibly could.

Limited

Small. Another word, which like 'intimate' reflects an anxiety to avoid losing face by saying 'small'. 'In addition to running a more limited bakery operation' (*D Tel*, 30.3.76)—a smaller baking oper-ation; '. . . has a limited number of vacancies in its buying team' (*S Times*, 16.11.75)—a small number of vacancies; 'Detached period farmhouse requiring limited internal refurbishment' (*Times*, 3.12.76)—a small amount of internal refurbishment; 'The Bicenten-nial carpet is now being shown at a limited number of fine stores' (*New Yorker*, 1.10.75)—a small number of stores. It is obvious that there must be some limit to the number of goods offered for sale–only opportunities and the grains of sand on the beach are unlimited–but many people with things to sell use the word 'limited' to give the impression that a quantity-line has been deliberately drawn to make what is available more precious, more valuable, and therefore more desirable. 'Hurry! this is a limited offer' (*Sydney Morning Herald*, 28.2.76). The commodity being new houses it would be surprising if the number were not limited. So, too, in a store in the American Federal Capital, where 'the selection is vast, but some items are in limited quantities' (*Washington Star*, 17.10.76). All are in limited quantities–the store buyers do not give their suppliers carte blanche to send as many as they like–but some lines cannot be re-ordered. All of the above examples together, however, are not an adequate preparation for teasing out the meaning of one particular advertisement, a collector's gem. It reads: 'The job is unquestionably the first of its kind in Britain–in a facet of business which our limited audience would not even have considered as a career' (*D Tel*, 17.12.76). What is 'our limited audience'? After discussion with other connoisseurs, this tentative explanation is suggested. The advertisement has been inserted by a firm of management selection consultants, which concentrates mainly on finding people for jobs carrying a fairly high salary. Men and women in the market at this level would, one might guess, constitute 'our limited audience', and these people would never have considered the job in question because, being 'the first of its kind in Britain', they would in all probability not have come across anything quite like it before. This obscurity and muddle would not have occurred if the writer had felt able to drop the posing and pretentiousness and to say something like, 'in a type of industrial work which our very specialised clientele would not previously have considered as a career'.

Limp

Flat, lifeless. 'Given the obviously provocative implications of the motif, his text is oddly neutral and limp' (*Art Journal*, XXXV/4, Summer 1976). The writer had not, in other words, risen to his subject. The painting was exciting and demanded attention; what he wrote about it was detached and lacking in liveliness and interest. Limp is a difficult word to use, in art criticism and in many other kinds of writing, because of its unpredictable associations. It is the hand with no grip when it shakes yours, the fish on the slab, the clothes removed from the body, the person who has fainted, the male organ which is no longer erect. The sexual connotation is never far away and there seems to be no doubt that it was present in the mind of this particular writer. The picture is the 'provocative' woman to whom the critic has remained indifferent ('neutral') and completely unexcited ('limp'). This, however, is a personal interpretation and one has no evidence that other readers would have responded in the same way. At this point one has to wonder if the article was intended for a closed audience of artists and critics who would have understood immediately what the author was getting at, or whether the periodical has a wider, more open circulation, in which case both intellectual and emotional communication might have been much less successful. Is this particular critic, in fact, trying to reach the feelings or the minds of his readers? Is the quotation something which other artists and critics will sniff at and sense a friend, or is it something which will worry and divide its readers just because they are a heterogeneous group? If the first answer is correct, clarity of meaning is relatively unimportant, but if the second, it is extremely important.

Lineality
Line of descent. A favourite Marshall McLuhanism, taken over by his disciples. 'Man's lineality was interrupted by Darwin, whose lineality highlighted a missing segment in the sequence' (McLuhan, 1962). An ugly sentence, which could be translated, 'Man's traditional idea of his line of descent was upset by Darwin, whose own theory gave prominence to a missing link in the chain'. Why does McLuhan feel the need for this word, which does nothing to ease the problem of communication, sets up unnecessary prejudice against the author, and introduces a bogus element of science into a sentence which has no need of it?

Liquid
Flowing like a stream. This is the charitable definition, but anyone who uses the word nowadays should bear closely in mind its regrettable alcoholic associations, as in 'a liquid lunch', from which no-one can wholly escape. To pretend otherwise is to confess insensitivity to the overtones of contemporary English. The critic responsible for 'his sleight-of-finger and his liquid lyricism in Stamitz's G Major flute concerto' (*Times*, 12.7.76) might have chosen a better adjective, such as 'gently flowing', to avoid the irreverent thought on the part of his readers that the flautist's lyrical playing may

have been due to his having taken a drop before coming on to the platform.

Literally

Exactly as the word says. In most cases 'literally' can be thrown out of the sentence altogether without the slightest loss or distortion. To allow it to remain is to invite trouble from people who know what the word means. 'The patented pulsing action literally dissolves stress from tired muscles' (*Signature*, Jan/Feb 1976). The 'patented pulsating action' is that of a shower and it does not and cannot 'literally dissolve stress from tired muscles'. Stress, unlike instant coffee, does not dissolve in anything, much as one might like it to. A classic instance of the same type of misuse is' "Crabs and lobsters are literally to be found crawling round the floor waiting for the order", reports an early nominator' (*Good Food Guide*, 1973).

Live

Up-to-date, stimulating, full of energy and creativity. 'It no longer provided a training as live as that which could be found in Venice' (*Apollo*, July 1966). Does this mean anything more than 'as good a training'? Or is there, perhaps, an ingredient of 'stimulating' in it? Was the training itself live, or did the liveliness come from the people whom the artist was able to meet and work with? 'Live' hinders rather than helps here. It makes the reader think too long about what should be a word of only moderate importance. To allow this to happen is to show that language has temporarily slipped out of one's control, and that, if not actually diseased, is certainly not a symptom of health.

Loaded

Full. 'This great house is loaded with charm' (Toronto *Globe and Mail*, 31.1.76). 'Loaded' implies weight and probably bulk, too, neither of which is a characteristic of charm, which is a light, airy quality. 'Loaded with money' has been with us for a long time, however, and is no bad expression. If one thinks of 'charm' as equatable with the things that money can buy, with material possessions, then a certain kind of establishment may well be 'loaded with charm', creaking and groaning with the sheer weight of all the charm placed upon its floors and walls and hanging from its ceilings. It is just possible that this is what the cynical advertiser meant, but one cannot be sure.

Loading
Allowance. Properly, the weight one has to put on one side of the scales in order to make them balance, and hence the extra ration of something a person has to receive in order to compensate for some particular hardship, like living in London, and to make all seem fair. 'Weighting' is used in the same sense. Often, as in 'liberal annual leave loading' (*The Age*, 28.2.76), the word has no meaning whatever, except possibly to make the leave seem more.

Loan
To lend. 'Loan' is the noun, 'lend' the verb, or so we in Britain were brought up to believe. But 'loan' is now widely used as a verb, following American practice. There is some evidence that 'lend' is continuing to be used where the transaction is informal and between friends – 'She lent me a pound' – whereas 'loan' is preferred where some more businesslike arrangement is involved – 'He loaned me money to carry on' (*D Tel*, 5.2.76). One cannot, as yet, imagine oneself asking one's friends, 'Could you loan me a pound', although 'loan' would upgrade the transaction and possibly add an extra note of respectability to it.

Location
Site, place, factory. Until the 1960s, 'location', 'locate' and 'located' were usually considered slightly vulgar Americanisms in Britain, but since then the American usage has gained ground rapidly, especially in business and industrial circles. One reason for this has certainly been the wish to avoid using the word 'factory' wherever possible. 'Environment' (q.v.) and 'location' are now the most popular euphemisms for the nearly unspeakable 'factory'. One company requires recruits 'to join our Engineering team at this location' (*D Tel*, 27.11.75) and there is reference elsewhere to 'a public company employing 1500 people in three manufacturing locations' (*D Tel*, 17.12.76). A 'manufacturing location' is what our more straightforward ancestors called a 'factory'.

Locum
Stand-in. For generations, the word 'locum', an abbreviation for 'locum-tenens', has been used almost exclusively by the medical profession, meaning a doctor engaged on a temporary basis to do the work of someone who is ill or on holiday. It has now been taken over

by the pharmaceutical and medical supplies industries, giving the completely erroneous impression that people employed by such firms form part of the medical profession. Reference to 'locum medical representatives' (*S Tel*, 4.7.76) would certainly put such a thought into the heads of most readers.

Logical

Able to reason logically? A word from the business world. 'The ideal candidate will be logical and numerate' (*S Times*, 20.6.76). The meaning of the word in such a context cannot be established with any certainty, because there is always the possibility that the firm either had nothing precise in mind at all or that it could not bring itself to utter the simple requirement that was in its mind and so covered up the blunt truth with something more impressive and obscure. Was the person being sought to be, perhaps, 'able to think and speak clearly'?

Long

Making its presence felt in the mouth for a long time? A wine word. 'The 1970 is a profound, long wine' (*Times*, 19.6.76); 'Long and with a fine, clean, finish, it would be a wine for spring lamb' (*Times*, 20.3.76).

Love

Make love. 'Come love me in Room 11' (*Montreal Star*, 16.10.76. A film title). One can never be sure what this sadly mistreated word means. Usually the imperative means 'make love', not 'love', although civilisation has not yet declined to a point at which the two cannot co-exist. The possibility that one may, however, love someone without making love to him or her seems to be steadily less acceptable.

Loving

Gentle, like a caress from a loving hand. 'Ondine with loving lanolin gives the soft touch that a woman's skin needs' (*Vogue*, Dec 1975). Lanolin never loved anybody or anything, but it can possibly be 'kind', in the sense of 'beneficial'. Beneficial, however, would be far too cold and impersonal to serve the advertiser's purpose. Once the manufacturer can implant the message that his product loves you, the customer has yielded and the sale is made.

Lovingly
Slowly, carefully and sensitively. Furniture, for example, is no longer polished, but 'lovingly hand-rubbed to antique sheen' (*New Yorker*, 21.6.76), just as the patient, old, skilled craftsmen used to do it in far-back Colonial days.

Low-budget
Cheap to make. 'Low-budget' has come into existence for the same reasons as 'low-cost' (see below). 'A series of low-budget violent Westerns . . .' (*Radio Times*, 31.1.76) can be screened without any sacrifice of propriety or B.B.C. professional standards. 'Cheap Westerns' would arouse much more hostility.

Low-cost
Cheap. 'Cheap' is a word that no really well-bred person can use nowadays, except possibly in inverted commas. The implication is that if something is 'cheap', the quality must be low and the design poor. 'One has to pay for quality' is the motto, and 'cheap' has suffered as a result. It is no longer acceptable to be offering and seeking somewhere cheap to live. It has now to be 'low-cost furnished accommodation' (*D Tel*, 27.11.75). A person, too, can be 'low-cost'; 'There is no cheaper way of running a radio-station than sitting a low-cost young man in a studio to talk about his breakfast and his fan-mail' (*N Statesman*, 11.4.69). In skilled hands, 'low-cost' can be a new instrument to play, with possibilities that were lacking before its arrival, such as the delightful counterpointing in 'The holiday with the low-cost high-life' (*Radio Times*, 15–21 Jan 1977).

Low-key
Modest, not assertive. 'A low-key shopping and office centre' (*AFR*, 4.3.76). Unfortunately, 'low-key' can also be a euphemism for 'mean, skimped', which many projects certainly are, and without actually going to look for oneself the precise meaning of the word is not clear. Politicians are now given to making 'low-key speeches'. Following a reference in *The Times* to something Mr. Harold Wilson had said 'in an unusually low-key speech', Sir Thomas Armstrong was moved to write to the paper (7.1.76). 'What,' he asked, 'does it mean? Pitch can be low. Metaphorically, I suppose, the tone of a speech can be low. Key can be major or minor, but never low. This catch-phrase, so uncritically used, like its friend, "the grass-roots", is

spreading like a weed and should be eradicated. Low profile also.' (q.v.)

Low-popular

Unpopular. 'The low-popular children included untreated isolates' (*JEP*, 59/3, 1968). 'Low-popular' is considered by social scientists and psychologists to be more objective, less emotional than 'unpopular'. It is undeniably a euphemism for 'unpopular', and to that extent a barrier to straight thinking. Cf. High-popular.

Low-profile

As inconspicuous as possible, quiet. 'The Nixon doctrine of "low-profile" involvement, in other words a maximum of aid and a minimum of U.S. troops . . .' (*Guardian*, 24.8.70). The phrase can, however, mean 'doing nothing or next to nothing', as well as 'doing something, but not allowing it to be seen'. Politicians, companies and governments do not like the suggestion that they are doing nothing. 'Adopting a low profile' is more dignified and better for the reputation. 'The company's low profile over the elections . . .' (*Times*, 20.1.76) may have concealed either considerable activity behind the scenes or equally notable sloth and apathy. Mole-like energy, however, is undoubtedly referred to in a reference to a decision 'to concentrate on only the most visible militant activities to the neglect of equally effective low-profile tactics' (Corwin, 1974). How our ancestors managed without 'low-profile' it is difficult to imagine. Their words 'concealed' and 'secret' seem so indiscreetly blunt to modern ears and eyes.

Luminous

Throwing light on, making something shine? A critic's pet word. 'His swift and luminous treatment of the scherzo' (B.B.C., Radio 3, 8.2.76). 'Swift' is clear enough: the pianist played the movement fast. But what was this 'luminous treatment'? Is the meaning that his playing caused the music to glow and sparkle with light? Or that the way the scherzo was performed was the result of light having shone into the brain of the pianist? 'Luminous' would in that case be a synonym of 'intelligent'. A third possibility is that the interpretation allows the listener to hear the music in a new way, that it is illuminated for him. It is a pity that a word so bound up with light should leave the reader so much in the dark.

Luxe

Luxury, de luxe. The word has made something of a comeback since 1950. There does not appear to be any significant difference between 'luxe' and 'luxury', although by pretending that 'luxe' is an abbreviation of 'luxury', as many younger people give the impression of thinking, it can be given an up-to-date, democratic and put-in-its-place feeling, whereas 'luxury' tends to be associated with yesterday's tastes and affluence. 'How luxe the feel of polyester satin' (*New Yorker*, 1.10.75). 'He looks around his palace of a house with a sniffly and quite unfair resentment, considering its comfort and luxe' (*New Yorker*, 3.6.74). 'Luxe' slightly pokes fun, in a way that 'luxury' does not.

Luxurious

Suggesting a film star's home, an oil-king's palace or an expensive cruising liner, with plenty of mirrors, gilt, heavy upholstery, small table-lamps and chandeliers. 'International cuisine served in luxurious surroundings' ('Evangeline' dining room of Nova Scotian Hotel, Halifax).

Luxury

Costing a good deal more than the average; better than it need be to do the job; making one feel like a princess at the very least. 'This beautifully finished luxury sleeping-bag' (*D Tel*, 21.8.76) – exceptionally warm and soft; 'A luxury tour to the four corners of the world' (*Good Times*, T.H.F., Summer 1975) – with the best hotels available, no night travel, and no roughing it; 'Luxury bathroom with shower' (*Obs*, 30.11.75) – with bidet and coloured tiles; 'Newly built luxury house' (*SMJ*, 27.11.75) – 4 bedrooms, properly heated, 2 lavatories. It is difficult to disentangle the various elements of 'luxury'. At its best, the word means that something is properly fitted, equipped, organised and designed to modern standards. At its worst, it hints at the dream-world inhibited by successful actors, opera-singers and the chairmen of large companies. In most contexts, there is more of the worst than the best.

M

Maintenance

Keeping in existence; in working order; preserving. The two meanings illustrated by (a) 'the maintenance of law and order', on the one hand, and (b) 'the maintenance of a car' on the other are not normally confused. But the sociologists' wretched habit of clamping two nouns together can create serious problems for the reader. What, for instance, is meant by 'Could a society develop a set of mores sufficient for society maintenance' (Cardwell, 1973)? Is this sense (a) or sense (b)? Does it mean 'sufficient to preserve the framework of society', or 'sufficient to carry out running repairs on society'?

Major

A window-dressing word, which sometimes means large, sometimes nothing at all. Politicians are fond of publicising the fact that they are about to make 'a major speech', fearful, no doubt, that the public and the newspapers would not recognise it as a major speech if it were not clearly labelled, and the dream of every chairman is to have his business officially described as 'a major engineering company' or 'major printing group', or whatever. 'A big engineering company' would not be the same at all; 'major' conveys the idea of importance, as well as size. 'This French subsidiary of a major international company' (*D Tel*, 27.11.75) shows the correct and pleasing form, and so, up to a point, does 'A major hospital products subsidiary' (*D Tel*, 27.11.75). The impressiveness of the latter example suffers somewhat, however, by leaving readers in the dark as to whether 'major' refers to the hospital products or to the subsidiary.

Make

'Make' is such a simple word and has been around for such a long time that one might reckon that hardly anyone could come to grief with it. But this is not so, as seen from the example of the company which offers 'an opportunity to make career progress and development' (*D Tel*, 28.1.76). This is, one supposes, an opportunity to progress in one's career and to develop in the way the person concerned wants to develop. One cannot, however, 'make development'; it is not even clear if the development is that of the individual or of his employers. 'Make development' could quite conceivably mean 'bring about developments in the company'.

Mandatory
Obligatory, binding. This word was, until recently, used almost exclusively in connexion with the operations of national or international government. It is now, for some reason, a popular and supposedly grander equivalent of 'essential'. The firm which tells applicants for a job that a 'knowledge of languages is an advantage, but not mandatory' (*D Tel*, 6.1.76) is doing its best to elevate itself to the level of a government department, where such talk is normal and fitting.

Manipulative methods
Bribery. A superb euphemism, totally confusing to those who have not been initiated. 'The Chinese use manipulative methods' (B.B.C. Television, 1.1.77) might well be thought to refer to the skill shown by the Chinese in osteopathy.

Man-manager
Skilled at handling people. Industry and commerce appear to work on the assumption that business requires two broad groups of skills, one concerned with things and the other with people. The people, to judge by the frequent requirement 'must be able to control staff', are commonly thought of as dangerous animals, and 'man-manager', too, has something of a lion-taming flavour about it, especially when it is used in contexts such as 'experienced sales trainer and man-manager' (*S Tel*, 14.12.75).

Manpower
Staff. 'Manpower' is an unwelcome hangover from two world wars, when people were turned into fodder for statisticians and civil servants. A great many problems would solve themselves if this and similar words were dropped and something more human substituted. 'The Hospital and Health Services Commission recognised that all these activities have manpower implications' (*Health*, 1975) would be, with its bureaucratic ending replaced by what it really means, 'all these activities need people to run them'. Once the translation has been effected, the need for the sentence disappears. What one needs to know is the number of people that are likely to be required, not the

fact that staff are necessary, which should be obvious.

Marine residence

House by the sea. An estate agent's word. 'A beautifully fitted marine residence of recent construction' (*Times*, 20.5.76). No owner of such a house is likely to tell his friends that he has just bought a marine residence. No one seems to know just how near the sea a house needs to be in order to qualify for the accolade of 'marine residence'. Must it be right on the sea-front, with nothing but a road or path between it and the beach? Or will a view of the sea from the upstairs windows or a smell of the sea in the garden be enough?

Market penetration

Share of the market. The fondness of businessmen for sexual imagery is remarkable. Manufacturers ('producers') are, of course, always male, but markets are female, to be attacked, seized, and, with luck, penetrated, with all resistance overcome and all competitors beaten off. 'A progressive Australian owned manufacturing company, enjoying excellent market penetration both nationally and export (sic).' (*Sun*, 2.3.76) illustrates the point. Since markets are female, salesmen are naturally male, and advertisements frequently specify that 'aggressive', 'thrusting' men are required for such posts.

Marketing oriented

Making things that sell. This extraordinary phrase is either meaningless or reveals a state of affairs that one could hardly believe to exist. If the purpose of a factory is not to sell its products, what is it for? Why should it be necessary to say that a firm, or any part of it, is 'marketing oriented'? Yet apparently it is. 'The Director will be solely responsible for the profitable organisation of the Cider Division, which is marketing oriented' (*Economist*, 14.12.76). What this must surely mean is that the Cider Division first takes pains to find out what kind of cider its customers and potential customers prefer, then makes such cider, in the quantities required, and finally delivers and sells it and gathers in the money. All this is so elementary and so obvious that the lay reader takes his eyes up from the advertisement once again, convinced that he must have missed something. He can reassure himself. The sentence quoted above should have ended at 'Cider Division'. All the rest is padding, put in, like so much artistic material, for the sake of the colour and the rhythm.

Marque
Make. A piece of motoring snobbery. It has been customary for many years to refer to racing cars and the more expensive sports cars by the French term 'marque', instead of the normal English 'make'. The practice has been extended by motoring writers to perfectly ordinary production cars in the middle price-range, to encourage people to think that they would be buying something very superior if they were to decide to buy the model in question. A description of the new Rover, for instance, praised 'the *marque*'s reputation for safety' (*S Tel*, 4.7.76).

Mass
A highly-emotive adjective, roughly equivalent to 'the working-class, considered as a closely-knit collective body'. So 'a revolutionary party, united in its aims and engaged in the mass struggle' (*Comment*, 29.11.75). 'Mass' is never used in a pejorative sense by the extreme Left, but it very frequently is by people of other shades of political opinion, e.g. 'There is an argument for introducing rationing in London, where some form of mass hysteria seems to have occurred' (*Times*, 7.12.73), the implication here being that people in the mass can be dangerous, something which Communists would never accept. It is, of course, perfectly possible, even in today's highly charged political climate, to use 'mass' in a neutral sense, as in 'The monetarists fear that some unemployment may be the necessary price of avoiding mass unemployment' (*Times*, 5.11.74). The difficulty in many contexts is to decide whether 'mass' is carrying any attitude or not, and this will usually depend on the prejudices with which one arrives at one's reading.

Massified
Totally absorbed into the mass. One might believe this to be impossible, but we have, on good authority, 'the massified negro, i.e. the negro who thinks of himself only as a section of the mass, with no personal identity' (*B J Soc*, June 1969). This term does not seem particularly flattering, although it is certainly intended to be objective, and it is unlikely that black people would use it about themselves. The danger is that once one has seen the word in print one may begin to believe in it, as one does in 'the fully institutionalised patient', who is also supposed to have lost his personal identity. And

then one finds oneself talking to such a person and the theory begins to crack.

Master

The master of the household. 'Master bedroom with dressing room' (*SMJ*, 27.11.75). A ludicrous attempt to make everyone believe that he owns a castle or a mansion, with servants at his beck and call and he is the master of them all. It means, whatever its size, that it is the biggest bedroom in the house, and quite probably the only one large enough to take a double bed.

Master-crafted

Skilfully made or prepared. A popular piece of American nostalgia, expressing a longing for the good old days of long apprenticeships and patient hand-workmanship. There are many instances where it does not seem appropriate at all. One such is, '16 of the world's finest fillets master-crafted from selected beef' (*New Yorker*, 8.11.76). A chair can be master-crafted, and so can jewellery, but steak certainly cannot. A butcher, however skilled and experienced, can do no more than select meat, cut it and trim it. He cannot make it, which is what 'crafted' means.

Master-mind

To plan or direct. The noun, in the sense of someone with an outstanding or commanding mind, has been used since the eighteenth century, the verb only since the early 1940s. There is nothing wrong with either the noun or the verb when they are properly used, that is, when the mind in question really is a master-mind, as in 'a ruthless master-minding conspirator' (*Guardian*, 29.6.73). The word has unfortunately been seriously debased by puzzle-games and quiz programmes, notably by the B.B.C.'s *Mastermind* series, where the successful competitors merely have exceptionally good memories and quick wits, and are not, so far as one can judge master-minds at all, with great planning and directing brains. The series would be much more accurately called *Master Memory*. The person who draws up the school timetable does just that. He does not 'mastermind' it. One should view every use of 'master-mind' with the greatest suspicion, and ask oneself what level and type of mind is really involved. 'And to mastermind all aspects of the project' (*S Times*, 30.11.75) would probably pass the test.

Mature
With a fair amount of experience, adult. It is not considered polite to say in an advertisement that candidates should be 'adult'. 'You will be a mature thinker' (*S Times*, 25.4.76) sounds much better.

Maturing
Nearly ready for attention. Business English. 'A department which is still pioneering, but in a maturing marketing environment' (*S Times*, 25.4.76). This example means, 'The department has found the going very rough and has met with little success so far, but the market situation seems to be improving and we think it should soon be worth our while to make a serious effort to start selling'. This, of course, would reek of amateurism and such words would never be uttered in public.

Maxi-length
The maxi-midi-mini series of compounds began to hit the world in the 1970s and it shows no sign of fading away. It can refer either to length or to size, and replaces such out-of-date forms as 'full-size', 'medium-length', 'short' and so on, which are reckoned to be dull. Such words give no more than a rough guide to how big the object in question is, and one has to use one's hard-won specialised knowledge to decide what kind of measurement is referred to. 'Add a touch of luxury to your leisure hours with this maxi-length robe' (*New Yorker*, 8.11.76) refers to a garment which may or may not actually sweep the ground, but cannot be far away from it. What is 'maxi-length' one year may, of course, be a slightly different length from what is 'maxi-length' the next. 'Maxi' is always relative to 'midi' and 'mini'. There is no absolute definition.

Maximise
To make as big, easy, efficient, profitable or anything else as possible. A very lazy word, useful when one has to say something and cannot be bothered to find the exact expression. Very useful, too, for staving off awkward questions, since obviously nobody has a right to expect more than the maximum. 'Sales Administration has been separated from the selling function in order to maximise customer service' (*S Times*, 27.6.76)–to give customers the best possible service; 'our homes are set amidst quiet meadows and woodlands and access to the outdoors has been maximised' (*Boston Sunday Globe*, 10.10.76)–easy

to get out into the fields and woods; '. . . has just introduced a unique service and we need a small number of professional sales people to maximise this situation' (*D Tel*, 30.9.76)–to push the service as hard as possible.

Meaningful

Useful, fruitful, real. A jargon word which first began to become really tedious in the 1960s, when everything had to be 'meaningful' to have any value. It is a perfectly respectable word, with a long history of service as the opposite of 'meaningless'. There can be no objection to 'All of us see a need to be related in a meaningful way to the black experience' (*Sat Review*, 18.12.71) or 'The Federation met again last month to try to get meaningful talks going again on a new disputes machinery' (*D Tel*, 9.9.76). In both cases something has to have a real meaning for the parties concerned. Irritation and bewilderment arise, however, at the point where one realises that the value of the sentence remains exactly the same after 'meaningful' has been thrown out. 'This,' one says, 'is mere trendiness'. A sentence containing 'meaningful' evidently has more appeal in certain quarters than one without it. Three such examples are: ' . . . a meaningful teaching relationship can emerge in which student and teacher are equal in terms of the recognition of their respective worth' (Rubinstein & Stoneman, 1970); '. . . thus allowing the encumbent to contribute towards corporate goals and provide objectives in a meaningful way' (*Sydney Morning Herald*, 28.2.76) and, even worse, 'a meaningful creative experience that enlarges our awareness' (Mueller, 1967). The non-trendy 'real' or 'significant' often does the job just as well as 'meaningful' and is less distracting and socially divisive. 'It is still useful to continue with a certain categorization of new music. Not only are there meaningful distinctions between Old World and New . . .' (Salzman, 1974) is a case in point.

Means-oriented

Dependent on the resources available. Most things unfortunately are, but there are those who still find the point worth making, always provided suffciently 'professional' language is employed to spread a veneer over the obvious. 'Most teacher preparation sequences are decidedly means-oriented' (*JER*, 63/3, Nov 1969) or, in other words, when teachers prepare their lessons, they have to do so with the resources they have to hand.

Media behaviour
The amount of attention one pays to newspapers or television as a source of news. At first sight, it might appear that one was concerned with the manner in which the media behave, but it is not so. What the phrase is trying in such a clumsy fashion to convey is that people behave in different ways towards the media. 'Using Media Behaviour as a crude index of political participation' (Hyman, 1969).

Mediate
A psychological term, meaning to achieve a result by acting as an agency or middle-man between an idea and its realisation. Often used more in the sense of 'influence' or 'help to bring about', which are perfectly acceptable translations of the jargon word. 'We shall return later to personality factors as they mediate these more general processes' (Hyman, 1969), i.e. as they influence these general processes; '. . . evokes an anticipatory goal response which should mediate avoidance behaviour' (*JEP*, 61/2, 1970), i.e. which should bring about the kind of behaviour which leads people to avoid difficulties and problems.

Mediated
Made available, organised, provided. Any one of these alternatives would be preferable to 'mediated' in 'Medical services in the urban community are mediated through a multiplicity of institutions' (Nosow & Form, 1962). What was it that drove these authors to use 'mediated' here when a simpler term would have done equally well, if not better? Why was there this need to impress?

Melodic
Possessing a melody, tuneful. This, one might think, would be an essential characteristic of a song, but sometimes there appears to be a necessity to spell it out. 'Having worked with Paul, whose songs are so melodic . . .' (*Melody Maker*, 29.1.77).

Memorialise
Remember, commemorate. 'Memorialising someone's grand-father . . .' (Schlebecker & Petersen, 1972). This is a very ugly and totally unnecessary word, which will certainly suggest different things to different people and therefore gets in the way of communication, rather than helping it. 'Remember', 'Erect a

memorial to' and 'commemorate' are three possibilities, any one of which may be equally correct, other information being lacking.

Memories

Mementoes? Reminiscences? The advertisement for a 'Sales Manager, Military Memories' (*S Times*, 20.6.76) suggests more than one possibility. Is the person appointed to be responsible for selling old badges, medals, pistols and shakoes, or is he to be on the lookout for retired generals with good stories to tell?

Metaphor

The expression of one thing in terms of another, in order to create a more striking effect, a highly condensed comparison. Dylan Thomas's 'lake-eyed cows' have big, wet eyes, and Bessie Bighead sleeps 'until the night sucks out her soul and spits it into the sky'. A musical metaphor is not impossible, but, if such things exist, they are likely to make enormous demands on any listener bold enough to contemplate the task. The degree of knowledge required to recognise and appreciate a musical quotation is great enough, but the concentration, study and re-study which would be involved to understand the musical equivalent of 'lake-eyed cows' would surely make music the preserve of an extremely small élite with a great deal of time on its hands. What, then, are we to understand by 'The disparate elements are brought together in very close, tight forms which are also intended to serve as analogies or metaphors' (*ABC Radio Guide*, 6-12 March 1976)? Is this an elegant swindle or do we go struggling on until we identify the metaphors, persuaded that we may be missing something if we fail to make the effort?

Middle-class

Traditionally, the class which values security, comfort and independence. No term in English is more argued about, abused and defended, none more socially divisive or more likely to engender bad feeling. It is no longer possible to use it in a way that is likely to produce common agreement, but no other word exists to express the concepts which lie behind it. Among a large proportion of the young, it is a term of contempt, an encapsulation of everything that is reactionary, cowardly and despicable. 'One might as well be dead as middle-class' sums up this attitude. On the other hand, the English-speaking world contains tens of millions of people who are prepared, if not to go to the barricades, at least to sacrifice a great deal in defence of what they would conceive to be their 'middle-class values', the most important of these probably being the right to own a house of their choice, to educate their children in a way which they feel to be satisfactory, to spend their money as they please, to save, to make provision for their old age, and rely on the law to protect them and their families from theft, violence and attack. All this adds up to setting a high value on independence and on the rule of law, and to be permanently suspicious of collectivist and socialist solutions to their own and the world's problems. No definition of 'middle-class' which fails to understand and explain its complex, explosive background and associations is of much use, which is another way of saying that there is and can be no satisfactory definition of 'middle-class', except perhaps the negative one, 'not working-class'. One can only take each instance of its use as it comes, measure it against its context, and enquire privately what it means, if indeed it means anything. What, for example, is to be understood by 'the pseudo-revolutionary middle-class totalitarians' (Lipset, 1971)? Who are these people? Where does one find them, frightening and loathsome as they may appear in the abstract? But, unless there is some kind of working agreement as to at least the outline of the middle-class, much of our sociological writing must remain unintelligible. The only measure that seems possible is to say, 'The members of the middle-class receive a salary, not a wage', and for the time being to leave matters there. We can then try to interpret most of the references to the middle-class in a dispassionate and, one hopes, sensible way. In the three sober and typical sentences which follow one may usefully experiment with replacing 'middle-class' by 'salary-earning class' and see how satisfactory the result seems to be, or in what ways it is unsatisfactory. 'The West Country, he found, has much the highest proportion laying claim to middle-class status' (Allen, 1968); 'Within the fringe of middle-class permissiveness exists a hard core of inflexible demand' (Craft, 1970); 'It is not that working-class children do not have in their passive vocabulary the vocabulary used by the middle-class children' (Rubinstein & Stoneman, 1970).

Mind
Mind. 'Like nothing your mind can imagine' (*The Age*, 20.3.76). 'Mind' is obviously redundant. 'Like nothing you can imagine' does everything required: one can hardly imagine with one's feet.

Mind-bending

Stupefying, incredible. 'A kaleidoscope of mind-bending sound' (*The Age*, 20.3.76. Film review). It is not easy to envisage this. The thought of having one's mind bent by sound or anything else is not pleasant, but what does it all mean? Music of overwhelming intensity or variety? Sound of such subtlety that the mind cannot comprehend it? In some contexts the word appears to mean nothing whatever and can safely be dropped, as in a reference to a campaign 'to raise money for Release, which has done such a lot to help those whose tastes in mind-bending lie in this direction' (*Melody Maker*, 29.1.77).

Mind-power

Intelligence. Fashionable business English. 'The Company's very high regard for scientific mind-power' (*D Tel*, 27.2.76). 'Mind-power' was presumably coined by analogy with 'man-power' and 'brain-power', but whether the idea behind it is of quantity or of quality is not clear. Should we translate 'The Company's high opinion of scientific intelligence', or 'The Company's strong wish to have plenty of scientists about the place'?

Mini-pétillance

Slight sparkle or crackle? ' . . . the mini-pétillance possessed by many young wines of quality' (*Times*, 29.5.76). No reference book can help us and the attitude of the wine-writers themselves is that one either recognises mini-pétillance when one sees it or one does not.

Minstrel-gallery

Gallery. From the house-agents' vade mecum. 'Gallery' sounds too ordinary to have much appeal, so 'Two further minstrel-gallery bedrooms' (*S Times*, 23.11.75). In any old house, no matter how radical the conversion or modernisation, an upper-storey where a band can be tucked away out of sight is automatically a 'minstrel-gallery'. 'An extremely fine old barn converted to music or dance room with minstrel gallery' (*Country Life*, 26.2.76).

Mix

Range. 'The Company's research mix encompasses consumer and retail research including product and advertising testing, retail audit evaluation and the normal mix of projects associated with fast moving packaged goods' (*D Tel*, 27.2.76). This particular sentence is a little unusual in containing 'mix' twice – one can have too much of a good thing—but it does at least illustrate industry's present fondness for this word, which is supposed to indicate a faster-growing, more vigorous concern than those concerned with mere 'range'.

Mobilise
A favourite left-wing synonym for 'kick and push into some degree of activity'. 'We shall work to mobilise the labour movement . . .' (*M Star*, 20.2.76) illustrates the technique of regarding the adult population of a non-socialist country as a reserve army of soldiers, eager to wage the class-war to overthrow the capitalist tyrants.

Mobilizeability (sic)
Ability to be found, rounded up and employed. It is not only applied to troops. Anything and anybody can be 'mobilized', including, in the academic world, facts and information. 'A high degree of mobilizeability' (*B J Soc*, June 1969).

Modality
Procedure; method; attribute. 'Everyone involved in the peace talks here agrees that the military modalities of a cease-fire are more easily negotiated than the political modalities' (*New Yorker*, 17.10.70) is reasonably understandable. Since the date is 1970 and not 1870 a political and strategic specialist naturally puts 'modalities' instead of 'procedures', but the word is under control and causes no trouble. It does, however, very often get out of hand, as in '*Big Doll* is a fetish of very different modality' (*Con.*, Vol 186, May/Aug 1974). Does it mean anything more than 'of a very different type', or 'with very different characteristics'? Or does it mean that the writer imagines himself to be writing for a modality-circle of people?

Model
Can legitimately mean a simplified description of a system or situation, put forward as a basis for further investigation. Used in this special sense, the word is useful and causes no problems. 'Forrester has designed a model of the world system to try to discover the long term effects of pollution and overpopulation' (*D Tel*, 3.12.71). 'Model' is often used more loosely, however, so that we are left in doubt as to whether, in a particular context, it means either (a) 'recipe', 'method', 'pattern', or (b) as defined above, 'provisional description to make further research possible'. The difference is fundamental and

important. In the following example, are we being given (a) or (b)? 'The medical model of diagnosis and treatment of drug-dependent people is not always helpful or desirable' (*Am J Psy*, 128/2, 1971).

Modern living

The way we have to live today. 'Modern living' is a trendy phrase, which has changed its meaning in a subtle way during the past twenty-five years. In the 1960s, when money was plentiful, unemployment was very low and there was a great deal of optimism about, 'modern living' was 'progressive living', 'good living', 'Habitat living', 'colour supplement living', to which everybody was moving. Today, 'modern living' has changed its emphasis and now stresses pressure, the need to cut costs, to make do and mend. All references to 'modern living' have to be related very carefully to the prevailing mood at the time they were made. 'Modern living and the pressures that have combined to make an expensive luxury of space' (*Con*, Vol 165, May/Aug 1967) was written at a time of general bustle and business. The same words could have been written today, but the implications would be very different.

Module

Properly, a standardised or clearly defined unit. A building, for example, can be constructed of 'modules' and so can a course. But something different is presumably intended in the following industrial outpouring, although precisely what this may be is a matter for argument. 'Practical involvement in management training is essential and exposure to presentation of financial modules would be an added advantage' (*D Tel*, 25.2.76). Would 'financial modules' just possibly be accounts, and would someone who had undergone 'exposure to presentation' have had experience of presenting them?

Momentaneous

Covering a single moment. 'What can be more world-wide, more ego-transcending, more all-embracing, more universal and more momentaneous than the broadcasts, which in *Kurzwellen* take on the guise of musical material?' (Wörner, 1973). What 'momentaneous' means here must unfortunately remain a mystery. 'Immediate' is one possibility, but only a possibility. so, too, alas, is 'nothing but a word'.

Mono-linear

Along a single track. A McLuhanism. '. . . proneness to look for mono-linear causation' (McLuhan, 1962). To look for causes along a single line for related facts or possibilities?

Monopolist
Any large industrial concern in a non-socialist country. A Communist term. ' . . . the monopolists, such as British Leyland, I.C.I. and English Electric' (Matthews, 1975). 'Monopolist' and 'monopoly' are interchangeable terms of abuse. There is, in left-wing literature, an abundance of such references as 'People and policies committed to struggle against the monopolies' (*The British Road to Socialism*, 1977).

Moral Decay
Collapse of the traditional system and foundations of right and wrong. The phrase is also used by the right wing to describe the state of mind of those who subscribe to left-wing opinions, deny any allegiance to ·Christianity, or criticise the capitalist form of society. The persons concerned may in fact have, according to their own lights, a very strict code of morality. ' "Moral decay" is the popular explanation for these phenomena' (Miles, 1971). The 'phenomena' are black revolt, drugs, and drop-out cultures, all of which are, ironically, forms of protest against a form of 'moral decay' which has been found intolerable.

Morish (or Moreish)
That makes one want more. A nauseatingly cosy word. 'I should love another piece of that cake. It's so delightfully morish'. Picked up, unfortunately, by the wine-writers and added to their vocabulary. 'The smoothness and length of flavour make the wine artfully morish' (Hedges & Butler's *Wine News*, Aug 1976). But surely any decent wine should make one want more of it?

Most
Biggest. In the following example, one the sequence of 'mosts' should be replaced by 'biggest' and it is a test of literacy to be able to say which. 'We have the most resources of any removals firm in Britain. The most men, the most fleet, the most specialised equipment and the most branches' (*Times*, 30.1.76). Those used to grammatical English may find themselves held up for a while over 'most fleet', wondering if 'fleet' means something different from what they imagined at first sight.

Motion discomfort
The airlines' wonderful euphemism for travel sickness, puzzling to raw recruits to flying. 'Motion discomfort bag. Call stewardess' (National Airlines flight amenity, 1974).

Motivate
Persuade to work harder. No modern manager can be asked to make people work hard. If the fact were ever to be revealed, there would be a strike of major proportions. But he can quite safely, as yet, have 'motivation' added to his list of duties. 'You will be expected to motivate and stimulate as well as organise the technical resources under your control' (*S Times.* 16.11.75).

Motivated
Driven on. 'Candidates must be money motivated'. (*Montreal Star*, 16.10.76), i.e. anxious to earn as much money as possible and willing to do almost anything to achieve this. The old-fashioned word was 'greedy'.

Motivation
The act of inducing men to work harder, especially those categories of men whose income is at least partly dependent on their efforts. One prospective sales manager must have 'a substantial success record in sales force control and motivation' (*D Tel*, 27.11.75) and another 'will be responsible for the control and motivation of the company's sales force' (*S Times*, 30.11.75).

Motivational variable
One of several factors which may motivate a person. 'Involvement in a career may be conceptualised as a motivational variable' (*JER*, 60/2, Oct 1966) or, in simpler terms, 'Feeling involved in one's career is likely to drive one on to work harder', which most of us knew all along.

Mouthfilling
Either (a) which makes one want to swallow mouthful after mouthful of it, or (b) which fills the mouth with its beautiful taste. Or perhaps something quite different from either of these. Wine words do not abide by ordinary rules or logic. 'The Vino Etrusco is a mouth-filling sunny red' (*Times*, 20.3.76).

Mouthwatering
Enticing. 'While you browse through the mouthwatering menus' (Copthorne Hotel, Gatwick, brochure). Restaurant menus have a way of being more mouthwatering than the food itself, as many an eater has found to his cost. The brochure speaks truer than it knows.

Movement
A convenient but highly misleading portmanteau term for people who happen to belong to the same organisation, which may well be totally static and not moving anywhere. 'Movement' is much used by the trade unions and the political left to convey the impression of an irresistible force, conscious of its unity, strength and destiny. 'A call to the trade union movement to resist . . .' (*M Star*, 20.2.76) gives the flavour.

Multi-disciplined (or **Multi-disciplinary**)
Combining a number of academic fields, approaches or methods. The advantages of using the term are not always apparent. 'A multi-disciplined team of architects, engineers and quantity surveyors' (*D Tel*, 30.4.76) is a team of architects, engineers and quantity surveyors. They are the disciplines involved, and, if they are working as a team, the team is inevitably multi-disciplined. 'Multi-disciplined' has been added as a make-weight, so that nobody can be in danger of missing the point.

Multi-faceted
Making or doing a number of different things. A company which made dog-food and semi-conductors and ran a publishing business and a travel agency could fairly be described as multi-faceted. The metaphor comes, of course, from diamonds, and one can easily understand what pleasure it gives an industrial concern to think of itself as a large-cut diamond, with each facet sparkling in the light. The reality, unfortunately, is apt to be rather different, but there is no harm in seeking inspiration and comfort in this way, even if the force and brilliance of the metaphor sometimes fails to strike the world in general. 'A multi-faceted U.S. Company seeks an experienced results orientated Product Manager' (*D Tel*, 17.9.76) brings the flight of fancy down to earth a little.

Multi-issue
Concerned with a wide range of issues, a meaning which might not be immediately obvious to readers of such sentences as 'The danger of a multi-issue organisation is that, as it grows . . .' (Teodori, 1969).

Multi-segment
Not homogeneous. Marketing people see the world in terms of segments, each inhabited by its own special kind of person, buying different things from the people living in the segments on either side. 'He will service a multi-segment market through his suitably structured sales team' (*Sydney Morning Herald*, 28.2.76). 'Multi-layered', it should be observed, is never used, since it would imply that some parts of the market are above others, superior to them, and that would not be sound commercial practice. 'Segments' avoids this, by keeping everybody on the same level.

Multi-years
Lasting for a number of years. 'Project managers for multi-years technical assistance advisory services in developing countries' (*D Tel*, 27.2.76). This is so diseased that it is barely English at all, but we pay it the compliment of inclusion.

N

Native-protested
Opposed by the natives. A Germanism which may cause difficulties for anyone not accustomed to this barbarous type of idiom. 'They then struck northward and succeeded in making a native-protested landfall at Calicut in India' (*Con*, Vol 164, Jan/Apr 1967).

Natural
Which looks or tastes like the real thing. If an advertiser uses the word 'natural' in any context, one should be immediately suspicious. So, 'a seamless bra with a front panel for superb natural body shaping' (*Washington Star*, 17.10.76). The natural shaping of this part of the body is as it appears without a bra. The whole point of wearing a bra, in fact, is to prevent the bosom from looking natural. What can be

achieved with care and good fortune is stylised–natural, which can be and probably is a considerable improvement on the natural. All that 'natural' means is 'soft and gentle looking'.

Neat
Noticeable, but not too prominent. A wine frolic, as in a reference to 'the neat finish' of a Chablis (*Times*, 6.3.76). The word maddens or pleases the reader, according to the social and cultural world he inhabits, but in either case it means very little.

Negative
Hostile. Psychologists never 'like' or 'dislike' anything. They have either a positive or a negative attitude towards it. 'A negative attitude is defined as an implicit anticipatory pain or frustration response' (*JEP*, 61/2, 1970). One dislikes something, in other words, if one has reason to expect that it will hurt or cause feelings of frustration. If one speaks of 'the possibility of creating a negative attitude to C.A.I. (Computer assisted instruction) by poor programming . . .' (*JEP*, 61/1, 1970) one means 'causing people to be suspicious of C.A.I.', 'causing people to say no to it and to refuse to buy or use it'. A negative attitude in this case is the customer's 'no' to the salesman. To 'arrive at a negative assessment' of anything is to be opposed to it, to refuse to admit its usefulness or validity. 'India and Sunnite Islam arrived at a negative assessment of intoxicants long before alcohol was distilled' (*BB/NZ*, 1975).

Negatively privileged
Poor. The absurd phrase 'negatively privileged' suggests that one is in some way blessed as a result of one's poverty, which is almost certainly not what the writer intended at all. There is a distinct flavour of 'Blessed are the meek, for they shall inherit the earth'. In a typical example, one is advised to 'prevent any attempts at community closure by the negatively privileged' (*B J Soc*, June 1969).

Neo-Georgian
The modern builder and architect, trying to achieve a style which is more Georgian than anything else. The result will only rarely look Georgian, partly because the genuine Georgian house was either designed to form part of a continuous street elevation or to stand on its own as a mansion, flanked by buildings which led the eye gradually downwards from the roofline of the house, and partly

because the Georgian facade has to be adapted to modern requirements. A group of 'magnificent new neo-Georgian detached homes'
(*Times*, 30.4.76) all have a garage, of course, which is enough to kill
the Georgian balance and appearance stone dead, and give the
impression of a vaguely eighteenth century terrace chopped up and
pulled apart where the cuts were made. One can, of course, buy kits of
fibre-glass components now to allow one to add Georgian features to
the front of one's existing house. The effect of this would, in some
cases, be very neo-Georgian indeed.

New
Extra, of a different kind. 'Bauer goose-down adds new warmth'
(*New Yorker*, 8.11.76). If this means 'extra warmth', well and good,
but if there is any suggestion that the warmth is of a kind never
experienced before,one is entitled to object. Very few of the things
claimed to be 'new' are really entitled to the accolade and warmth is
certainly not one of them.

Non-imitate
Not to imitate. One cannot easily imagine Hamlet saying 'To be or
non-be. That is the question', but the psychologists and sociologists
talk in precisely this way, e.g. '. . . to imitate or non-imitate a peer
model' (Hoppe, 1970), and then wonder why polite people are
baffled and irreverent people laugh.

Non-purposive
Aimless, lacking in ambition and determination. 'The satiated person
tends to be non-purposive and inefficient' (*Business Horizons*, Dec
1973) means 'The person with everything has no good reason to want
any more', or, conversely and more poetically, 'The lean tiger hunts
best'. The businessman who has achieved all his goals can hardly be
compared to a slothful zoo-fed lion, however. 'Non-purposive and
inefficient' makes the point in a more civil fashion, always assuming
that one understands the full implication of the words.

Non-racist
Which treats people of all races and colours in exactly the same way.
There is no evidence that such a paradise exists anywhere in the
world, but the belief appears to exist. 'A few of us have already left for
non-racist African countries' (Mullard, 1973). It would be interesting
to know which these highly-favoured countries are.

Normal-admit
Admitted in the normal way. 'An equal number of normal-admit children matched for sex from the same classrooms' (*JEP*, 63/3, Nov 1969) are not, as might seem at first glance, children who need no medical attention to their admit, but children whose educational standards are normal and who have entered the school at the level which is usual for their age.

O

Objectivate
Express as a general truth. 'Language objectivates typical experiences' (*Sociology*, Sept 1975). What lies behind this ill-sounding sentence is the truism that, if it is to exist as a general means of communication, language has to be based on the assumption that one person's experience is the same as another's, that the word 'runs' always means the same, no matter whether the running is being carried out by A, B or C and ignoring the possibility that A may hate running, that B may enjoy it and that C, who suffers from arthritis, can run only with great pain. To iron out these differences is to 'objectivate experiences'. A more elegant and less confusing way of making the same point would be to say that 'language, in order to function at all, has to assume that all experiences are typical'.

Observational
Of observation. The passion for sounding as Germanic as possible and for avoiding prepositions at all costs leads to such wretchedly befogged forms of expression as 'Photography can permit improved observational effectiveness' (Michelson, 1975), i.e. 'Photography can help one to see and interpret certain things more clearly'.

Obstructed
Prevented. 'Obstructed from enjoying . . . ' (*D Tel*, 7.1.76) is the product of a badly clogged mind. One's enjoyment can be obstructed, and one can be prevented from enjoying, but one cannot be 'obstructed from enjoying'. The writer has two concepts, 'obstruction' and 'enjoyment' floating loosely about in his brain. He assumes

that he has only to utter them for the relationship between the two to become apparent. Any convenient linking word will do, and careful attention to syntax is élitist. So, too, is precision of meaning. In these democratic days, a rough and ready association of ideas should be good enough for anybody.

Officer

Can this possibly, in view of the source, be only a misprint for offer? Or, as seems more likely, does it mean 'is responsible for', in the way that an officer is responsible for the men under his command? Readers must be left to make up their own minds. 'The discipline presently officers the normal range of courses in English Studies' (*Times*, 21.3.75). (The reference is to a department of the Flinders University of S. Australia.)

Olde-worlde

Old-world, but more so. The use is more or less confined to the lower grade of estate agents and to the proprietors of inns and hotels. It is an unintentional warning to approach the establishment concerned with more than a touch of discretion. 'The Hotel, originally a coaching inn some 300 years old, retains a great deal of olde-worlde charm and character' (1976 brochure of Swallow Hotels). 'Olde-worlde' can be removed from this sentence with no loss of meaning and a considerable improvement in elegance.

Old-fashioned

Characterised by un-modern quality and reliability. More used in the United States, where nostalgia is exceptionally highly valued by the advertising profession, than in other parts of the English-speaking world. 'Vanilla Ice Cream floating in a frosty goblet of old-fashioned root beer, topped with a blanket of whipped cream, chopped nuts and a cherry' (Howard Johnson menu, Dallas, 1973). The root beer is, of course, an ordinary factory product. There is nothing old-fashioned about it whatever. Although, for such an innocent drink as root-beer, 'old-fashioned' might suggest extra strength.

On-going

Continuous, continued, continuing. A Germanism, developed and popularised in the United States and which is felt, for some reason, to indicate more energy and determination than the equivalents given above. 'Continuing' change suggests, to those who feel this way, that the change merely happens, whereas 'on-going' change is willed, directed and controlled by the right kind of forward-looking people. Examples are widespread and legion. 'The on-going progress of science' (Ruddock, 1972)–the continued progress of science; ' . . . research to inform the on-going action' (*N Soc*, 4.12.75)– the action in progress; 'the on-going development of our staff' (*D Tel*, 9.12.75)–the continuous development; 'readiness of an immediate on-going role' (*PNGUT*, 1975)–an immediate and continuing role; 'And there was promise of an on-going dynamic–a duel just begun' (*Listener*, Auckland, Vol 80, No 1886, 1976); the reference is to a runner–a hard-fought race; 'The successful candidates will provide a vital on-going link between the company's design and development team and the engineers of major motor companies' (*D Tel*, 16.9.76)–a vital link.

On-target
Achieved. Modern industry is much given to thinking about targets, which are to be aimed at, reached and, if possible, exceeded. Logically, the only things one can do to a target are to hit it or miss it, one's excellence as a performer being determined by the closeness of one's arrow or bullet to the centre of the target. Those whose pursuit is archery or rifle-shooting know very well that no marks whatever are to be obtained from shooting over and beyond the target, but industry thinks otherwise and reserves the highest praise and reward for those who exceed their target. There is, even so, something not quite right about 'a generous bonus for an on-target performance' (*S Times*, 30.11.75), since to be merely 'on-target' does not strike one as particularly good. Only bullseyes or, at the very least, inners, would seem to deserve a bonus.

On-task
Following instructions or the pattern laid down. A social science term of no special value or merit. 'On-task behavior improved in the class receiving instructions' (*JEP*, 64/1, 1973). 'On-task behavior' is our old friend, now in disgrace, 'doing what one was told to do'. Children cannot be told to do something nowadays but 'on-task behavior' is perfectly acceptable.

Opaque
Not easy to follow? Not sharp or clear? A word used by music-critics,

who can tell us, not very helpfully, that a piece of music 'emerged as a heavy, opaque piece of academic counterpoint' (*Fin Times*, 7.2.77).

Open

Frank, easy, as in 'loyal, capable of open communication' (*Times*, 22.7.76). This advertisement, from an organisation based in San Francisco, suggests that a secretive, introspective person would not be appointed. A friendly, honest, heart-on-sleeve extrovert was evidently being sought, although 'capable of open communication' certainly grades up the requirement.

Open out

Reveal the beauties within? A wine word, with the usual amount of inexpressible mystique. 'Château d'Issan Margaux is beginning to open out agreeably' (*Times*, 31.7.76).

Operant conditioning

The Pavlovian conditioning of operatives or workers, carried out by giving or withholding bones and gravy. A management euphemism. 'Motivation is based on operant conditioning, or contingent management principles, through which desirable behaviour is positively reinforced with tangible rewards' (Corwin, 1974).

Operates

Is. 'This major company operates in the paper packaging field' (*D Tel*, 27.11.75) is a pretentious way of telling anyone who is willing to listen that the company 'is in the paper packaging field', or that it 'makes paper packaging', both of which would be insufficiently grand. The second, indeed, might be considered rather coarse.

Operation

Usually means nothing, a word inserted for padding and, supposedly, grace. A firm of wine and spirit bottlers, for instance, can speak of its 'production operation based at Harlow, Essex' (*D Tel*, 17.11.76), meaning its 'bottling-plant at Harlow, Essex'. 'Operation' has a fine military flavour and its popularity in recent years may be partly due to this.

Operationality

Whether it works or not. 'Scientific rigor must be traded off against operationality' (Michelson, 1975), i.e. the perfect design is of no use unless it can be put into production and be made to pay.

Operations
Manufacturing, marketing and selling. 'An international soft-drinks company is seeking a Director of Operations for Europe' (*Times*, 17.4.76). Such a man is a Field-Marshal at least, and the thought of a soft-drinks Field-Marshal is ludicrous in the extreme. The person concerned is, in fact, General Manager, Europe. 'Director of Operations, Severn Trent Water Authority' (*Times*, 21.1.77) is only slightly less grandiose and Gilbertian.

Oppression
Pressure. 'We can develop our sense of middle-class oppression by remembering how passionately we do not want to be like our parents, what we revolted from' (Teodori, 1969). This is a tedious, long-winded way of describing the phenomenon of the children of middle-class parents who long to throw off what they feel to be their middle-class chains. 'Middle-class oppression' in this sentence means 'oppressed by one's middle-class origins, by middle-class character-istics and values', not 'tyrannised by the middle-class'. The writer wishes to be thought of as if he were a Jew in the Soviet Union or a coloured person in South Africa, a member of a persecuted class, a second-rate citizen. It is a ridiculous pose.

Optical excitement
Visual excitement. The phrase, as in 'the importance goes far beyond optical excitement' (*Apollo*, May 1966) is strangely pretentious. 'Optical excitement' suggests that the eyes themselves are excited, whereas all they can do is to transmit to the brain and the nervous system what they see. The eyes are mere agents, and 'optical excitement' is just an art critic behaving in an upstage manner.

Optimise
Force to the highest possible point, make as successful as possible. One of the most popular words in business English. A typical example is the 'leading leisure footwear manufacturer determined to optimise overseas sales' (*D Tel*, 17.11.76). Purists in the business world insist that 'optimise' does not mean simply 'bigger and better', but rather 'yielding the best possible results in view of all the circumstances'. In the case quoted, for instance, it might be that, in a particular year or period, exports should be played down and domestic sales played up,

so that the overall strategy of the company would have to be interpreted in this way. In practice, however, 'optimise' nearly always does mean just 'push to the limit'. It is therefore a term which adds an overtone of quality to a concept of mere quantity and is, in that sense, misleading.

Optimisation

Using to the best advantage. This, however, is not thought to be very dignified or scientific, so 'optimisation' it has to be, as in 'the optimisation of engineering, manpower, and raw material resources' (*D Tel*, 9.12.75).

Option

Something one can have and use if one wants to. Car manufacturers are particularly fond of mentioning their 'options', the idea being to make the sale by offering the basic car at the lowest possible price and then persuading customers to buy the 'options'. The word used to be 'extras', but that was felt to make the public think first of its pocket and only second of the benefits that the 'extras' conferred. 'Options' is much more genteel and less frightening. Occasionally the advertiser's enthusiasm runs away with him, so that one becomes a little unsure if one is acquiring 'options' or not. 'The limited edition Audi isn't a stripped down car. In addition to the special options, it's loaded with standard features you might have to pay extra for on some other cars' (*New Yorker*, 27.9.76). Not infrequently, the 'options' are there anyway and one has only to decide whether to use them or not. The difference between an 'option' and a 'facility' then becomes blurred to the extent that one wonders why 'option' is there at all, e.g. the recording studio which 'has many options and facilities which have made it very popular' (*Melody Maker*, 7.2.76).

Oral

Talking, using the mouth. 'The oral time budget takes a great deal of interviewer time' (Michelson, 1975) is not for beginners in the art of interpretation. It means that the kind of interview in which the subject has to tell the interviewer what he did takes a lot of time. 'The oral time budget' is the number of minutes the interviewer has to allow for this.

Oral incorporation

A baby sucking a nipple or bottle teat. 'These attachments are manifest in the motoric behaviour of oral incorporation' (Hoppe, 1970). The 'motoric behaviour' is the baby moving his sucking muscles, the 'oral incorporation' means that he has the teat in his mouth. A ridiculously complicated way of describing a simple fact within the experience of everybody.

Order
'In the order of' is a longer and therefore preferred way of saying 'about'. 'In the order of 6 million' (*D Tel*, 6.2.76) is 'about 6 million' or, equally probably, '6 million', with no 'about' involved at all.

Organic
(a) grown without the use of chemical fertilisers. Health fanatics are much given to extolling the superior quality of 'organically' grown foodstuffs, although the difference is wholly in the mind, with no scientific basis at all. A carrot is a carrot, and no laboratory test can reveal the slightest distinction between an 'organic' carrot and a 'non-organic' carrot. If, however, one believes that 'organically' grown carrots have a better flavour, contain more vitamins and do not poison or contaminate the human system, one is expressing a religious or cult point of view. It does nobody any harm, adds a certain interest to life and forms a bond of friendship between like-minded people. 'Fresh organic vegetables' (Notice outside *Harvest* shop, Bath, 1.4.76) is a rallying call, as well as commercial advertisement. (b) Belonging to a living organism. Many companies like to think of themselves as biological, rather than commercial entities, and are fond of using the word 'organic' to indicate their belief, which is, of course, a metaphor, not a fact, however passionately and devotedly they may hold to it. 'Through organic and acquisitional growth, UCAN is expected to achieve eight-figure turnover by 1978'(*S Times*, 20.6.76).

Organismic
Considering something as a living organism. 'They tend to be inspired by organismic perspectives' (*BJ Soc*, Sept 1966) means, presumably, 'They tend to see everything as if it were a living organism', which is what the businessmen referred to in the previous item do.

Orientated, oriented
These two words are interchangeable. Whether one uses the first or the second seems to be entirely a matter of personal preference. The

basic meaning is 'inclined towards', as a Moslem turns towards the East and a sunflower towards the sun. 'Orientated' or 'oriented' are great savers of time and effort, since they avoid the need to search for the precise word one needs, and sound sufficiently impressive to avoid any accusation of mental laziness. 'Motorway orientated industrial estates' (*Times*, 26.1.76) – close to the motorway; 'Applicants should be practically orientated' (*D Tel*, 27.11.75) – should have a practical turn of mind; 'A cost-efficient house oriented to today's life-style' (*New Yorker*, 15.9.75) – suited to the way we live today; a suit which is 'oriented to embrace both style and elegance' (*Vogue*, 1.3.76) shows style and elegance.

Orientation
Attitude, adjustment. Much more common on the American side of the Atlantic, where people of all ages tend to be seriously concerned about their orientations and where psychologists encourage them to think that way. 'Those students whose primary orientation to college is vocational' (*JEP*, 60/4, 1969) – who see college as a way to a better job; 'The middle-class mother's response is dependent upon the question, not upon the mother's general orientation to her child' (Pride & Holmes, 1972) – the mother's general attitude; 'This problem is avoided by sufficient interviewer orientation before the actual interviews' (Michelson, 1975) – getting himself mentally adjusted to what he is going to do.

Outgoing
Extroverted, warm, friendly. the 'outgoing' person has great prestige nowadays and the word is often slipped in for no particular reason at all, as in 'an outgoing flair for getting along with people' (*The Age*, 20.3.76). Either one has a flair for getting along with people or one has not. 'Outgoing' makes no difference to the flair, although it is possible that the outgoing person may have more flair.

Outlets
Shops, stores. 'This large, well-known manufacturer operates a chain of retail outlets' (*Sydney Morning Herald*, 28.2.76), which can only be shops, and the man required to possess 'a flair for selling to retail outlets' (*D Tel*, 7.1.76) is unlikely to call on anything but shops and stores. But, no doubt for reasons of morale, it is nearly always, to the manufacturer, the classier 'retail outlets' nowadays.

Outreach
Ability and willingness to go out to find and meet people; the analogy presumably being with someone extending a helping, welcoming hand. 'As he continued in the church, it reflected the work of the Holy Spirit in its worship, ministries and outreach' (*Listener*, Auckland, Vol 80, No 1886, 1976). In this context, 'outreach' is a synonym for 'pastoral care', which no doubt would be somewhat difficult to use in a country such as New Zealand, where there are far more sheep than people.

Outstanding
Distinguished. By putting 'most' in front of it, the attempt is frequently made to turn an ordinary mountain into Everest, to make the object in question stand up or out even more. An establishment in New York therefore becomes elevated into 'one of the most outstanding restaurants in the world' (*New Yorker*, 15.1.76), instead of 'one of the world's outstanding restaurants', which is a claim of doubtful validity, anyway. To be outstanding is surely all that any restaurant or person could reasonably hope for.

Over-commit
To use too much. The 'unnecessary fixed partitioning which over-commits floor-space' (*BB*/NZ, 1975) merely takes up too much room, wastes space. A person with extravagant, spendthrift habits can over-commit himself, but it is difficult for partitioning to do the same.

Overly
Too much? On the whole? Over the whole field? All these are possible in 'the overly generalised extrapolation from simpler to more complex organism' (Hoppe, 1970). The probability is that the author is trying to say 'over-generalised', but has lost his academic nerve.

Over-size
Of above-average size. An over-size pair of shoes would be larger than one really needed, so that there would be room to wear extra-thick socks if the weather turned cold. The implications of 'twenty-four custom-styled houses, carefully sited on over-size, well-tilled lots' (*Axiom*, Oct 1976) are different. The agent would never be so

unwise as to suggest that the building site was bigger than one needed. On the contrary, the extra-large acre on which one's house is to stand is entirely suited to one's position in society. One deserves it.

Overview

Survey. A Germanism adopted with gusto by the social science and management professionals in the United States and exported from there all over the English-speaking world. 'Overview' is reckoned, wrongly, to have more status and style than 'survey'. 'The Centre relies both on a national overview . . .' (*N Soc*, 4.12.76); 'A concentrated overview of the latest strategies and techniques' (*Times*, 27.1.76) – Manchester Business School advertisement; 'The author presents a well-measured overview of business information systems' (*Business Horizons*, Aug 1974); 'A definitive overview of intelligence testing in childern' (*JEP*, 64/3, 1973). In all these examples, is 'overview' really so much more forceful and scientific than 'survey', or does it belong to the new dream world of power and professionalism?

P

Painterliness

Appears to mean pride and pleasure in being a painter, but it is used by art critics as a pejorative, and implies that the person concerned is superficial, lacking in social purpose, insufficiently interested in theory and obsessed with technique. 'In order to wallow in painterliness and opticality . . .' (Walker, 1975) sums up the attitude.

Palate

Taste. A wine word. Properly, the drinker, not the wine, possesses a palate, a fact not understood by the Australian author of 'It shows excellent Riesling characteristics with a full fruity bouquet and well-rounded palate' (*National Times*, 1.3.76).

Palette

'A clean palette' means, for the painter, a fresh start, a new picture. The use of the phrase in music criticism illustrates the problem of being compelled to describe and analyse one art in terms of another.

The results are rarely satisfactory but, in order to be able to work at all, the critic has to make the attempt. He lives in a world of never-ending metaphor, but it does no harm to draw consecutive metaphors from an approximately similar field, if one wishes to avoid giving the impression that one is desperate for images and that no reasonable offer will be refused. 'Prokofiev seems to represent, in the Russian music of its (sic) time, a clean palette and a breath of fresh air' (*Times,* 4.3.76).

Panache
Style, flourish. 'A delicious selection of haute cuisine dishes, all served with a panache that only the finest cuisine can equal' (1976 brochure of Swallow Hotels). A restaurant's 'cuisine' is the style and repertoire of its cook, who ceases to have responsibility for the dishes once they have left the kitchen. Whether they are 'served with a panache' or not has nothing to do with either the 'cuisine' or the cook. Service is the business of those who wait at table and it is just possible to imagine this being carried out with 'panache', although most eaters would probably prefer competence and speed to the flamboyance and slight arrogance which 'panache' suggests.

Paradigm
Pattern, example. Many modern users of the word appear to have little idea of its meaning and choose it, so far as one can judge, for its impressive sound and appearance. Sometimes it should be replaced by 'situation' sometimes by 'theory', sometimes by 'framework of argument'. More frequently, the whole sentence needs re-casting, in order to avoid using the word at all. 'Here we find ourselves in a new paradigm whose implications have this potential to reap (sic) havoc in our universities' (*THES*, 13.2.76). The absence of a much-needed comma after 'paradigm' and the use of 'reap' instead of 'wreak' increases one's suspicion that this particular writer is not fully at home with his own language. For others, 'paradigm' is just another way of getting lost. 'The researcher using photography seems to make an explicit, replicable statement of fact, to substantiate, embellish or overthrow a paradigm' (Michelson, 1975).

Parameter
Originally a purely mathematical term, it is now used figuratively, in the sense of 'limit', 'constant quality', 'fixed and recognised frame-work'. The meaning is often elusive, and one fervently wishes the

writer had had the courage to choose another word. 'In searching for the parameters of adult development and functioning . . .' (Ruddock, 1972) leaves one a little gasping for air and sense. Presumably one translates, 'in searching for the pattern of adult development', and throws away both 'parameters' and 'functioning' as useless mental lumber. Similarly, 'The post will involve specification of process and machinery parameters' (*D Tel*, 17.12.76) means 'the specification of processes and machinery parameters'. The word is frequently confused with 'perimeter', as in 'For Benninck, the perimeters of the kit dissolved years ago' (*Melody Maker*, 29.1.77)

Partialed

Parcelled. 'When abilities were partialed out . . .' (*JEP*, 65/3, 1973). This is a particularly interesting example. The periodical from which it comes is a respected professional journal, with an editor to match. It is an excellent source of psychological jargon and, given the linguistic atmosphere in which both its editor and contributors move, any English word can be taken over to serve as a technical term. 'Partial' exists as an adjective and it is a simple matter to form a verb 'to partial' from it. Once this is put in a convincing 'professional' context, nobody takes the trouble to enquire if it means anything or even if it is correct. Everyone concerned, editor, referee, proof-reader, is bewitched by the context and possibly by the author's name and reputation, so that the fact that he cannot spell 'parcelled' has never become apparent.

Participant

Someone taking part in. 'Participants in a linguistic event' (Pride & Holmes, 1972) are simply, but incredibly, people talking and listening to one another. A conversation has become a 'linguistic event', which had to come, but which flatters some conversations.

Participate

To work. 'Secretaries who are keen to participate in the fast-moving oil business' (*Times*, 27.5.76). The word is dishonestly used, because it implies that the people concerned will influence the way in which the business is run, that their voices will be heard, whereas what in fact they do is to carry out precise orders to the best of their ability. They 'participate' only to the extent that a cog participates in a machine and a raindrop in a shower.

Participatory democracy
One in which everyone plays a part in deciding policy. Bearing in mind the meaning of 'democracy', this is equivalent to saying 'a democratic democracy', and it is a sad comment on our times that such repetition should be necessary. 'These are the legitimate rights to be expected in a participatory democracy' (Rubinstein & Stoneman, 1970).

Party-on
To go to a lot of parties, to go from one party to another. '. . . and generally partying-on in a way that must have left little time for anything else' (*The Australian Women's Weekly*, 7.1.76).

Passionate
Deep; from the heart. In the cliché language of our time, passion can be only deep, flaming, raging, or simmering, but the interpretation of the word in a particular context is often far from simple. 'Mood stone watch displays time and emotion at a glance. The mood stone face changes as your emotional state does, from nervous black to passionate purple' (*Delta Flightline Catalogue*, 1976). Which 'passionate' is one to choose here? Deep seems the most reasonable, but the contrast with 'black' is not sufficiently great, so it will probably have to be flaming, although quite what shade that is leaves room for argument and doubt.

Past participle
A social scientist's trick, aimed at increasing the scientific flavour of his writing. Ordinary mortals say 'eating either a little or a lot of a vegetable one dislikes'. The sociologist or psychologist, however, in his eagerness to prove his status and complete objectivity, prefers 'eating either a little or a lot of the disliked vegetable' (Cohen, 1964).

Peace
A political state of close friendship and alliance with the Soviet Union. '. . . the Soviet Union, which has worked tirelessly to initiate peace policies' (*Comment*, 29.11.75).

Peacefully
Threateningly and with intimidating words and gestures, but without actually using physical violence. '. . . where pickets peace-

fully approach a lorry driver' (*TUC Report*, 1974).

Pedigree
Properly, with a recorded line of descent, but increasingly and fraudulently used as a classy replacement for 'record'. 'Candidates should have a good product management pedigree' (*D Tel*, 27.11.75) can only mean, to anyone who considers the meaning of the word, that they must belong to a family which, generation by generation, has bred good managers. The man who 'came to Downsway with a good pedigree' (*Fin Times*, 14.1.76) was not in quite the same situation as the bull who came to the agricultural show with a good pedigree. His record, not his breeding, was the relevant point. At one time only living creatures could have pedigrees, but now it is possible for anything from cars to houses and pictures. An American wine-producing concern can assure the public that 'our grapes are pedigreed' (*New Yorker*, 5.4.76) and an article in an art magazine can say of a chimneypiece, 'Family tradition gives it a fairly detailed pedigree' (*Con*, Vol 161, Jan/Apr 1966). The swindle-element in this use of the word 'pedigree' is the implication of quality which it is made to carry. Everybody and everything has a pedigree, if the details could be discovered, but only the pedigrees of the well-born and expensive are likely to be fully documented. 'Pedigree' and 'high quality' have consequently become almost inseparable.

Penetration
Sales, selling. The aggressive sexual symbolism used by today's marketing organisations is very widespread, and, to outsiders with a sense of humour, often ludicrous and childish. A straightforward example is provided by the firm which talks of its 'commerical strategies for rapid market penetration' (*D Tel*, 7.1.76), but the metaphor gets confused in the reference to the fact that 'penetration of their consumer products in Middle Eastern markets is not yet at the high levels achieved elsewhere' (*S Times*, 8.2.76), since penetration is measured by its depth, not its height. One can penetrate even an environment, as shown by the mention of 'an environment with great potential for further penetration' (*S Times*, 30.5.76). Cf. Market penetration.

People
Staff, customers. The person who is required, for a job with a Montreal bank, to have had 'experience in lending and people

management' (*D Tel*, 22.1.76) may be expected to display his talents with either the bank's staff or its customers–'people' leaves the question open. Whether the customers would appreciate the thought of being 'managed' is open to doubt, although there could be no objection to management of the lending side of the bank's activities.

Perceive

Become aware of. Writers on educational and social science subjects, in their never-ending attempt to keep their books and articles as cold and impersonal as possible, have become very fond of 'perceive', partly, no doubt, because it corresponds in a satisfying way to 'perception'. So, 'Teacher satisfaction will be significantly higher for locals who perceive a high degree of bureaucratization than for cosmopolitans with similar perceptions' (*JER*, 60/2, Oct 1966). 'Perceive' is only 'notice', 'are aware of', but both these alternatives would be too colloquial to be acceptable.

Percentile rank

Percentage score, number of points out of a hundred. In 'estimate his own percentile rank on each variable' (*JER*, 60/3, Nov 1966), no question of rank is involved, since the subject is not comparing himself with other people. He is simply asked to work out what his score is under each heading.

Perceptive

Given to noticing significant details. A book reviewer's terms. Publishers like their novelists to be called 'perceptive'. The word is easily and cheaply quotable in advertisement and looks impressive, even if one is not quite sure what it means. 'Jackie Gillot's *A True Romance* is a perceptive, intelligent novel about personal re-lationships' (*Times*, 7.8.76). This probably means something like 'a novel written by someone with a good eye and ear for the finer points of human behaviour', but this would be to consign the author to the popular category.

Performance contracting

Agreeing to pay by results. A phrase from the educational world. 'Performance contracting represents a modest step toward creating alternative forms of schooling' (Corwin, 1974). The contract is with a firm, which engages people, qualified and unqualified, to teach the children. The firm is paid a specific sum for every pupil whose performance, especially in reading and mathematics, improves by an agreed amount. The phrase is misleading, since the firm does not contract to raise a child's level of performance–this it could never undertake to do–but the school agrees to pay for every boy or girl who does improve.

Period

Dating from more than fifty years ago. We have become used to having 'period houses', 'period dresses', 'period plays' and 'period furniture', but, until one specifies which period it is, the word is largely meaningless. It is not even a recommendation or enticement, since one can and probably does enjoy the products of one period and hates those of another. 'The beautiful period décor' (*High Life*, Dec/Jan 1975/6) comes from either an ignorant or a lazy mind.

Personal

Should mean used by oneself; belonging to oneself. 'One of America's finest personal luxury cars' (Toronto *Globe and Mail*, 9.10.76) raises some questions. In what sense is this car to be regarded as 'personal? Is it the non-business car, the car one uses for shopping, holidays and running round the district? Or is it an all-purpose vehicle, meeting one's need for personal luxury at all times? The confusion, which is, of course, deliberate, could have been avoided by rewording the sentence. 'Cars for your personal luxury' or 'cars for your private purposes' would have made whichever point was intended clear.

Personal involvement

Throwing oneself wholeheartedly into a task; becoming absorbed; never indulging in clock-watching. In the days before the phrase was invented, one wonders how people managed. What, fifty years ago, was a job which 'will entail a high degree of personal involvement' (*D Tel*, 27.1.76)? Was it one which demanded 'hard work' or 'constant attention to detail' or 'wholehearted application'? The most likely explanation is that our ancestors took 'personal involvement' for granted and therefore never mentioned it, whereas, in these unin- terested, 9 to 5 days, 'personal involvement' is such a rarity that one has to specify it as an unusual but necessary requirement, in order to sift out those potential applicants who make no pretence of possessing such a quality.

Personalised

(a) Given a special appearance or characteristics to meet the wishes of one particular person; (b) personal. A shirt which had one's initials embroidered on the pocket would be 'personalised'. So, too, would a motorcar with the Christian name of oneself and one's girlfriend plastered across the top of the windscreen. The essence of 'personalisation' is that one starts with a standard object and then, by adding details to it, makes it slightly different from all the others in the same range. This is probably not what has happened in the case of 'the popular Dave and Shirley Harris Trio, a favourite with their personalised song styling' (*Key*, Dallas, 1973). This must mean 'personal style of singing', with the singing styled, not the songs.

Personality

(a) Person, well-known performer; (b) group of characteristics which distinguishes one person from another. A 'television personality' is someone who is frequently seen on television; a 'self-effacing personality' and a 'strong personality' are exactly what these phrases suggest. But persons, not personalities, apply for jobs, and one does not know, therefore, if the 'excellent opportunities for a self-motivating personality' (*D Tel*, 7.1.76) are for a self-motivating person or a person with a self-motivating personality.

Personal relationships

A portmanteau word, including love, friendship, parent-child relationships and the more or less authoritarian links which exist between employer and employed, and between colleagues at work. It describes, in fact, the whole of life, and is a useful cover for those who feel unable to use the various specific terms. When we read a review telling us that a book is 'an intelligent novel about personal relationships' (*TLS*, 12.2.76), our inclination is to say, 'Of course. What else could it be about?'

Personhood

The state of being an individual person. 'It is wrong to think of personhood as something simply given, like bipedhood' (Ruddock, 1972). 'Personhood' appears, so far as one can judge, to be a highly developed stage of human existence; one has reached it when one is conscious of being a person in one's own right, essentially different from other people. In any group of people of various ages, some will have reached personhood and some will not, although it is difficult for an outside observer to know which is which. In view of such complications and possible misunderstandings, it seems better to avoid the term, although with the Sex Discrimination Act now a feature of English life, it does have certain advantages of ambiguity.

Persuasion

Pulling and moulding into shape. An American advertisement for brassières promises 'gentle underbody persuasion' (*Washington Star*, 17.10.76), and no-one could ask for more.

Petite

Tiny. At one time only women could be petite in English, and the feminine ending is there to prove it. No man, however small, was ever 'petit'. This restricted use of the word no longer seems to apply and it is possible to have such linguistic oddities as a necklace 'with petite jade and ivory pendants attached' (*Panorama*, Boston, Oct 1976). The intention, if there is any clear intention, is presumably to convey the impression that the pendants are not only tiny, but delicate and feminine as well, like the most petite and dainty of women.

Pharmacological treatments

Drugs. A verbose piece of professional respectability and pretentiousness. ' . . . existing means of reducing anxiety, such as behaviour therapy, removal of threatening cues, and pharmacological treatments' (*JEP*, 61/2, 1970).

Phase

Branch, aspect. The essential feature of a phase is that it forms part of a sequence. On the analogy of the moon, anything which changes can, at least theoretically, pass through phases, but without the concept and reality of change there can be no phases. The following Australian sentence is therefore either illiterate or puzzling. 'The attractive working environment and a small staff allows exposure to all phases of the direct response business' (*The Age*, 2.3.76). What is probably meant is 'all aspects' or 'all branches', but there is just the possibility that the direct response business proceeds in phases and that employees can gain experience of each of these phases.

Philosophy
A coherent body of ideas, serving to illuminate human thought and activity. 'Philosophy' and 'policy' are not at all the same, and much contemporary use of 'philosophy' is ignorant and unscrupulous. 'The company commitment to a philosophy of profitable sales attainment' (*D Tel*, 27.11.75) is, if anything, 'the company's commitment to a policy of profitable sales attainment'. Since this must necessarily be the aim of any commercial undertaking, the point does not seem worth making, but in any case to dignify such an aim by the name of 'philosophy' is an impertinent degradation of the word.

Picture window
A window made up of a large single pane of glass, so that what one sees through it resembles a picture in its frame. What cannot be guaranteed, however, is that the picture is worth looking at, and in many cases drawing the curtains is a wise precaution. The 'picture window' has become a status symbol, the equivalent of the Victorian piano. No self-respecting home is complete without one, a fact fully recognised by the estate agents, who are constantly advertising such attractions as 'large dining room with picture window' (*Times*, 27.5.76). The great disadvantage of the 'picture window', that it is all or nothing, is conveniently overlooked, except by those who have been unfortunate enough to have one broken.

Place
Come, rank. 'It would place second to the Canadian Post Office' (Toronto *Globe and Mail*, 31.1.76), shows confusion between 'It would come second to' and 'it would come in second place to'.

Plain
Ordinary? Homely? Another baffling wine word. 'The full but plainer Langoa' (*Times*, 17.7.76).

Planfulness
The ability to plan? 'Planfulness' suggests an Indian who is unable to speak English very well, but the word is unfortunately in common use among psychologists who count English as their mother tongue. 'Planfulness and formal reasoning best discriminated among grade point average groups' (*JEP*, 65/3, 1973).

Plantagenet
Thirteenth to fifteenth century, from Henry II to Richard III. 'An opportunity to live in a gracious Plantagenet manor' (*Times*, 8.7.76). 'Plantagenet' is one of the estate agents' higher and newer flights of fancy. Even the fifteenth century, to say nothing of the thirteenth, was a very long time ago, and the number of domestic buildings which date from that period and are in anything resembling their original condition must be exceedingly small. It was, in any case, a rough age, in which construction was functional, rather than elegant, and home comforts were few. Certainly no building of the Plantagenet period could be described, even by the most enthusiastic historian, as 'gracious'. Pressed to explain himself, the agent could probably be forced to admit that the house he is doing his best to sell is a modernised, restored and considerably altered version of something which stood on the site in the fifteenth century at the earliest, if indeed he had any concept of dates at all.

Plebiscitarianism
Voting, holding plebiscites. If a vegetarian practises vegetarianism, and a Presbyterian Presbyterianism, there is clearly no reason why a plebiscitarian—a man who pins his faith to plebiscites—should not devote himself to plebiscitarianism. But the word is as difficult to pronounce as to spell and there seems to be little necessity for it. 'A compromise between plebiscitarianism and the principle of functional representation' (*B J Soc*, Sept 1966) – all the writer is trying to convey is 'a compromise between plebiscites and functional representation', which makes the meaning perfectly clear. The –ism and 'principle' are just academic padding and fluffiness.

Plethora
Large quantity. 'We want an accountant who can ingest a plethory (sic) of information and succinctly report the facts pertinent to Wimpey operators' (Toronto *Globe and Mail*, 7.10.76). The accountant who has to swallow his professional raw material by the plethora must be of a very exalted rank indeed, and no doubt his salary matches his quality.

Plurality
More than one, several. 'We thus had the direct experience of a *lasting* meta-personal inspiration, expanses of calm dimensional plurality,

freedom, spaciousness, and of a medial self-renunciation transcending all our previous experiences' (Wörner, 1973). Anyone with the stamina to plod through this sentence to the full stop and to emerge intact at the end might feel inclined to attempt a translation of 'expanses of calm dimensional plurality'. As an encouragement, one could suggest 'calm multi-dimensional expanses', but without any great confidence that the new version corresponds to what was in the writer's mind or that it conveys any more meaning than the original.

Portable
Able to be carried. Some things are admittedly more portable than others but there would seem to be no doubt about the portability of a tube of foundation cream, even when its owner is very small. Yet, 'it comes in a portable tube to go anywhere . . . everywhere with you' (*Vogue*, 1.4.76). Not just a tube, a portable tube.

Portfolio
List of clients. 'Our portfolio is comprehensive and expanding' (*D Tel*, 29.4.76) reports a firm supplying equipment to the computer industry, thereby putting itself on the same pompous level as the people who talk of 'portfolios of investments'. A portfolio is a file, which brings a mundane commercial fact out of the skies and down to earth with a beneficial bang.

Position
Require to live. One 'positions' a vase on a shelf or a piece of machinery on the floor, and a house can, if one wishes, be 'positioned on the outskirts of this most attractive and unspoilt village' (*SMJ*, 18.12.76), but one does not normally do the same to one's employees, unless they are policemen reconstructing a murder. The firm which makes it known that a newly appointed member of its staff will be 'positioned in or near Lagos' (*D Tel*, 17.12.76) seems to be thinking of a most unattractively static situation, especially in the Nigerian heat. 'Based in or near Lagos' would be more comfortable and more efficient.

Positive
A word which, in nine case out of ten, means nothing at all, and from which we could do with a long rest. Very occasionally it helps. 'We do receive very positive management direction' (*S Times*, 4.4.76), i.e. the management tells us what we should do, not merely what we

should not do, and 'The personal style of the successful applicant should be positive, yet diplomatic' (*Fin Times*, 1.4.76), i.e. the candidate should give the impression of knowing his own mind. In a great many more cases, however, 'positive' can be dropped from the sentence without the meaning suffering in the process. 'Recent graduates with a positive desire to make a career in the field of market research will certainly be considered' (*D Tel*, 30.3.76); 'What positive measures could be implemented to encourage girls to study a wide range of subjects' (*Sydney Morning Herald*, 28.2.76); 'Their 50-year-old tradition of positive tolerance' (*Con*, Vol 165, May/Aug 1967). Some instances of 'positive' are plainly absurd. One firm makes it known that 'as a member of the management team, the Foundry Manager will be expected to make a positive contribution' (*D Tel*, 18.6.76). Can one think of any concern which would want one of its managers to make a negative contribution? 'A real contribution' or 'a special contribution of his own' must be meant. 'Growth', says another firm, 'has been positive and exceptional' (*D Tel*, 8.1.76). Nobody would publicise negative growth, and, since 'exceptional' clearly indicates success, why use 'positive' at all? The same question can be asked of the Hotel Bristol, which 'takes a positive pride in personal service' (*Economist*, 14.2.76), although here there is admittedly a certain charm in the alliteration. 'The Authority has a positive attitude to the role of the Psychological Service' (*TES*, 9.1.76) means that it thinks the Psychological Service is a good thing, and 'On balance we were positive to the idea' (*Boston Sunday Globe*, 10.10.76) means that we said yes. The word is used so automatically in some circles that it is often difficult to decide if any real meaning should be attached to it or not. The person who says 'There are so many positive things I want to do' (*Melody Maker*, 29.1.77) may be saying merely 'There are so many things I want to do', or 'There are so many positive things I want to do' instead of smashing shop windows or sitting around in the sun.

Positively
'Positively', plus a verb, can nearly always be replaced by a single verb, with great benefit to the reader. 'Desirable behaviour is positively reinforced with tangible rewards' (Corwin, 1974), i.e. encouraged by; ' . . . the decision by the shop stewards to reply positively to the Government proposals' (*Voice*, 1975), i.e. to agree to.

Post-atomic
Presumably, since the first atomic bomb was dropped. We are, unfortunately for mankind, not yet in the true post-atomic age. One periodical, even so, finds it possible to refer to 'the new post-atomic fundamentalism and pragmatism' (*Con*, Vol 165, May/Aug 1967).

Post-painterly
Related to the stage reached by artists after they have turned their backs on the possibility of expressing themselves by 'pure' art, i.e. art not rooted in social considerations. 'More important, however, than his rejection of post-painterly preoccupations, is what is becoming for him, and for other younger artists who continue to paint, a revaluation of painterly and expressive abstractism' (*Arts Canada*, July/Aug 1976).

Potent
Important; likely to lead to results. 'The most potent effects in the data are rated ability, grade, and Lindamood subtest' (*JEP*, 64/3, 1973).

Potentiate
Make possible or likely; cause; encourage. 'Etrafon may impair alertness or potentiate response to alcohol' (*Arch Gen Psy*, Mar 1976). 'Cause' would do perfectly well here, although the psychiatrists would undoubtedly consider it low.

Powerful
(a) Stirring the emotions? Making a powerful impression? A favourite word among book reviewers, committing them to nothing but very quotable. 'This powerful new novel' (*Times*, 27.11.75).
(b) With a higher than average alcohol content? 'Powerful, full-bodied flowery wines of great elegance' (1976 catalogue of Lay and Wheeler, Colchester).

Practically
Within the range of your pocket. 'Choose from 372 practically priced rooms' (*New Yorker*, 14.1.76). This hotel advertisement is trying hard not to say in so many words that its rooms are not the most expensive in town, without actually saying how much they cost, which might frighten off some potential customers. Since

nobody, including the management, knows just what 'practically priced' means, one cannot very well pick a quarrel by arguing that one's room is not 'practically priced'. Anything one is willing to pay is presumably practical.

Pragmatic

Properly, concerned with practical consequences or values; making decisions step by step on the basis of their probable effects. The word is very loosely used, and often seems to mean nothing more than 'practical'. Someone may describe himself, for instance, as 'a pragmatic sort of person', meaning that he is not greatly concerned with theories or principles, but does what seems best at the time. Sir Harold Wilson raised no objection to being called 'pragmatic'. Some uses of the word do, even so, give rise to a certain amount of head-scratching. 'The fourth and less pragmatic pursuit encompasses creative production experiments' (*Mus News*, Jan/Feb 1974). 'Production experiments' would seem to be as 'pragmatic' as anything could well be, since the whole nature of an experiment is to see if something works or if some improvement can be found. What is probably meant here is that run-of-the-mill museum work is 'pragmatic', a practical activity by which museum staffs earn their living, whereas those responsible for 'creative experiments' are concerned with chances, possibilities and hopes, with their feet less firmly on the ground.

Pragmatism

Practical ability; judging everything by its immediate effects. A technical representative, for example, can be required to have 'the qualities of diplomacy, selling ability, pragmatism and toughness' (*D Tel*, 21.1.77).

Precision

Careful design and manufacture. Americans in particular are fond of thinking that they are about to buy something made to meet the exacting standards of a lunar probe, which is often suggested but rarely the case. 'Robert Indiana's famous sculpture precision—scaled to $3'' \times 3'' \times 1\frac{1}{2}.''$ (*Delta Flightline Catalogue*, 1976) is simply a scale-model of the original.

Predicated

Based, dependent. 'A client/counsellor relationship is one of growth predicated on trust' (*Times*, 27.7.76). The Californian company responsible for this whole-page and extremely expensive advertisement for a confidential secretary was clearly concerned to tell the world that it represented the very highest standard of financial counselling, and pulled all the most stately and flowery language out of the bag to prove it. Other and lesser organisations might be content to say that their business was 'founded on trust', but not this one.

Pre-empt
To forestall, literally 'to buy something before anyone else has a chance to do so'. Military leaders are much given to talking of 'preemptive strikes', i.e. hitting the enemy before he has a chance to hit you, and the word is also popular in the business world, which likes to sound military whenever it can. A firm can be looking, for example, for someone trained and equipped 'to pre-empt production difficulties' (*S Tel*, 1.2.76).

Premier
Of the best quality available. 'The premier 2-storey residence' (*AFR*, 2.3.76) so highly recommended by the agents was no more than a detached house in one of the more expensive Australian suburbs. One could certainly think of many better places to live, a possibility not allowed for by 'premier', which means the first, the very best.

Premised
'Is premised on' means 'assumes', which is too ordinary a word for a social scientist with his reputation to protect. 'The authority system is premised on teacher-compliance' (Corwin, 1974).

Premium
More, extra. In some instances, it is difficult to decide if the word is being used as a noun or an adverb. 'We pay premium for all wood brought in at this time of the year' (*New Yorker*, 22.11.76). The important thing, for anyone engaged in a high-class business, is to avoid using the low-class, commercially dangerous word 'extra'.

Premium-priced
The most expensive. A snob-word and a commercially attractive euphemism which implies that one is buying the best and would naturally wish and expect to pay for it. If one can, by some miracle, get premium-priced goods at a bargain rate, one has both the cachet

and a welcome saving. The wily merchants of an unknown whisky, for instance, saw distinct advantages in offering it as 'every bit as good as better-known, premium-priced scotches', (*New Yorker*, 29.3.76).

Prescind

Cut off, strip away. Liked by social scientists because of its Latin, scholarly flavour, but quite unnecessary as a technical term. It serves, however, to keep the ignorant laity gaping and marvelling on the other side of the fence. 'Knowing the watch consists of prescinding its accidental qualities and seizing upon its essential form, its "watchness".' (Brubacher, 1969).

Presence

Having somebody there. Industrial management is fond of having or establishing presences. 'What you need is a local marketing presence; a real strategist who can beat him at his own game' (*High Life*, Oct 1976), i.e. someone who lives where his market is, a local man, in fact. There are also 'Professional and commercial concerns ready to establish a management-presence in Europe' (*High Life*, Oct 1976), i.e. ready to set up offices.

Presently

At present. The British say 'at present', the Americans 'presently', continuing a usage which has been obsolete in Britain, except in dialects, since the seventeenth century. For a British writer to use 'presently' in the American sense, instead of with the traditional British meaning of 'shortly, very soon', is to be guilty of a special form of snobbery. The 'presently' people in Britain, are mainly, but not entirely, to be found in the industrial and commercial fields. Consciously or unconsciously they use the word as a means of showing that their hearts beat with their American brothers, whose methods, philosophy and success they admire so much. They are willing to commit linguistic treason in order to cement the spiritual alliance. 'Their joint American/English company presently fabricates stainless steel products' (*D Tel*, 27.11.75) comes from the main group of users, but even educational writers have been contaminated: 'Daniel Stewart's and Melville College is presently a grant-aided school' (*D Tel*, 6.2.76). In Britain to throw away 'at present' is to abandon a precision-tool. Cf. Currently.

Pre-shopping
Before one shops. A shopping service is provided by a shop, a pre-shopping service by some form of consumer organisation. Why it cannot be called, honestly and simply, a 'shoppers' advisory service' is difficult to understand, unless there is supposed to be something more clinical about 'pre-shopping service', by analogy with 'pre-natal service'. In London, the Borough of Lambeth announces that it makes 'provision for pre-shopping services' (*Times*, 22.1.76).

Prestige
Owned, occupied or operated by socially desirable people. Estate agents make much use of the word, offering such enticing possibilities as 'an elegant fourth floor flat in a prestige modern block' (*S Times*, 30.11.75) and, even better, 'a superb third floor flat in a prestige luxury block' (*S Times*, 30.11.75). A senior executive would expect to drive 'a prestige company car' (*D Tel*, 9.12.75)—this, in Britain, would be of the Rover or Jaguar type—and any housewife would be proud to know that she was cooking, not with any old saucepan, but with 'a prestige product' (*D Tel*, 27.11.75).

Prestigious
Enhancing one's social standing. One can have, in today's jargon, a prestigious job, a prestigious wife or 'a superb prestigious home of distinction' (*Times*, 3.3.76). In our consumer society one earns prestige not so much from one's personal qualities as from one's possessions.

Prime
Best. In the United States meat is always 'prime'. Something else must happen to such meat as is not 'prime'. It never finds its way to the shops. It could be that it ends up as fertilisers or cat and dog food. When a shop talks of 'all the prime beef we've got to sell'. (*New Yorker*, 27.9.76) it means 'all the beef we've got to sell'. In the sense of 'highest quality', 'expensive-looking', the word can be applied to anything offered for sale. Furniture, for example, can possess 'the prime upholstered look, but at only a fraction of the cost' (*D Tel*, 16.1.77).

Primeval
Primitive. The two are often confused, and it is not always easy to

decide which the author has in mind. If a group of musicians plays with 'a rumbling, almost primeval violence' (*Melody Maker*, 29.1.77), are we to think of conditions on earth before man appeared, or a good deal later, say in the Stone Age?

Principled

Following a principle. Until recently one could refer to a person or his actions as 'high-principled', or 'unprincipled'. Modern business, taking its linguistic cues from the psychologists, has gone a stage further, with such remarkable statements as 'the keynote of British Leyland's industrial relations style is being made principled consistency' (*Times*, 20.1.76). British Leyland was obviously after a slogan which could be waved at its employees and used as the theme of conference lectures by members of its industrial relations and personnel departments. 'Principled consistency' fits the bill very well —'Ladies and Gentlemen. Mr. Jones of British Leyland will now address you on Principled Consistency.' Slogans, however, have a way of hardening into a thick crust, which conceals and stifles the once-living idea below. The idea is presumably 'having principles and sticking to them', which is admirable, but there is something close to a natural law which says that slogans drive out sense, and one has fears for British Leyland under the rule of Principled Consistency.

Proactive

Is it 'pro' in the sense of 'previous to', or 'in the place of'? If one decides on the first possibility, the meaning could be something like 'before action is decided on'; if the second, then 'instead of taking action'. 'The planners must consider time skip not only in historical perspective, but also in a proactive way' (*Business Horizons*, Aug 1975) shows the word in a typically baffling context, and it is highly probable that not one reader of *Business Horizons* in a hundred either had the slightest idea of what 'proactive' meant or was able to find it in any available dictionary.

Problem

Anyone who is unable to do or get something, or who has too much of a good or bad thing, nowadays has a problem. It may be a drink or alcohol problem, a sex problem, a housing problem, a husband problem or a weight problem. The essential thing is to have a problem. Nobody is credible or complete without one. So, 'Kelly has a communication problem' (Toronto *Globe and Mail*, 31.1.76) or, in plainer terms, he is a poor talker and finds it difficult to put pen to paper; 'A long time ago I used to have a weight problem' (*Good Housekeeping*, Feb 1977). 'Problem,' in either the singular or the plural, keeps everything decently vague. 'You will be expected to become·involved in the recruitment and problems associated with female staff' (*D Tel*, 5.2.76).

Product-initiation
A course to familiarise an employee with the firm's products. 'He's had product-initiation' (Shell executive, in the course of a conversation overheard on British Airways flight, Bucharest-London, 4.6.76).

Production
At one time farmers bred and reared animals. Now, like any other industrialist, they produce them. 'The animal production industry' (*Obs*, 15.12.76) degrades living creatures to the level of cars or cans of soup.

Product-training
Training in the details or use of the firm's products, with pronounced echoes of 'toilet-training'. 'He'll need product-training' (Shell executive, in the course of a conversation overheard on British Airways flight, Bucharest-London, 4.6.76).

Professional
Traditionally a profession is a self-governing corporation of people with recognised qualifications. Doctors are, in this sense, a profession, and so are lawyers. But in recent years, with so many experts anxious to be considered 'professionals', the use of the word has widened to a point at which it has ceased to be of any great value. If one tries to establish an acceptable definition of 'professional' to fit today's situation and produces something that looks tidy, simple and comprehensive, one is faced with insuperable difficulties. To be a 'professional' nowadays, is it necessary to have followed a recognised course, obtained paper qualifications at the end of it and devoted oneself to earning a living in the same field? If so, what is one to do about 'professional actors' and 'professional criminals'? Should one pare away the definition still further, until one is left only with 'earning a full-time living by the occupation in question'? This would certainly not help to interpret 'the necessary equipment of pro-

fessional workers in many fields' (Ruddock, 1972), where the workers would not wish to be confused with actors, broadcasters or cracksmen, who have simply learned their respective skilled trades on the job. But it would apply to 'become Sales Professionals with NCA' (*D Tel*, 22.1.76). A firm as well as an individual, can be 'professional', although one has to work hard to discover any meaning in such sentences as 'We are looking for young men or women who are seeking an opportunity of joining a young professional and dynamic brand leader' (*D Tel*, 21.1.77). What the reader is probably intended to gather from this is that the firm has not been established very long, that its products are well-known and that its staff are on the young side and very keen on their jobs.

Profile
(a) Outline specification; (b) graph. 'The job profile and form will be sent to you immediately' (*S Times*, 20.6.76), i.e. the specification of the job. 'To improve our customer profile by gaining new accounts' (*D Tel*, 28.4.76) is more difficult. Does it mean, 'a graph or diagram showing the number of customers we have', 'the general appearance of our customers as a social and statistical body', or 'the impression the outside world has of our clients'? Profile is an immensely popular word these days, but it is usually employed in contexts where an alternative would make for speedier and more effective communication.

Profit responsible
Responsible for profits. To be 'profit responsible' is, for some reason, reckoned to be superior and more impressive than to be 'responsible for profits'. A manager can now expect to be held 'fully profit responsible for the district served' (*D Tel*, 27.1.76).

Profound
Capable of being savoured and enjoyed for a long time? A wine word. 'The 1970 is a profound, long wine' (*Times*, 19.6.76). There is also profundity, meaning, perhaps, the depth which comes from experience? 'People who like to sense summer and the profundity of a great estate in certain white wines' (*Times*, 6.3.76).

Programming
Planning, organising. 'Programming' has become more widely used since the introduction of computers, even when the application

referred to has nothing whatever to do with either computers or mathematics. 'We are at the beginning of a new era in mental health programming' (Duhl, 1963). One cannot, unfortunately, draw up a programme for mental health. The only possibility, as yet, is to plan and organise treatment for mental ill-health.

Progress

Both the noun and the verb—never used transitively until recently—are sadly misused, largely as a result of confusion between movement and improvement, both of which are supposed to be included in 'progress'. 'A desire to progress your career' (*D Tel*, 8.1.76) is a wish to help you to make progress in your career; 'to indicate sales projects and progress them to successful conclusions' (*D Tel*, 22.1.76), i.e. to carry them to successful conclusions. 'The officer with progress amenity development proposals' (*D Tel*, 2.1.76) is having some difficulty in communicating what he has in mind, perhaps 'proposals for carrying the development of local amenities a stage further forward'. The cult of the word 'progress' is such that 'climbing the management ladder' has become 'progressing up the management ladder' (*D Tel*, 6.2.76), and 'we are offering an enlightened attitude to career progression' (*S Times*, 30.11.75) forecasts the death of the useful but old-fashioned 'promotion'.

Progressive

Not following traditional, conservative methods, moving onwards to something better. Used particularly by people active in Left-wing politics and in the educational field. All activities of socialists and communists are, in their own eyes, necessarily 'progressive'. The word is used mainly for emotive reasons and has no particular intellectual meaning. One reads, for instance, of 'the progressive foreign policy demands of the labour and trade union movement' (*Comment*, 29.11.75) and of 'a fight that is the responsibility of all progressives' (*Comment*, 29.11.75). 'Progressive educational methods' are methods employed by progressives, i.e. by people who have turned their backs on formal ways of teaching. Or, as one writer has put it, perhaps with a certain regret, 'Many people equate progressiveness with lack of form and shape'(*Times*, 7.5.76). The theory of 'progressive' education is perhaps easier to comprehend than its practice, or, as one authority has put it, 'The theory of progressive education can hardly be faulted' (*Times*, 7.5.76). 'Progressive music' is experimental music, which in its aims and techniques marks a break with tradition. 'The rumours that have been buzzing around progressive jazz circles these last few years' (*Melody Maker*, 29.1.77). Nearly everybody is glad to be thought 'progressive' nowadays, since the alternative labels are usually 'stagnant' or 'reactionary'. So, in business, we have 'our client, part of a highly progressive, multi-national group' (*Times*, 26.1.75) and 'a leading and progressive firm of solicitors' (*Times*, 18.6.76). Sydney has 'one of the most beautiful harbours in the world, surrounded by a modern progressive city' (*Australia Welcomes You*, 1976), and 'the United States is a progressive country, one which accepts reform and change' (Lipset, 1971). 'Which accepts reform and change' is certainly one definition of 'progressive', but it does not, alas, explain more than a small proportion of the uses of the word. For some people, it means something closer to 'growing steadily', for others 'anti-capitalist', and for others again, 'non-authoritarian'.

Proletariat
Originally manual workers owning no property. The word is still used to produce an emotional response, although it has little meaning nowadays in Western countries. Attempts 'to convince teachers that their true interests lie with the laboring proletariat' (Brubacher, 1969) sound curiously old-fashioned, a cry from the Marxist-Leninist deep past.

Proliferation
When things proliferate there are a lot of them. It is a strong word. Half a dozen are not enough to justify the word. It may be true that 'a proliferation of small ships using Currie would be preferable to the provision of one large ship' (Hooper, 1973), but it is unlikely that the author had more than a handful in mind. 'A number' would have expressed his meaning, and avoided misunderstanding.

Promotional
Used in two quite different senses, which are easily confused. The first is concerned with promoting, i.e. advancing the career, of a person and the second with promoting, i.e. advertising and selling, commodities. Sense (a) is to be observed in 'For the right candidate promotional prospects do exist' (*D Tel*, 30.3.76), and sense (b) in 'The job holder will be responsible for promotional programmes' (*D Tel*, 1.4.76). One 'promotes' a boxer by arranging suitably

profitable fights for him and an impresario may well consider a man's 'promotional prospects' in this light, but an executive has to reach the very top of the management tree before the company's public relations department becomes seriously concerned with promoting him or with his 'promotional prospects' in this sense.

Propagandise

Propaganda is not the same as publicity, at least in Britain, and 'propagandise' and 'publicise' are not interchangeable. For most people, 'propaganda' and 'propagandise' have sinister connotations. Those with power and knowledge are trying to bend ordinary people to their will, and to make them accept ideas which are not likely to benefit them. We are always faced with the problem of deciding how undesirable the propaganda is in a particular context; with 'publicise' we do not have the same difficulty. In the following sentence, the author seems to have made a misleading choice of word. 'Our college catalogues propagandize this or that institution as preparation for success' (Green, 1968).

Propulsive

Of a musician, pushing his listeners, himself or the music forward? 'Mr. Antal Dorati, who made every note taut and propulsive, a riot of disciplined colour' (*Times*, 4.3.76). The mixture of metaphors is unfortunate. Mr. Dorati appears to be propelling us into a flower-crowded garden, which is probably not what the author intended.

Prototypical

Typical. 'The prototypical childhood experience of being dressed up and dragged around museum corridors' (*Mus News*, Jan/Feb 1974). A fair number of children, no doubt, have been dressed up and dragged around in this way in their time, but most children have not, certainly not sufficient to make it reasonable to call the experience 'prototypical'.

Proud

Reflecting national or personal pride. It is difficult for a piece of furniture or glassware to be proud, a quality generally reserved for living creatures, although their owners may well be proud of them. We can therefore give no marks for communication to 'these proud Williamsburg reproductions' (*Washington Star*, 17.10.76), or to 'Each 4 inch high tumbler proudly bears the Seal of the Confederacy' (*Delta*

Flightline Catalogue, 1976). Proud cheese is even stranger to con-template: 'Holland Gouda. Full-flavored, mellow, proud' (*New Yorker,* 22.12.75).

Proven
The old word 'proven' was, until recently, almost obsolete in Britain, except in the legal phrase 'not proven'. It has now been taken up in a big way by business and is often used as a substitute for 'good', which is not reckoned to be sufficiently impressive or dignified. In each of the following instances 'proven' can and should be replaced by 'good'. 'A proven communicator' (*D Tel,* 27.11.75); 'A proven selling record' (*D Tel,* 27.11.75); and 'a proven record of achieve-ment in negotiating at national account level' (*S Times,* 8.2.76). In 'Candidates must be able to demonstrate a proven high level of management ability' (*Times,* 5.3.76) 'proven' can be dropped and not replaced without the slightest harm to the sense.

Provocative
Exciting. 'We'll explore some of the most provocative monuments of the Mayan civilisation' (*New Yorker,* 6.10.75). In what way, one wonders, are these monuments likely to provoke the cruise passen-gers who are taken to see them? Will they be provoked to murder, wild dances or unbridled lust, or will they, as one suspects, simply be provoked to photography?

Pseudo
Something one believes should not exist, something which one feels is bogus. 'This elaborate pseudo-measurement' (Rubinstein & Stone-man, 1970). The 'pseudo-measurement' referred to here is the well-tried habit of awarding marks in examinations. 'The pseudo-revolutionary middle-class totalitarians' (Lipset, 1971) are, one supposes, unfortunate members of the middle-classes who are deluding themselves by believing that they hold democratic and revolutionary ideas, when they are in fact of a dictatorial turn of mind.

Psychodynamically
Concerned with getting people to work out their own solutions to problems? 'A supportive group using psychodynamically orientated case-work skills' (*N Soc,* 4.12.75). One could translate: 'A group of people helping one another to solve their problems, under the

guidance of case-workers who are skilled in persuading people to work out solutions for themselves'.

Psychological
Properly, determined by the mind and the emotions. The word is used ad nauseam, but not always with the care it deserves. What, for instance, is the reader supposed to make of 'the psychological difficulties in getting acceptance for the use of processed manure as an animal feed' (*Times*, 8.6.76)? Are the psychological difficulties to be found among the animals themselves, in which case all that is meant is that cows or pigs find chicken-manure unpleasing as part of their diet, or does the problem lie with the people who tend the animals or who eat them afterwards? Whose 'acceptance' is required?

Punctuation
The really busy, dedicated executive has no time for such frivolous niceties as punctuation, and those who serve him follow his example, like courtiers imitating the King of Spain's lisp. So readers have to be baffled and exhausted by the galloping progress of such sentences as 'Applicants should have the use of a car as there is a considerable amount of travelling entailed for which an "essential user's" car allowance will be paid' (*SMJ*, 5.2.76), and 'The applicant must be able to compose and type own letters which they will be responsible for and will sign' (*Times*, 4.2.76). Non-punctuators like these should be compelled to read their sentences aloud several times in succession. There might then be a gradual realisation of the fact that punctuation is a great help to communication.

Q

Quaint
In a bogus, old-fashioned style. 'Unwind in one of the quaint cocktail lounges' (*New Yorker*, 14.1.76). Why anyone should wish to do this is not immediately apparent, but quaintness takes many forms and some may suit cocktails better than others.

Quality
Good quality. In the commercial world nothing is ever of bad

quality, so that the use of the word 'good' is unnecessary. One can, however, say 'exceptional quality' for something which has no ascertainable faults. 'The most sought-after quality cruises from New York' (*New Yorker*, 13,12,75) are likely to be without the grosser kinds of heartiness and get-togetherness which characterise ordinary cruises, and they will be correspondingly more expensive, to keep the louder and more vulgar elements away. 'A bungalow of quality' (*B & WEC*, 2.12.75) has slightly bigger rooms than the average and better workmanship and is almost certainly on something rather larger than a pocket-handkerchief site. Candidates for a post who are assured that 'a quality company car is provided' (*Times*, 16. 11.75) will be given something in the middle price range and 'an extensive range of quality meat products' (*D Tel*, 16,11,75) probably means nothing more than 'an extensive range of meat products', the minimum quality of such things being controlled by law and the top quality found only in a relatively few very expensive shops. 'If you are planning to build a quality house' (*The Age*, 28.2.76), choose your architect carefully and allow him a lot of money to play with. 'Elegant shoes carefully crafted to Lotus quality' (*Vogue*, Nov. 1976) are made to the standard the public has come to expect from this firm.

Quantitative

Usually, capable of measurement. Sometimes, however, the word appears to mean 'careful, well thought out'. 'The candidate should be qualified to draft quantitative written reports of these meetings' (*Times*, 22.7.76). The San Francisco company inserting this advertisement cannot surely have meant that these reports would be quantitatively assessed, i.e. given marks out of 10?

Quartiles

Originally, an astronomical term, meaning the aspect of two heavenly bodies which are 90° equidistant from one another; the word has been taken over by the social scientists, to mean something like 'group of scores', not necessarily 'a fourth part of the total possible score'. 'Academic and nonacademic achievement quartiles' (*JER*, 63/3, Nov 1969).

Queen-size

Somewhere between the smallest and the largest versions available. This is so far used only for beds or bed-like furniture, not for cigarettes. A typical instance would be 'a Simmons sofa that converts into a queen-size inner-spring bed' (Catalogue of Woodeward and Lothrop's store, Washington, 1976). Cf. King-size.

Querist
Person asking a question, enquirer. An amusing piece of social science professionalism. 'The future querist will use A on A . . . An in his retrieval' (Perreault, 1969).

R

Ramifying
Branching out in many directions. The word was virtually obsolete until the social scientists, grateful for another Latinism, seized on it recently, and were able to revel in such phrases as 'the full and ramifying effects' (*Sociological Review Monograph* 13, 1969). 'Ramifications', by a curious trick of Fate, has continued in common use and is in the normal vocabulary of people who would never say or write 'ramifying' and almost certainly have no idea of its meaning.

Rapport
Sympathetic relationship, understanding. One must, however, have 'a rapport' with something or somebody; one cannot simply have 'rapport'. 'The dynamic rapport of Tony's vocals is infectious from beginning to end' (*New Yorker*, 14.6.76) raises the question, 'Rapport with whom'? Since no-one is specified, the answer is presumably, 'With everyone who hears him', which seems a trifle arrogant and unlikely.

Reactionary
A favourite term of left-wing abuse, automatically applied to any non-socialist activity. 'A reactionary backlash to legislation on equal pay' (*M Star*, 20.2.76) is typical, meaning, presumably, when one digs beneath the jargon, that there are certain people who are opposed to legislation on equal pay. A similar flavour is to be found in 'the activity of the right wing, led by a reactionary Madison radio commentator' (Teodori, 1970).

Readable
Easy to read; not likely to tax the brain; good to read in bed. A

critic's favourite term of praise, sure to be quoted in publishers' advertisements. 'Latest Giles Yeoman adventure novel, as usual highly readable, fast moving and accomplished' (*D Tel*, 20.1.77). 'Highly readable' means that little effort is required to read it, which is praise of a sort, but surely not the highest, although considerable skill and experience is certainly required in order to produce such a book. The phrase is an expression of gratitude on the part of a reviewer forced to read far too many books in order to earn a living, quite as much as a recommendation to the reading public.

Readability
The quality of being readable (q.v.). To say of a book that it represents 'the acme of readability' (*D Tel*, 20.1.77) must mean that it is impossible to imagine a book which is easier to read, which suggests the lightest of mental fare, a possibility not always supported by the titles and subjects of many of the books so described.

Realistic
Relatively cheap, not outrageous. An estate agent's word. 'A pleasant part of the Midlands, where housing is still realistically priced' (*D Tel*, 27.1.76). 'Realistically priced' in the sense that the prices are in line with what real people in the district can and will pay. The estate agent who found it possible to say that any part of his stock of houses was 'relatively cheap' or 'sensibly priced' would be a very unusual man. 'Realistic' is considered a generally acceptable euphemism.

Real-time
Any version or reproduction which is described as 'real-time' takes exactly as long as the original event or series of events. It is debatable if 'real-time' can be properly or usefully applied to a pictorial representation, although the attempt is made. 'Since many of those who design our environments are visually oriented, the visual real-time image permits a much more effective communication than reams of words and intellectual abstractions' (Michelson, 1975). 'A visual real-time image' is a trendy way of saying 'a photograph', or 'a glance'. A painting would not, one supposes, be a 'real-time' image, since the subject would have taken longer to paint than to see.

Reasonable
Which people can afford to pay. 'Sea foods, meat and poultry at reasonable, inexpensive prices' (*The 4th Estate*, 13.10.76) says it twice

over, which suggests that the writer has no clear image in his mind of what 'reasonable' means. The word is dead for him.

Reasonably priced
Cheap, fairly cheap. 'One of England's most reasonably priced housing areas' (*D Tel*, 7.1.76). 'A wide range of accommodation is available at Great Barrier Reef resorts, from sophisticated luxury hotels to simply furnished beach cottages and lodges. All are reasonably priced.' (*Australia Welcomes You*, 1976). There is, of course, no standard by which 'reasonably priced' can be measured objectively, so that the term is a very safe one to use.

Recency
The state of being recent. A seventeenth century word, which continued to be used until the nineteenth and then, to all intents and purposes, fell out of use until the sociologists re-discovered it. 'There are many conditions under which recency will operate' (Cohen, 1964). 'Recency', in this kind of context, means something like 'an attitude caused by something being recent'. One form of this might be expressed by saying 'it's good because it's new'. Translated into simple language, the quotation given above does not appear to contain any very profound truth.

Reconceptualisation
Thinking of something in another way. '. . . his discussion of the reconceptualisation of child socialisation as cultural contact' (*Sociology*, Sept 1975) could be profitably rephrased. ' . . . his discussion of the possibility of thinking about childern's acquisition of social habits as a form of cultural contact with people who had such habits already', which seems a fairly obvious thing to say.

Recontouring
Reshaping the body, slimming. 'Recontouring. 10 day course' (*Vogue*, Jan 1977).

Rectitude
In correct usage, moral straightness; integrity. To the Left, or parts of it, however, 'rectitude' seems to mean something rather different, a mixture of 'thinking the same way as we think', 'honesty' and 'fairness'. 'Students evaluations of the legitimacy of faculty demands and the rectitude of professors' (*JEP*, 60/1, 1969). It has clearly

become a highly emotive word and one to be used with great watchfulness, since it certainly does not have the same meaning for different groups of people.

Regal

Associated with royalty, always a popular and nostalgic concept in republics such as Germany and the United States. 'It's unique, expressive, regal. It's Royal Copenhagen Musk Oil Cologne, regal because it exudes the essence of royalty' (*New Yorker*, 11.10.76). And what precisely, one subject of an old-established monarchy feels able to ask, is 'the essence of royalty'? Which particular set of royal persons? The essence of Swedish royalty, if such a thing exists, would certainly not be the same as the essence of royalty in Britain or Tonga. Is 'the essence of royalty' a certain subtle, indefinable smell of kings and queens, perhaps? 'Exquisite cuisine and impeccable service, in a regal atmosphere' (Toronto *Globe and Mail*, 7.10.76) is easier— high prices and plenty of gilt, plush and mirrors.

Regimen

A set of rules or a diet, but, in the world of business, what the job involves. This is seen as a discipline in its own right, fully worthy to be placed beside the monastic rules of the past. 'As this regimen is likely to involve travel throughout the U.K. . . . .' (*Times*, 27.6.76).

Reification

The turning of a person or an abstract concept into a thing. The word does not always seem to be well understood by those who use it. What, for example, is the meaning of 'The reification of "economic man" met with considerable resistance' (*Soc Ruralis*, 6/2, 1966)? 'Economic man' has surely never been anything other than an abstraction, even in such contexts as 'He's economic man personified'. In what sense could 'economic man' ever be converted into an object, a thing, even by the most wilful sociologist or economist? It is possible, however, that the writer saw 'economic man' as the thing into which man was being converted and that the confusion is caused by the preposition 'of'. In that case, 'The reification, economic man', although not elegant, would make the point clear.

Reinforce

Strengthen. The analogy is probably with reinforced concrete, but some uses of the word amount to saying 'strengthen further something which is strong already'. The difficulty of interpretation lies in the fact that concrete, like the heels of socks, is reinforced from the beginning—one cannot reinforce it after it has set—but other things may be reinforced to prevent them collapsing, once a weakness has been revealed. Which form of reinforcement are we to understand in 'reinforcing brand image' (*D Tel*, 5.12.75)? Is it a shaky brand image which requires buttressing in order to stop it from crashing into ruins? Or a fine strong brand image which is going to be made even stronger in order to allow it to meet the growth and greater responsibilities which lie ahead?

Relations
Contact. Nowadays, no very clear distinction seems to be observed between 'relations' and 'relationships'. This is a vague border country where one may expect either word to be used indiscriminately. But there are times when one wishes that some quite different word had been chosen, as, for example, when one tries to disentangle 'a few scattered Jesuit priests had but mildly succeeded in establishing limited access to more intimate Chinese relations' (*Con*, vol 164, Jan/Apr 1967).

Relationship
Friendship? Everybody has relationships nowadays, instead of the old-style friends and acquaintances. But, with the fading out of the old words and the old distinctions, adjectives are needed to qualify the relationships–'a close relationship', 'a not very close relationship', 'a permanent relationship', 'a platonic relationship', and so on. When these adjectives are not provided, the reader can be faced with problems. What, for instance, is one to make of 'Excellence in teaching means a successful series of relationships' (Rubinstein & Stoneman, 1970)? Is it any more than 'A good teacher gets on well with his pupils'? What sort of 'relationship' can or should a teacher have with pupils? What, if any, is the difference between 'a successful series of relationships' and 'a series of successful relationships'?

Relative deprivation
Some people getting less than others. A popular euphemism in these envious days, when 'parity' and 'differentials' are such important motivations. 'The expansion of the new middle class will also pose material questions of status and income. These will be matters of "relative deprivation"' (Miles, 1971). Or relative advantage. The

situation can be viewed through both ends of the telescope.

Relaxed

Not tense, fully in control of the situation, with plenty of energy in hand. In these days of high-pressure and demanding work, to say that someone looks relaxed is very high praise. A 'relaxed' person is one who has fought his way through the jungle of competition and emerged intact and still a human being on the other side, a superior human type. A group of successful musicians, for example, can be characterised by 'their relaxed, unpressured approach to it all' (*Melody Maker*, 29.1.77).

Relocate

Move. The American term 'relocate' is now almost universal in the business world. Ordinary mortals move, businessmen relocate. The ambitious man is quite used nowadays to being told that he 'must be prepared to relocate to Switzerland' (*D Tel*, 22.1.76). Having got the job, does he say to his wife, 'Darling, we shall have to relocate to Switzerland', or 'We shall have to live in Switzerland'? To keep its end up, the company, of course, will pay 'generous relocation expenses', not 'moving expenses'.

Remediation

Improving matters, raising someone's standard of performance. This social science word has a distinctly clinical flavour – 'medication' is not far away – which no doubt adds to its prestige. 'Remediation should consider variation in need as related to sex and type of underachievement' (*JER*, 63/1, Sept 1969), or in other words 'Attempts to help the pupil to improve should bear in mind the kind of weakness they show and the fact that boys are different from girls in some respects'. The translation is clear, but would not increase the author's reputation a great deal, since the thought is fairly banal. Dressed up in its psychological clothes it sounds much more impressive, at least to those who are content to allow their minds to remain on the surface.

Remit

Brief, instructions, job specification, task. 'Task' and 'instructions' sound altogether too plebeian for a company in a substantial way of business, and 'brief' is too political. 'Remit' is felt to meet the case reasonably well, once one is committed to sounding grand. 'The initial remit will be to assess training skills for the company' (*Good Housekeeping*, Feb 1977).

Remuneration

Pay, a low word used only by the John Lewis Partnership, which is almost alone among large concerns in never having shown signs of any inhibition in the matter. Otherwise one finds such painted-up ways of saying 'money' as 'The company will offer a good remuneration' (*D Tel*, 5,12,75). With 'pay' or 'salary', one knew where one stood. This was the amount of money one could count on getting each month. The difficulty with 'remuneration' is that it may or may not be just money. Various fringe benefits, some of them substantial, may be included in it, although some concerns have thoughtfully adopted the habit of making a distinction between 'remuneration' and 'remuneration package' (q.v.).

Remuneration package

Everything a person receives from his employer in exchange for his services. This can include a car, a loan to buy a house, help with school fees and many other attractions. What, one should always say to a prospective employer, is the remuneration package? The answer may be, 'The remuneration package is most attractive' (*Sun*, 2.3.76).

Renowned

A synonym for 'famous', a definition with which all users of the word are obviously not familiar. 'One of the most renowned and famous country house hotels in England' (*S Tel*, 1.2.76) could cause some people to wonder if their intelligence was equal to the demands of all the reading matter placed before them. They should not worry. The author, for some reason best known to himself, is simply saying 'famous' twice.

Replicable

Able to be duplicated, copied or repeated. Social scientists much prefer to 'replicate' things, rather than copy them. 'The researcher using photography seeks to make an explicit, replicable statement of fact, to substantiate, embellish or overthrow a paradigm' (Michelson, 1975). Such a person has not so far, however, reached the point of refinement and academic altitude at which he speaks of Xerox replications, but that will no doubt come.

Replicate
The academic word for 'repeat'. 'We failed to replicate the finding that . . .' (*JEP*, 61/1, 1970). 'The present study directly replicated earlier research in two aspects' (*JEP*, 69/4, 1968).

Report
'Report to' is the fashionable synonym for 'is responsible to', and implies, fraudulently, a more active, more energetic kind of relationship. 'Report' has military and police overtones and implies that the industrial executive concerned is a patrol-car radioing back to base. Not infrequently one comes across cases in which not the man but the 'position' reports to a superior. There is also, for many people, the unfortunate association with the occasions on which one had to report to the headmaster or some other person in authority for some alleged misdemeanour. 'Is responsible to', or 'is directly responsible to' avoids all misunderstandings, but instead we have such saluting and heel-clicking sentences as 'You would report to the Project Manager' (*D Tel*, 9.12.76) and, with the man himself completely suppressed, 'The position reports to the General Manager' (*D Tel*, 9.12.75).

Repressive
Exercising a certain amount of discipline; orderly. Any organisation which fails to yield immediately to left-wing demands is automatically 'repressive', resulting in immediate demands for 'desanctifying and rendering disfunctional the administration's repressive authority' (Teodori, 1969). The administration referred to here is that of a university.

Reserection
Pouring into a decanter? The word has not been found in any dictionary published in Britain. It may possibly come from a Latin verb meaning 'to open up', and hence to pour into another container. Or it may be a wine-writer's joke, thought up in the certain knowledge that many, perhaps most, of his readers will pretend to understand it. 'Perignon is a good wine, fully flavoured and well suited to reserection' (*Nation Review*, 6/20, 1976).

Reserved
Virginal? Yet to blossom? Not fully mature? 'As yet, the wine is a bit

reserved' (*Times*, 20.3.76). Its confidence will come in due course, and it will learn the art of making its charm and its merits fully known to the world.

Reside

Live. It was for a long time accepted that the lower orders lived in houses and the better-off people had residences. This peculiar snobbery has been taken over by those arch-snobs, modern business enterprises, who are all too apt to insist that their executives, the descendants of the Victorian middle-classes, 'must reside in one of the above areas' (*D Tel*, 6.2.76).

Residual

Left behind, still around, sticking it out. Social science jargon. '140 residual families, tenants and licensees living in the clearance area' (*Soc Work Today*, 3/10, 10.8.72). The word is extremely unflattering and surely best avoided, carrying as it does overtones of residue, rubbish and sediment. A 'residual family' suggests something left in the bottom of the barrel, when all the good, drinkable liquid has been run off but, in fact, such families may well be exactly the opposite of this, the people with courage and stamina who have refused to let bureaucracy shift them.

Resolution

Settling, dealing with. One resolves a problem and settles a complaint, but 'settle' is nothing like grand enough for certain concerns, who display something like an instinct for 'the resolution of consumer complaints' (*Times*, 22.1.76), showing, perhaps, that they do indeed consider every customer to be a problem.

Resource

Something one makes use of. In the industrial world people are one 'resource', to be ticketed, stocked and used like any other. It is not an agreeable concept and as an indication of a habit of mind, it may quite possibly be a root cause of trouble between employees and management. 'Responsibilities include human resource management' (*Boston Sunday Globe*, 10.10.76).

Resourcing

Concerned with resources, either of things or of people. 'Candidates should be graduates under 35 with resourcing experience gained in a

professional personnel environment' (*Times*, 14.12.75). There is no
need for 'resourcing' at all here, nor, for that matter, 'environment'.
'With professional personnel experience' says everything required.

Results-oriented
Concerned with getting results. 'The successful candidate will be
dynamic and results-oriented' (*D Tel*, 7.1.76). 'Energetic and eager to
get results', which is exactly what it means, is mere layman's stuff and
strikes the wrong note altogether.

Reticence
Not asserting oneself. Easy to understand where people are concerned, but not very comprehensible for non-living things. How
does one interpret 'the almost capricious way in which wines go
through periods of reticence' (*Times*, 17.7.76). Do they temporarily
become tasteless or without aroma? Or call a short halt to the process
of maturation? Is 'reticence', perhaps, the equivalent of 'marking
time'? The adjective is also used, and the following example gives a
clue to at least one possible meaning: 'This Montagny is still very
reticent, its aroma hardly noticeable' (*Times*, 21.2.76).

Retinal experience
Seeing things. A very trendy phrase, popularised by McLuhan.
'Number and visuality, or tactility and retinal experience, split quite
asunder' (McLuhan, 1962). On the same pattern, 'lingual experience'
would be tasting, and 'digital experience' would be feeling. But one
has to allow for another possibility. 'Seeing', in the strict sense of the
word, involves recognising what one sees. A 'retinal experience' in
the physiological sense of the term, on the other hand, can be simply
an experience, with no additional meaning. One has a 'retinal
experience' in the course of a migraine attack—whirling wheels of
light—but this is hardly 'seeing'. McLuhan *may*—one stresses
may—mean this, but the pairing of 'tactility and retinal experience'
surely suggests 'the ability to touch and to see'? Is he, in short, being
perverse or profound? His friends, no doubt, would say the second
and his enemies the first. The innocent layman is left to puzzle it out
for himself, or to give up.

Retinal reaction
Seeing things, visual appreciation. Another piece of trendy nonsense.
People who favour this kind of phrase find it possible, for instance, to

refer to a theory 'which substitutes intellect for retinal reaction' (*Con,* Vol 167, Jan/Apr 1968).

Rewarding
Worth eating. 'Holland Edam. Tangy, firm, rewarding' (*New Yorker,* 22.12.75). 'Rewarding' here may also mean 'worth the investment, worth the price one paid for it'.

Rewardingness
Helping one to do better. A very nasty social science coinage, found, for instance, in 'The rewardingness of a peer model was positively associated with imitation' (Hoppe, 1970). This means, for the lucky band of initiates who have been provided with the necessary clues, that children found they did better if they imitated some figure admired by others of their own age.

Rich
Containing a lot of? A person can count himself rich in his blessings or good fortune, but it is doubtful if the same can be said of inanimate objects, such as chair and bed covers. Such an anthropomorphic attitude exists, however: 'Easifit have produced a totally unique cover rich in the luxury of wool' (*D Tel,* 16.1.77). This causes problems for the reader. Is the cover made entirely of wool and does its rich luxury lie in this fact? Or does it contain a mixture of fabrics, with the wool supplying the luxury element?

Riddled
Full of holes. Generally speaking, something can only be 'riddled' with unpleasant features, e.g. 'riddled with bullets', 'riddled with woodworm'. To use 'riddled' in a general, non-pejorative sense is incorrect, and is likely to make the reader go in search of sinister possibilities where none in fact exist, e.g. 'The game is riddled with such stories' (*Signature,* Jan/Feb 1976).

Right-minded
Serious-minded, untainted by hippy or leftist ideas. It has become almost a synonym for 'right-wing' or 'not interested in politics'. 'In an airport interview, Reagan commented that right-minded students should be assured of educational security' (Miles, 1971). 'Right-minded students' are those who think as the college authorities think, whose behaviour is correct.

Riveting
Presumably, which rivets one to the spot. The word is also used in the sense of 'fascinating', 'hypnotising'. 'All the riveting magnetism of avant garde design' (*New Yorker*, 25.10.76). 'Riveting magnetism', an interesting scientific concept, is no more than 'fascination'.

Robust
Strong; able to stand up to rough treatment. But in what sense can it be made to apply to a wine, as in 'the 1972 Mercurey is a firm, moderately robust red' (*Times*, 21.2.76)? The basic meaning must be 'strong', but how can a wine be strong, except in its alcoholic content? If this is not the writer's intention, what is? Will the Mercurey travel well, perhaps? Does it possess stamina, i.e. will it remain in drinkable condition for a long time? What is a reasonably intelligent reader of the *Times* supposed to think?

Room-excitement
The feeling one gets from an unusual room. Another example of the bogus-combination disease. Cf. Native-protested. Species characteristic. 'The Couristan Experiment introduces Kafirimar . . . creating room-excitement with Olde-Worlde mystique set to the beat of today's modern' (*sic*) (*House Beautiful*, Oct 1976). 'Creating room-excitement' is probably best translated 'livening up a dull room', which rugs might conceivably do. 'Room-excitement' is clumsy and misleading, suggesting an excited room, rather than excitement from a room. 'An exciting room' would be much more straightforward and satisfactory.

Rounded
Smooth? With round edges? A word from the wine world. 'Those who prefer a wine to have the rounded, gracious style' (*Times*, 19.6.76).

Rugged
Strong, rocky, tough. The exact meaning of 'rugged' is often difficult to disentangle, partly owing to the deliberately cultivated 'masculine' overtones. 'Rugged' not infrequently means, 'with strongly male characteristics', 'calculated to appeal to women'. There is certainly something of this in 'the rugged beauty of Wewak' (*Sydney Morning*

Herald, 28.2.76), where 'rugged' is a hybrid of 'rocky' and 'masculine'. Features, sweaters and tyres can all be rugged.

S

Salience

Prominence. Most English-speaking people recognise the phrase 'Salient point', and many of them use it more or less correctly. Of the two corresponding nouns, 'salient' and 'salience', the latter is probably not in the vocabulary of more than a tenth of one per cent of the adult population of either Britain or the United States. It belongs to a very select group, among whom must surely be every psychologist and sociologist with English as his mother tongue. Since it is easily replaceable by words which are more widely understood, the use would seem to argue a wish on behalf of the tenth of one per cent to use it almost as a private code word, a bond between equals, a choice which could be described as wilful, pharasaical or anti-social, according to choice. 'Wider creativity-control issues would have no, or negligible salience in workers' consciousness' (Mann, 1973) or, in words which everyone can understand, the workers care less than a bag of beans about such issues. 'High in salience', a great favourite among salience-people, means 'outstanding'. 'Negatively evaluated stimuli are high in salience' (*JEP*, 61/2, 1970).

Salient

To use the adjective 'salient' as a synonym for 'outstanding' betrays ignorance. One can only use it figuratively, as in 'a salient point'. 'The salient actor in the play' is a silly affectation, and so is 'This difference holds for both salient and non-salient students' (*JEP*, 60/1, 1969). 'Outstanding' and 'average' are possibly avoided here, because, being used in ordinary conversation, they are felt to be emotionally loaded, whereas 'salient' is cold and therefore scientific and safe. This is an illusion, since a word which causes the reader to become irritated by the writer has explosive possibilities and is not, for this reason, cold or neutral.

Satisfactory

Progressing favourably. If one telephones a hospital to ask how a patient is, one may well receive the answer 'Quite satisfactory'. This does not have the same meaning as 'satisfactory' on a school report, which is an indication to parents that their offspring's work and conduct are satisfactory. A hospital patient does nothing and therefore cannot be marked for hard work or good behaviour. He simply lies there at the mercy of the doctors and nurses and waits for an improvement to happen. The most unsatisfactory people can be in a satisfactory condition. The B.B.C. is a particularly bad offender in its persistent misuse of 'satisfactory'. Its news bulletins contain examples almost daily. 'She was taken to Poole General Hospital, where she was said to be satisfactory' (*B.B.C. News*, 12.2.76). The B.B.C. was in no position to comment on her character in this way.

Scenario

Orginally an outline libretto for an opera. Now any plan, scheme, project or sequence of events. Those who use it, and they are very numerous, especially in business and politics, could hardly live without it now. It is imposing and defies detailed or ruthless examination, invaluable assets to any politician or businessman in his public dealings. A very run-of-the-mill example is: 'The scenario is an explication of possibilities in the manner of exploratory forecasting' (*Business Horizons*, Aug 1975). 'Scenario' here is simply 'plan'. 'Scenario' can also be used in the sense of 'the way things have turned out'. Outlining his belief that, for most people, life is better now than it was 25 years ago, Dr. Michael Young says, 'Economic setbacks are actually favourable for this kind of scenario' (*S Times*, 30.1.77), i.e. this kind of development.

Scientific

A Communist term, meaning approximately 'shaped and arranged in a way which pleases us'. It is therefore possible to refer to 'the scientific theory called Marxism-Leninism' (Matthews, 1975), as if Marxism-Leninism could be tested by normal scientific methods.

Script

Code, set of rules. A social science takeover of a word which most people still take to mean 'a written document'. 'Kirk thus analyses adoption, seeing it as an emerging measure and one for which the cultural script has not prepared parents' (*B J Soc*, Sept 1966).

Seafood
Fish, with or without shells. What is now a seafood restaurant used not so long ago to be a fish restaurant, although we have not yet reached the point of seafood and chips. 'Seafood', like 'fish', would not seem a difficult word to use, but it can go very wrong, as one can see in a magazine reference to 'the Cameo Restaurant, which specialises in maritime seafoods' (*The 4th Estate*, 13.10.76). The possibilities arising from this are interesting. If—and it is only a possibility—'seafood' now means 'creatures living in water', one could have 'freshwater seafood' and 'salt-water seafood'.

Sedimented
Sediment in any solid matter, usually of an earthy nature, which sinks to the bottom of liquid; mud in various forms. The following use of the word does not therefore seem particularly happy: 'With language as a cultural product embodying the typification sedimented in the history of the society' (*Sociology*, Sept 1975). Words can fairly be described as typifications, but to suggest that they sink to the bottom of the history of a society as a sediment is true only if they are dead. Living language is closely intermingled with the texture of society or, if one prefers the liquid metaphor, floats constantly about in it. All the writer is probably trying to express is that language is a social legacy which has survived and can be seen in something like solid form, after the water of history has evaporated or been drained off.

Selected
A retailer's word, which usually means nothing at all. 'Buy a selected raincoat now' (Stone-Dri shop advertisement, Bristol, Apr 1976), means 'Buy a raincoat now', or possibly, 'Select a raincoat now', or 'Select and buy a raincoat now'. It all comes down to 'Buy a raincoat now', however, unless, as a fourth possibility, attention is being drawn to the management's powers of selection, not the customer's. In that case, one could translate, 'Buy one of our selected raincoats now'.

Self
'Sense of self' is a trendy phrase for 'personality'. 'Fashionable attire for the man whose sense of self demands expression' (*Panorama*, Boston, Oct 1976).

Self-disciplined
The 'disciplined person' has been with us for many years, but it has usually been assumed that the discipline came from within. 'Disciplined', in other words, meant 'self-disciplined'. This, apparently, can no longer be taken for granted, so we have such demands as 'the successful candidates will be dynamic, self-disciplined professionals' (*D Tel*, 27.11.75).

Self-generating
Making one's own electricity, able to function without being connected up to the managing director's mains? 'You will need to be articulate, self-generating, ambitious for personal development' (*D Tel*, 30.9.76).

Self-motivating
Not needing to be given day-by-day, hour-by-hour orders from a superior. A favourite business English term. A salesman, for example, is told that he must be 'totally self-motivating and able to operate from a home base' (*D Tel*, 6.2.76), and a middle-range manager that he should have 'the ability to self-motivate' (*D Tel*, 17.12.76), i.e. to work on his own initiative.

Self-organisation
The ability to organise oneself. 'Self-organisation and diligence are essential' (*Sydney Morning Herald*, 28.2.76). Both of these qualities could surely be assumed in candidates for a senior management post. Spelling them out in this way is merely a form of ritual; the very rhythm of the sentence has something of a religious flavour.

Self-starter
A person able to work on his own initiative. An exceedingly popular requirement in job advertisements, and usually found in such contexts as 'the ideal applicant must be a self-starter' (*D Tel*, 27.11.75). Occasionally someone with even more initiative is called for and we consequently have the 'strongly motivated self-starter' (*S Times*, 30.11.75), which presumably means a man who is eager actually to go somewhere once he has started himself. Evidence that the metaphor, which comes from motoring, is dead for many of those who use it is provided by a vintage example: 'You must be an

enthusiastic self-starter, preferably with a motor manufacturer' (*D Tel*, 23.1.76).

Self-styled
Bogus. 'These self-styled fighters for education' (Rubinstein & Stoneman, 1970) implies that the author disapproves of their particular fight and considers them dangerous and anti-social figures. The phrase is nearly always used by members of the Left when holding up the opinions of the Centre and Right to ridicule.

Semantic differential
A complicated term for a simple thing. It means that different people are likely to use different words to describe what they see when they are looking at something. One therefore speaks, for example, of 'the use of the semantic differential in architectural research' (Lowenthal, 1972).

Semesterisation
Organising the academic year in semesters or terms. An absurd piece of 'professionalisation' and striving for effect. 'The commencement of semesterisation has introduced a greater element of flexibility' (*PNGUT*, 1975).

Sensitive
In a potential trouble-area. 'This is a sensitive role, and, to be successful in it, the appointee must be capable of maintaining the existing close co-operation with other Divisions' (*Sydney Morning Herald*, 28.2.76). Since the appointment is for an executive to organise the supply of materials, the 'sensitivity' is probably connected with the difficulties caused in other departments when supplies fail to arrive, and 'sensitivity' means 'trouble'.

Sensual
Sexual. 'A sensual triangle' (*The Age*, 20.3.76) is the familiar eternal triangle of two men and one woman or two women and one man.

Sensuous
Sunny, and food and sex loving. 'She was cut off from all contact with the sensuous Mediterranean world' (*Con*, Vol 163, Sept/Dec 1966).

Serendipitous

Happening fortunately and by accident. It is not infrequently used to mean simply 'fortunate', as in 'the main finding of this experiment was serendipitous insofar as the experimenters let the data lead them to the unavoidable conclusions' (*JEP*, 59/1, 1968). One can only suppose that the 'happy' context of the definition has proved so attractive that the 'accidental' element has been forgotten or never known.

Serene

Quiet. One is 'serene' when one has peace of mind, but one is often quiet because one is oppressed by doubts and troubles. To those with any feeling for words at all, 'serene' and 'quiet' are certainly not synonymous. When Americans are recommended to 'adapt the serene lifestyle of colonial Williamsburg to your own way of life' (*Washington Star*, 17.10.76), they may wonder in what way that lifestyle was 'serene'. Was it merely slow-moving, easy-going and free from the noise and perils of motor-traffic, or did the inhabitants of colonial Williamsburg really have the peace of mind the word suggests?

Serenity

Peace and quiet and freedom from music, qualities which have little to do with 'serenity' in the proper sense of the word. 'The serenity of the hotel's main restaurant' (Royal Lancaster Hotel brochure, Jan 1976) is the lack of noise and clatter in the restaurant, and the same, no more or less is true of the Ritz Carlton, Chicago, with its 'serenity of environment only perfect service can provide' (*New Yorker*, 14.1.76).

Served

An absurd piece of restaurantese. All food has to be served, and there is no point in saying so. Yet one frequently finds it emphasised, as in 'Scallops in white wine and tomato sauce, served in the shell' (T.H.F. menu, Coventry, Feb 1976). The shell, which restaurants use over and over again like a plate, makes no difference either way.

Service

'Service' means bringing care and attention to the point where it is needed. There is no reason to add anything which aims at making this clear. 'The Area is committed to a high standard of service delivery to clients' (*N Soc*, 26.2.76). The Social Services Department which was responsible for this advertisement should have known better. It would have been quite sufficient to say that 'the Area is committed to a high standard of service', since this is what it exists to provide. 'Delivery' adds nothing and confuses the reader.

Shapely
Well-proportioned. The word is perfectly and traditionally acceptable when used to refer to the human body, but a shapely voice requires a greater degree of imagination. One critic has written of the singer, Lucia Popp, 'everything she does is shapely and often radiant' (*Fin Times*, 7.2.77).

Shirt-sleeved
Able and willing to do the practical part of the job himself. Sometimes the wording chosen leaves the reader in some state of bewilderment as to whether a particular individual does actually carry out these comparatively menial tasks himself, or whether he merely cultivates the appearance of someone who could carry out such tasks at any time, if he wanted to. How, for instance, is one to interpret the search for 'a mature, shirt-sleeved individual to be responsible for directing, supervising and co-ordinating the computer services' (*Boston Sunday Globe*, 10.10.76)?

Shortened Christian name
Publicising the Christian name of a senior official is a modern and spurious attempt to give a democratic and with-it flavour to the organisation for which that official works. If the Christian name is shortened, the image is considered to be super-democratic and even more with-it. An advertisement by the Royal County of Berkshire for a Senior Social Worker, for example, ends, 'Further information by telephoning Mike Stanier or Lyn Allaway' (*N Soc*, 19.2.76) and one from another authority says, 'Further information and application form from Larry Klein, Assistant Divisional Director, Social Services Department' (*N Soc*, 19.2.76).

Shut up
Which has not yet released its full aroma, flavour and bouquet? 'The Decru, which is a biggish wine, still shut up within itself' (*Times*, 31.7.76); 'The Palmer, still very shut up' (*Times*, 17.7.76).

Significant

Important. This is a fairly strong word, and its use in the wrong place can cause the sentence to collapse with a disquieting bump and possibly with some amusement to the onlookers. 'Our clients, who are a significant force to be reckoned with in the worldwide bathroom fittings market' (*D Tel*, 19.1.77) would have been slightly less ludicrous if 'significant' had been struck out.

Silky

Smooth? Another mysterious wine word. 'The long silky style of the great champagnes' (*Times*, 19.6.76). 'Champagnes' does not, somehow, seem an appropriate adjective to apply to champagne. It seems better suited to a sweeter and less bubbly kind of wine. Silkiness and bubbliness do not go easily together.

Sinewy

Tough? Full of muscle and inner strength? Repeated attempts to discover what this wine-word means have failed. The reader must do his best to work out an answer for himself from such clues as 'One that combines an inner sinewy firmness with a beautiful bouquet is a Coteaux du Layon moelleux' (*Times*, 3.7.76). The music critics, who also make use of 'sinewy', do little to bring us into touch with its meaning. 'The Adagio being full of a fairly unusual kind of sinewy yet lyrical melody that is never facile' (*Times*, 12.11.76).

Situation

A padding word from business English that can usually be omitted altogether, or a more specific word substituted. 'A real appreciation of the problem of implementing changes in the manufacturing situation is required' (*S Times*, 16.11.75), i.e. changes in manufacturing methods; 'decisive action in Management situation (sic)' (*N Soc*, 4.12.75), i.e. by the management; 'communication between people in work situations' (*Times*, 28.11.75), i.e. between people at work.

Size

Extent to which it fills the mouth? 'For a wine to get near it in size . . .' (*National Times*, 1.3.76).

Sizzling

Rushed at breakneck speed from the grill. It is common for American restaurants to advertise themselves as, for example, 'featuring sizzling steaks in an Old West atmosphere' (Brochure of Marriott Hotel, Dallas, 1977). A sizzle is a noise, which one can hear while meat is cooking. It disappears very quickly after the meat is removed from the source of heat and it is extremely unlikely that a steak will still be sizzling when it reaches a restaurant table, although one hopes it will be hot. In places where the grilling area forms part of the restaurant, customers sitting close to the grill may possibly hear the sound of sizzling, but the intention, in an advertisement, is to make eaters feel that they are around a camp-fire at dusk, or perhaps near their own barbecue.

Skilled
People are skilled, things are not. 'Tested in our own skilled workshops' (*S Tel*, 1.2.76) is nonsense. The workshops may well contain skilled people or depend on them, but they cannot themselves be skilled.

Sleekly
With a flowing line? Like a cat's back? 'Choose sleekly scaled lounge chairs' (*Washington Star*, 17.10.76). 'Scaled' means perhaps 'proportioned'. The chairs would therefore have 'flowing lines'.

Smile
To suggest sunshine and happiness? 'The 1971 Dom Scharzhofberger . . . a wine that smiles' (*Times*, 3.4.76).

So-called
A term indicating that one's adversary's attitude or activity is not what it seems or purports to be. A left-wing person can refer, for instance, to 'the so-called diagnoses of Britain's ills' (*Comment*, 29.11.75), with the implication that no capitalist government or economist is capable of making a sensible analysis of anything.

Social
Relating to the manners of an age. 'Not only has Clement made a film with a broad social comment' (*The Age*, 20.3.76). The English dramatists of the eighteenth century and some of the Victorian novelists made pungent comments on the society of their time, going to great pains to expose its rottenness, shallowness, and greed. But they did so without feeling obliged to·become 'involved', as is

demanded of the modern artist, to the extent of identifying themselves with direct political protest. Dickens and Sheridan did not march in processions or hand in petitions at No 10 Downing Street. Because the nature of 'social comment' has changed, it is difficult to know how one should interpret the phrase, or that of 'social protest', when it appears in a modern context. In some cases the writer or painter or film-maker or dramatist remains detached, in something of the nineteenth century way, but in others he clearly cares very deeply about his subject and identifies himself with it. How is the person thinking of seeing Clement's film to decide in advance if he is to be offered a crusading piece or a detached artistic reflexion, since 'broad social comment' covers both? He might well want to avoid one or the other.

Sociological stranger

An outsider, someone who decides to opt out of society or live on its fringe, a misfit. 'In many respects they are sociological strangers who remain outside the basic class structure of the community' (Corwin, 1974). An earlier period would have called such a person a 'man of an independent turn of mind', an 'individualist', or even an 'eccentric', and respected him. Our age, with its emphasis on the fully socialised, group-thinking man as the norm, sees anyone who fails to fit into the pattern or does not even attempt to, as the man on the beach, 'the sociological stranger', the foreigner in his own country.

Socialisation

The process of making people think of themselves primarily as group-animals, and to conceive their identity in these terms. This or that factor can therefore 'play an important role in the socialisation of teachers into either a professional or employee role' (*Educ & Soc Soci*, 1/2, July 1969). But some teachers can feel themselves to be professional people and some mere employees.

Soft

'Smooth; gently stroking the palate, velvety'? A wine word. 'Sichel's vintage report describes them as "soft and graceful, with no edges" ' (*Times*, 31.7.76).

Soiled

Dirty. Since, in these hygienic days, nobody and nothing can ever be dirty, some more suitable word has to be found, and 'soiled' does very well. 'Extra polythene bags (wonderful for soiled laundry)' (*Qantas* brochure, 1976).

Sophisticated
Complicated, complex, not simple or cheap. Anything and anybody can be 'sophisticated' nowadays, and the term is always taken to indicate praise, with the implication that what is described as 'sophisticated' must have had a great deal of money, care and attention devoted to it. We therefore have 'sophisticated capital cities' (*D Tel*, 28.1.76); 'sophisticated capital equipment' (*D Tel*, 27.11.75); 'sophisticated warships for the world's navies' (*D Tel*, 5.2.76); and 'sophisticated additives for the food industry' (*The Age*, 28.2.76). 'Sophisticated' is a flattering adjective, which can and often does cloak some extremely unpleasant and even dangerous characteristics.

Sophistication
The state of being sophisticated, highly developed, highly trained and educated, highly cultured. 'The degree of sophistication in this essentially applied work will be high' (*D Tel*, 5.2.76), i.e. complicated; 'obviously, considerable sophistication is required to see the difference between . . .' (Hyman, 1969), i.e. intelligence and training; 'such is the sophistication of the trade links between the U.S, and Europe' (*High Life*, June 1976), i.e. complexity; 'beautifully basic to every wardrobe, classic lines and pure sophistication' (*N Y Times*, 12.10.76), i.e. suggesting a cultivated taste; 'the contrast between inns steeped in history to the sophistication of modern hotels like the Lord Darebury' (Swallow Hotels brochure, 1976), i.e. looking and feeling modern in every way, highly refined and up-to-date.

Sound
Solid, dependable? 'When the occasion or circumstance calls for a sound, presentable bottle of wine' (*National Times*, 1.3.76). 'This vintage produced some very sound clarets' (Ellis, Son & Vidler, Hastings and London, 1976 catalogue). 'A sound background in planned selling techniques' (*D Tel*, 27.11.75). 'Sound' rarely means anything more than 'good'.

Soundly based
Good. 'The successful man or woman will have a soundly based education' (*D Tel*, 30.3.76). There will be considerable disagreement, of course, as to what constitutes a 'good' or 'soundly based' education.

The term is far from being absolute.

Spear-head
Head, lead. Part of industry's great penetration metaphor. A firm indulging in these violent fantasies finds it possible to refer to its 'dynamic team spear-heading further growth' (*D Tel*, 12.2.76), which suggests that the spear, having been driven deep into the enemy, sprouts and multiplies. To 'lead' is evidently felt to be insufficiently aggressive for some concerns, and we therefore find such violent alternatives as 'an additional Systems Analyst who will be responsible for spearheading a major segment of that development programme' (*S Times*, 30.1.77).

Special
Unusually precious, worthy of V.I.P. treatment. 'And because we think you, too, are special, we fly you as if your living depended on it' (*Good Times*, T.H.F., Summer 1975). British Caledonian Airways, from whose advertisement this comes, no doubt does its best to make its passengers comfortable, but it is engaged in mass transport, and the very special passenger, such as one seven feet tall, or eating only fruit, is frankly an unwelcome nuisance who, in the last resort, has to accommodate himself to the general level of provision.

Species-characteristic
Characteristic of the species. The inversion and the hypen are just a piece of pseudo-scientific tarting up. 'Species-characteristic behaviour' (Hoppe, 1970). Cf. Native-protested, Room-excitement.

Specifiers
Specialists? People who try things out and test them before specifying and recommending them to clients? This is undoubtedly from the technical wing of business English. A man is required 'with experience selling to specifiers and industry' (*D Tel*, 7.1.76).

Specifying
With the power to specify. A representative can be told that 'an element of calling will be required on premier specifying influences' (*D Tel*, 7.1.76) or, in other words, that some of his calls will have to be on people who can influence the decision as to whether this or that product is used in a contract.

Spend
Expenditure. A trendy word for a basic idea. There is, for example, the firm 'whose annual spend will be of the order of £6 million' (*D Tel*, 6.2.76). It is interesting to notice that the use of a simpler word is against the general trend of business, which is always to use a complicated word when a simple one would do. The reason is probably the throw-away overtones of 'spend', giving the impression that money is of secondary importance, with plenty more available when the next £6 million is required.

Staff
Servants.'Servants' is now an obscene word, and anyone who advertised in these terms would get no replies. 'Staff' it now has to be for anyone wanting domestic service. 'A staff flat over the garage block' (*Times*, 7.7.76) is the modern shorthand for 'Accommodation over the garage is provided for a married couple, the man to act as chauffeur/handyman/gardener, and the woman to cook and do odd jobs about the house'.

Stance
Attitude. A business-English word. 'The Group's positive stance towards growth' (*S Times*, 30.1.77) means that the Group is, not surprisingly, in favour of growth.

Standing
Well-known in his particular field? Respected by those who are in a position to judge? Of good presence? Well-connected socially and professionally? This is an extremely difficult word to translate, and one is bound to wonder if the people in the business world who use it always have a clear idea of what they mean by it. What does a company really want or expect when it insists that a new management recruit 'must be a well-proven administrator of high personal standing' (*Guardian*, 11.12.75)?

Start
Starting. In certain sections of the business world, 'start' is reckoned to be more vigorous, aggressive and competitive than 'starting'. It has helpful racing associations. A company will therefore refer to 'the start point for an ambitious expansion programme' (*D Tel*, 8.1.76), not to 'the starting point' of such a programme.

Statement

Anything one presents to the world, an assertion of confidence. A trendy designer's fashion-world term, which has been with us for long enough. One store offers women 'a sum of many compatible parts to communicate your personal fashion statement' (*New Yorker*, 13.9.76) and another, believing that the product itself is the message, tells potential customers that 'it's the best way to communicate beautiful fashion statements to the world' (*New Yorker*, 9.8.76). A piece of jewellery is presented in these terms: 'From every angle the Luciano chain becomes a stunning design statement' (*New Yorker*, 25.8.75). At one time it would have been just 'a beautifully designed chain', 'statement' being wisely reserved for something that is said in words, not in clothes or jewellery.

Status

(a) State, whether one is single, married or divorced. A curious use of the word, since no question of status is involved. 'The married state' has been with us for centuries; 'married status' is an idiotic nonsense, introduced during or just after the Second World War, no doubt by the same military genius who was responsible for the famous 'married families'. But 'status' has now settled firmly into business English and into the world of passport officials and hotel receptionists. 'This is a bachelor preferred status appointment' (*D Tel*, 12.1.76). (b) Social level. 'The West Country, he found, has much the highest proportion laying claim to middle class status' (Allen, 1968). (c) Social identity, the place a person sees himself occupying in the community. 'Another possibility open to the individual with a poorly crystallised status is that he will react to resulting unpleasant experiences by blaming himself' (Lazarsfield, 1972).

Status deprivation

Low esteem, small regard. Educational psychologists and sociologists, always in search of euphemisms and circumlocutions, have taken this phrase to their hearts. 'The low-ability child suffers from status deprivation in the school' (*JEP*, 61/, 1970) means, roughly speaking, that the child who is no good at his work is usually not thought very highly of by his teachers and fellow pupils, which is not particularly surprising. Cf. Status inconsistency.

Status inconsistency

Regarded as belonging to different levels of ability, maturity or reputation in different fields of activity. 'What types of status inconsistencies do youths encounter?' (Corwin, 1974). The problem behind the question is apparently that a person can be defined, by those who know him, as a child in some respects but an adult in others. There is nothing new about the problem. It is one of the perils and inevitabilities of adolescence. Only the term is new and suggests that the difficulty did not exist until modern psychologists discovered it.

Stereotypical
Monotonously typical? 'Stereotypical' is felt to sound much more scientific than the layman's word 'typical', and many social scientists have undoubtedly come to prefer it for this reason, even when 'typical' is a perfectly adequate equivalent. 'The stereotypical dissenter is popularly portrayed as both a bohemian and political activist' (Corwin, 1974). Most people would find it difficult to explain what a 'stereotype' is and how it differs from a 'type', but might prefer 'stereotype' because it sounds more impressive.

Stigmatised
Marked. Experiences undoubtedly do leave their mark on people, and in the course of one's life one is bound to have a lot of experiences, some pleasant, some not. 'Stigmatised' seems rather a strong word to describe such a process, however, although not to sociologists, who are able to wonder 'how much students are stigmatised by the system' (Corwin, 1974).

Stimulus
Anything which sets one's thoughts or feelings in action. A psychologist's word, much overused. Phrases such as 'the dimensionalisation of stimulus values' (*JEP*, 61/1, 1970) abound–this particular one means 'finding a way of measuring the effect of stimuli', and man is reduced to 'a hierarchically organised stimulus-response system' (Ruddock, 1972), meaning that he is nothing more than a machine which responds to stimuli in a certain order, determined by their relative importance to him. 'Questions' become 'stimuli' and the results are 'reflected in the written helper responses to the written student stimuli' (*JER*, 63/4, Dec 1969).

Straightforward
With no pretence of being better than it is? The contents matching up

to the label? 'The non-vintage, honest and straightforward' (*Times*, 19.6.76).

Strategy
Plans, methods. Both government and business obviously enjoy the word 'strategy' and use it, instead of the traditional and plainer alternatives, whenever they can. Part of its appeal is undoubtedly its military flavour. The most ordinary planner, supported and encouraged by 'strategy', can feel that he is helping to organise a major war. We have, therefore, such imposing statements as 'information processing strategies should differ with developmental level' (*JEP*, 59/4, 1968), where 'strategies' can disappear from the sentence altogether, without the slightest loss, and 'senior planners to undertake the highly important role of strategy developments' (*PNGUT*, 1975), i.e. deciding changes of policy. There is no doubt that both government and business feel that they are adding enormously to their stature if they reveal to the world that they have not just a plan, but a strategy, although the difference between the two often does not reveal itself even under the most powerful microscope. 'The Government's strategy aimed at stimulating manufacturing industry' (*D Tel*, 2.2.77) is a case in point.

Stressful
Carrying a great deal of responsibility? Exhausting? 'This work is extremely stressful' (*Times*, 20.5.76). Is this a threat, a warning or a promise? The question is a fair one, because today's executive is supposed to revel in pressure of work and to regard the heart attack which follows from it almost as a military decoration.

Strike rate
Proportion of successes to failures. To anyone not familiar with current jargon, 'Our sales force can boast a consistently high strike rate' (*D Tel*, 27.1.76) could be misleading. When an industry or the nation has a 'high strike rate', what is meant is that its workers are frequently on strike, but when a salesman is praised for his 'strike rate', he is receiving credit for having a satisfying proportion of successful calls on his customers. Although the advertiser may not realise it, this is a rowing metaphor. The strike rate is the number of times each minute that the oar enters the water. A salesman's strike rate, however, is presumably not the number of calls he makes a day, but the proportion of times that his oar gets properly into the water

and pulls his employer's boat along. It is a metaphor which obviously demands careful use.

Strong

Forceful? Courageous? Having a principle and sticking to it? A business English word. 'Candidates who have strong managerial styles' (*S Times*, 30.11.75) are possibly men with deeply cleft chins, a staccato way of speaking and a steely glint in their eye.

Struggle

Fight, campaign. An essential part of the Communist myth is that the working-class is always struggling, until the magic moment when socialism is finally achieved, after which it receives its just dues and struggle is at an end. 'No individual, no group, no class is genuinely involved in a revolutionary movement unless their struggle is a struggle for their own liberation' (Teodori, 1969). This, on the face of it, is perfectly true. What is misleading about it is the implied notion, first, that people act as cohesive social groups and, second, that these groups are involved in a never-ending battle to secure what they believe to be their rights. The militants and the theorists may indeed see the situation in this way, but the great majority of the workers in any country are much more likely to grumble and envy than to struggle. The use of the word 'struggle' to indicate a continous process is both flattering and unrealistic. It does not correspond with the situation as it is.

Student

Someone attending school or college, not necessarily someone who studies. To call every schoolboy and schoolgirl a student is, alas, both flattering and untrue. 'The character of a student's classmates' (Jenks, 1972) would be more accurately expressed as 'the character of a boy or girl's classmates', although if one calls a boy a student long enough there is always a hope that he may decide to study.

Sturdy

Of wine: strong? Peasant-like? Plebeian? 'The Corbières region, better known for its sturdy red wines' (*Times*, 2.7.76).

Style

A group of qualities which distinguish one from another? Yet another wine word. 'The clarets of this year have style and substance' (1976 catalogue of Ellis & Vidler, Hastings and London).

Subcompact
Since a 'compact' car is, in America, a normal European sized car, sub-compact is smaller than that, a European small car. A car cannot be 'small' in America; the word would make it unsaleable. 'Compact' is tolerable, and 'subcompact' is sufficiently ingenious to be attractive, so one can have 'a subcompact rental car' (*N Y Times*, 12.10.76) and still keep face.

Subordinable
Able to be subordinated. The one word is reckoned to be much more scientific and professional than four. 'All the contexts to which the individual event is subordinable' (Perreault, 1969).

Subpart
Section. A 'sub-part', a sociologist's jargon term, is presumably part of a part. 'The change agent hopes to work toward a broader involvement of community subparts as the change project moves along' (Havelock, 1973). What, one may well ask, is 'a community subpart'? Is it a family, a house or a flat, assuming the 'part' to be a street or an apartment block? Or, making the 'subpart' even smaller, is it perhaps an individual? Does anyone want to be called a 'community subpart'?

Substance
Weight. At one time a 'person of substance' was someone who possessed a good deal of property. It is unlikely that this is the meaning of 'substance' in, 'This is an outstanding opportunity directed towards sales managers of verve, integrity and substance' (*Sydney Morning Herald*, 28.2.76). The man the company is looking for is probably not a lightweight, a man with something to him. It may be that a wine can be thought of in similar terms, although 'substance' in wine is apt to suggest sediment. But, anyway, 'the clarets of this year have style and substance' (1976 catalogue of Ellis & Vidler, Hastings and London).

Substantial
Fairly large. It is not clear why the word 'large' sticks in the throats of so many industrial concerns. One possibility is an inferiority complex; they feel that, compared with the giants, they are not large

enough to be called 'large' and it hurts their pride to describe themselves as 'fairly large'. 'Substantial' is a vague word, which suggests considerable size and adequate funds, but discourages precise comparisons. 'A substantial and well-diversified group of companies' (*The Age*, 20.3.76). 'It is mandatory that candidates have experience of the control and motivation of a substantial work force' (*S Times*, 30.5.76).

Subsumed
An unnecessary and pompous academic alternative to 'contained', as in 'the maintenance of the nature and logic of a subject which is subsumed in a General Studies course' (*Educ & Soc Sci*, 1/1, Feb 1969).

Sulkiness
Refusal to speak or express oneself. A wine word, meaning, so far as one can judge, that the wine in question remained quietly marking time and thinking its own thoughts, while other wines were steadily developing. 'The 1961s never went through a phase of sulkiness or dumbness' (*Times*, 17.7.76).

Super-contemporary
More contemporary than contemporary, as contemporary as it is possible to be. 'Put together a super-contemporary apartment as geared to moving as you are' (Catalogue of Woodies' store, Washington, 1976).

Superior
Better built, slightly larger and more expensive. An estate agent's word, never used by the owners of the houses. 'Superior modern detached bungalow' (*Obs*, 30.11.75).

Supportative
Giving support and encouragement when required. A business English word, used especially when referring to secretaries and personal assistants, who should be 'non-aggressive, supportive, excellent personal appearance' (*Times*, 22.7.76).

Supportive
In favour. 'We were basically supportive of the idea' (*Boston Sunday Globe*, 10.10.76) means that, on the whole, we agreed with the idea.

Supraregional

Of more than regional size and importance. 'The running and development of a Supraregional Assay Centre within the School, providing measurement of hormones on a nationwide basis' (*Times*, 27.5.76). The title of the Centre may look good, but 'Supraregional' adds nothing to the meaning, since we are told that the Centre operates on a nationwide basis.

Supreme

The highest possible. Few things or people qualify for this adjective, yet at one hotel we are very rashly assured of 'the supreme enjoyment of delicious meals' (Copthorne Hotel, Gatwick, 1976 brochure).

Surely

In America 'surely' means 'certainly', but in Britain it aims to set a doubt at rest, e.g. 'Surely he'll come', after someone has suggested that he may not. 'Surely the results will be enlightening and useful' (*AAM 1971 Financial and Salary Survey*). 'Exhibition farming surely costs more than operating a museum' (Schlebecker & Petersen, 1972).

Svelte

Not heavy? How a wine can be svelte, i.e. slim, is not clear, but the wine-writers insist: 'The La Tour Bicheau has a balanced, close-textured, svelte style' (*Times*, 31.7.76).

Swedish

Plain and simple, applied particularly to furniture and domestic equipment, despite the fact that a high proportion of these articles, as made and sold in Sweden, are not plain and simple at all. 'Swedish style dining chairs, beautifully made on the Continent' (*S Tel*, 7.11.76). An illustration shows these to be very ordinary upright wooden chairs, with upholstered seats, and with nothing particularly 'Swedish' about them at all.

Sylph-like

Slim and goddess-like. There is no great difficulty with such phrases as 'her sylph-like appearance', but a sylph-like voice is another matter. Are we to understand from 'sylph-like vocals from Jane Relf' (*Melody Maker*, 29.1.77) that the lady's voice was thin, or that it was the kind of voice one would expect a sylph to have, whatever that might be?

Syndrome
Widely used as a synonym for 'attitude'. 'Part of the general anti-establishment syndrome' (Lipset, 1971).

Syntax
Relation of parts to whole. The word applies to the structure of language and, as with 'grammar', any attempt to extend its use to other fields is confusing and affected. Yet plenty of such attempts are made, e.g., referring to a sculptor, 'Fried was impressed by Caro's mastery of compositional syntax' (Walker, 1975).

T

Tactical
According to plan. Business English. 'Tactics' are as important to businessmen as they are to the military, and indeed a comparison between the methods and aims of the two can be illuminating. Many businessmen have, in fact, had a military training and have carried over large parts of the military vocabulary and attitude of mind into their civilian occupation. It is therefore perfectly natural to find 'tactics' in business and to hear about 'the highly important role of tactical implementation' (*PNGUT*, 1975).

Tangible
Able to be touched. It is not easy to think of any manufactured item which, given the opportunity, one could not touch, yet we read of the firm which is 'offering the customers a wide range of tangible products in the communications field' (*D Tel*, 19.1.77). One can imagine the intangible services, but what are the 'tangible products'? It seems sensible to decide that 'tangible' means nothing at all here, and to edit it out.

Tankard
A metal drinking vessel with a handle, in which draught beer is served. The reference to 'bottled beer by the tankard' (*The 4th Estate*,

13.10.76) is consequently somewhat puzzling and suggests that the writer has never seen a tankard. 'Bottled beer by the crate' would seem more appropriate.

Target
A disc covered with concentric rings at which one shoots, the highest scores being obtained by planting one's arrows or bullets in the inner rings. 'Target' has therefore become a synonym for 'aim' but, since real targets are still in use, i.e. 'target' is by no means a dead metaphor, the choice of the correct verb becomes important. Targets should not be 'passed', 'exceeded', 'lowered' or 'raised', yet there are innumerable examples of such nonsense as 'Xerox lowers profit target' (*Herald Tribune*, 28.1.76) and 'formulating and achieving his sales targets' (*D Tel*, 5.12.75). Cf. On-target.

Task-directed
Getting on with the job in hand, disciplined by what has to be done. 'Task-directed free-group discussion without the tutor' (Rubinstein & Stoneman, 1970).

Taste
What is conventional and accepted within one's social group as being of the highest standard. 'The small group of people with extraordinary taste' (*New Yorker*, 1.10.75). 'Taste' cannot be measured objectively, although wealthy and privileged sections of society may find it convenient to insist and assume that their taste is 'taste'.

Taxpayer
A fellow citizen. When right-wing people are trying to persuade people to band together in support of a cause, it is common to appeal to them as 'tax-payers'. Almost everyone is a 'tax-payer' in one way or another, but only the political Right uses the word as an emotional rallying-call. The 'tax-payer' is the individual defending himself and his rights against a greedy, all-demanding and quite possibly socialising state. 'The message his audience wants to hear; the defense of the "tax-payer".' (Miles, 1971).

Teach
Earn a living by instructing, by constructing and following a syllabus, no matter how bizarre the subject may be. 'The author has taught recreation and physical education' (*JER*, 61/8, Apr 1968). How does

one 'teach recreation'? Anything one is taught surely ceases to be recreation, which is a self-generated activity or hobby. One could conceivably teach people how to follow a wide range of recreational activities, from chess to karate, but it is quite another matter to 'teach recreation', which is an attitude of mind. It is also doubtful if one can 'teach' a wine, although one can certainly teach people to think about and explore its characteristics. 'Those teaching claret . . .' (*Times*, 17.7.76).

Tender
Eatable. Following the American example of adjectives with everything, British restaurants have been increasingly serving up words like 'tender' as anticipatory aids to appetite. These are not to be taken too seriously, but encourage customers to feel that they have come to the right place. In the old days, patrons of a restaurant were provided with a list of the finished products. Now they have the recipe book hurled at them, e.g. 'Small pieces of tender pork cooked with onion, white wine, capsicums and cream' (T.H.F. menu, Coventry, Feb 1976). One of the deliberately contrived sources of confusion here is whether the pork is supposed to be tender before or after it is cooked. Meat which is not tender enough to eat after cooking has been through inexpert hands, but, since nobody will eat it raw, its condition before cooking is not a matter of great importance.

Tertiary
Higher. The traditional stages of education have been primary, secondary and either higher or further. 'Tertiary' is an administrators' and educationists' affectation, which the general public has fortunately shown no noticeable sign of taking to its heart. An Australian company, for instance, requires 'someone in his mid-30s, probably with some tertiary studies' (*Sydney Morning Herald*, 28.2.76), i.e. he is expected to have followed some kind of higher education course since leaving school. An even nastier phrase is a 'tertiary educationist', i.e. a person who teaches in an institution of higher education. Our universities are staffed, whether they like it or not, with 'tertiary educationists', as indicated by handbook references to 'secondary and tertiary educationists' (*Sandwich Courses*, 1976).

Tessera
A small piece of anything, by analogy with tesserae, small pieces of stone which are used to make up a tessellated pavement. A

psychologists' word, not to be taken over-seriously. 'A behaviour tessera is a fragment of behaviour created or selected by the investigator in accordance with his scientific aim' (*JER*, 63/4, Dec 1969).

Texture

Weave, mixture. The metaphor has appealed to·many people who would have done well to resist the temptation to use it. Communication is not improved by referring to 'the close texture' of a Chablis (*Times*, 6.3.76) or to the 'very precisely calculated contrasts of texture' of Elliott Carter's Kaleidoscope Concerto (*Times*, 12.7.76). What can possibly be meant by 'problems involving cues concerning the probability texture of English' (*JER*, 61/7, Mar 1968) is anybody's guess. One takes it that the English language contains 'probabilities' and that these 'probabilities' are somehow woven into a mat or 'texture'. But what, in this context, is 'probability'?

That

The, a, your. An arch-confidence trick, implying, like the very similar use of 'this', that the writer and his reader are close friends, with a full knowledge of each other's habits, plans and possessions. 'Who can say where that quiet dinner will take you?' (*New Yorker*, 1.10.75)–a quiet dinner; 'That meal when everything else is closed' (*High Life*, Dec/Jan 1975–6)–a meal; 'Keeping that old car one more month' (Toronto *Globe and Mail*, 31.1.76)–your old car; 'For that Christmas gift' (*News Letter*, Belfast, 18.11.76)–a Christmas gift.

The

Your. By using 'the' instead of 'your', it is implied that something which is being advocated is already common, if not universal practice. 'You can use it every day for the family' (*Signature*, Jan/Feb 1976) has a different flavour and purpose from 'for your family'. 'The family' is something that everybody is reckoned to have, like some sort of accessory. 'Use it for the family', echoes 'feed it to the pigs', i.e. any pigs, all pigs. By saying 'the family' instead of 'your family', the possibility is removed of distinguishing between one family and another. 'The family' means 'all families, including yours', and if all families have adopted a certain habit, yours must necessarily have done the same, possibly without knowing it.

Theatre
The theatre, art of the theatre. One goes to the theatre, but, in the jargon of the dramatic world, one studies theatre, one talks about theatre. It is a convenient, but quite spurious way of suggesting that some people think about the theatre in a more serious way than others. Those who make a cult of the theatre omit the definite article, talk of 'the current experimental work in theatre today' (*Radio Times*, 10–16 Jan 1976) and proudly admit that 'We learned a lot about theatre' (Rubinstein & Stoneman, 1970).

Theatrics
Fooling about on the stage. This involves no dramatic ability whatever, although an audience may love it. Groups of musicians often indulge in 'theatrics'. 'Ronnie also has some thoughts on his costumed/theatrics oriented contemporaries' (*Melody Maker*, 29.1.77).

Thermal
Heated. The use of 'thermal' is a pathetic attempt at upstaging, as in 'thermal swimming pool' (*Vogue*, Jan 1977). There is, in fact, no difference whatever between a 'thermal swimming pool' and a heated swimming pool, and there cannot be.

This
The. A storytelling device to knock the listener slightly off balance and to persuade him that he and the storyteller have been in contact for much longer than he thought. 'At this health farm I go to twice a year' (*Good Housekeeping*, Feb 1977) illustrates the technique. One is not supposed to ask 'which health farm'? One is supposed to know. It is, of course, no more than 'the health farm', but to use only the definite article is to break the spell of bogus intimacy.

Thoroughbred
Perfectionist, with meticulous attention to detail, characteristic of a top-class performer. This bloodstock metaphor is often used with remarkably little meaning. 'His account of Prokoviev's eighth sonata (op. 84) on its own massive, thoroughbred terms, was nearly perfect' (*Fin Times*, 7.12.76). Apart from the contradiction between 'massive' and 'thoroughbred'–carthorses, not racehorses are 'massive'–what can 'thoroughbred' conceivably mean here? Does the writer think of

a race of pure-bred pianists and violinists whose technique and devotion to music is of a totally different order from that of the ordinary run of hacks and nags? If not, what interpretation are we to place on the word?

Those
The. A notorious and widely used piece of commercial cunning. Together with the other demonstratives, 'that', 'this' and 'these', 'those' implies that writer and reader, advertiser and customer, are both in the game together, fully in one another's confidence. Consider the difference between the fraudulent, impertinent 'And for those special nights . . .' (*New Yorker*, 1.10.75), said with a knowing wink, and the honest, straightforward 'And for the special nights'. The first is cosy and conveys the impression that the parties are already on good and knowledgeable terms with one another, the second is objective and impersonal, as communication between strangers should be.

Thoughtfully
Properly, with attention to the comfort and welfare of others, as in 'It was a cold night, and she thoughtfully put another blanket on my bed'. It is not, as so many people appear to think, a synonym for 'carefully'. 'A former farmhouse, that has been thoughtfully renovated' (*SMJ*, 5.2.76). To justify thoughtfully in this context, one would have to continue in some such way as, 'to make the occupants happy'.

Thugs
People who do not share one's political views. A term of abuse favoured by members of the Communist Party and its sympathisers. 'Trailing between the Trotskyite anti-Communist gangs of thugs' (Lipset, 1971). To be a 'thug', in this particular fantasy world, it is not necessary to be a violent or aggressive person at all, or, indeed, a member of a gang. The quietest loner qualifies, provided he believes neither in revolution, nor in Communism.

Time budget
'A time budget is very simply a record of what a person has done during a specified period of time' (Michelson, 1975). The phrase is a poor one, and misleading, since for most people 'budget' suggests money and 'time budget' should therefore connote not only what

one does with one's time, but what those activities and that length of time are estimated to be worth.

Together
Perfectly co-ordinated? Bringing performers and audience into close contact? 'Hines' mastery of the keyboard sets a compelling pace for a session that's so together, it's hard to imagine what they could do for an encore' (*New Yorker*, 14.6.76). 'Together' with whom or what?

Togetherness
The warm feeling of being all together, or both together. 'This great 3 bedroom brick home was planned especially for the family that enjoys togetherness' (*Washington Star*, 17.10.76). Exactly what the three bedrooms have to do with 'togetherness' is not clear. There would surely be more 'togetherness' in a one-bedroom house?

Toiletries
Anything that one uses to make oneself cleaner, sweeter-smelling and more beautiful. Women are allowed, indeed encouraged, to specify exactly what all these things are, but men are still remarkably coy about such matters, scent being such an embarrassing matter that it has to be concealed under such names as 'after-shave lotion' and 'freshener'. 'Toiletries' covers everything and causes no problems. 'The most exclusive range of toiletries for men' (*S Tel*, 14.12.75).

Tokenism
Token support. A pejorative, implying, rightly or wrongly, that someone's heart is not in what he is doing, and that, for this reason, the revolution is being unnecessarily delayed. 'We learnt to oppose tokenism and build up our own community rather than depend on the good intentions of whites' (Mullard, 1973). 'The tokenism of the Administration with respect to unemployment, automation, poverty and social stagnation is clear' (Teodori, 1969).

Top
High. 'The position is London-based and carries a top salary' (*S Times*, 30.5.76). Salaries nowadays can be 'appropriate', 'above-average', or 'top'. 'Top' is not, however, the highest, but within the range below the highest, and does not, therefore, really justify the name.

Total concept
'The recent opening of Dallas' first total concept hair styling salon' (*Key*, Dallas, 1973). 'Total concept' apparently means taking the head and face into consideration in working out the hairstyling, which one would have imagined any competent hairdresser would have done anyway, long before the phrase 'total concept' was invented.

Totalitarian
A meaningless but highly charged term of Communist abuse. 'The pseudo-revolutionary middle-class totalitarians' (Lipset, 1971) is not concerned at all with 'totalitarians', i.e. people of a dictatorial habit of mind, determined to crush the slightest sign of opposition.

Totality
All, for people who find the word 'all' too short, simple and vulgar to use. 'Breslaw does find that when the totality of social influences were conservative . . .' (Hyman, 1969) is only 'when all social influences . . .'

Tour-manager
A guide, a courier. The grading-up of 'guides' to 'tour-managers' does not change their old-established function, which is to escort parties of tourists and sort out their day-to-day problems, as the following quotation makes clear. 'We are looking for a number of tour managers to escort our American, Canadian and Australian groups on motor-coach tours through Western and Eastern Europe and Morocco' (*D Tel*, 21.1.77). The 'management' of these and all other tours is carried out at the company's headquarters and, in some cases, their local offices, not by the guides.

Town-house
An expensive terrace-house, not necessarily in a town. 'The magnificent $63,000 3 bedroom townhouses right on the river . . .' (*Sydney Morning Herald*, 28.2.76); 'A select development of luxury town-houses' (*S Times*, 23.11.75).

Track
Curriculum. 'A student's track' (Jencks, 1972).

Track-record
Record. Used throughout the English-speaking world within the

fields of industry and commerce. It has now almost replaced 'record'. A person with a 'track-record' is clearly a winning athlete, someone who is accustomed to breasting the tape ahead of his rivals. 'Candidates must have a successful track record of multi-brand marketing' (*S Times*, 30.11.75) is a typical example. Companies, as well as individuals, can have a 'track-record'. 'A totally British company', for instance, can claim to have 'an extremely good track-record in the manufacture and sale of high-quality blood transfusion and dialysis equipment' (*D Tel*, 20.1.77).

Trainer
Person concerned with training. Circuses have always had animal trainers, and now business has people trainers. One company requires an 'experienced sales trainer and man-manager' (*S Tel*, 14.12.75).

Transportation car
A car with no symbolic or prestige value, good only for getting you there and bringing you back. '63 Dodge. Runs good. Transportation car. Must sell. $100.' (Shrope, 1974).

Treasurer
Until recently, only used of the person in charge of the finances of a local government unit. Such an official carries titles such as 'the Borough Treasurer'. Lately, private corporations have begun to have their 'Treasurers' and 'Treasuries', as a token of their wish to have themselves regarded as almost indistinguishable from Civil Service departments. Corporation 'treasurers' usually, but not always, concentrate on specialised matters, such as foreign exchange and international banking; in other words, with the company's flow of funds. One such expert, required by a large company, is described as 'Assistant Treasurer' and is expected to have 'at least 3 years practical experience in the Treasury function' (*S Times*, 30.1.77).

Treasury
The department in a corporation which is concerned with its flow of funds. A pompous and unnecessary title, with governmental ana-logies. One company advertises for 'additional senior financial management to fill posts in a variety of functions, including the Treasury' (*S Times*, 30.1.77).

Trotskyite
Traitor to the working class and the revolution. Possibly the foulest term of abuse of a Communist can throw at anyone, roughly equivalent in meaning to 'Judas', but with a much greater force. 'The Trotskyite anti-Communist gangs of thugs' (Lipset, 1971).

U

Ultimate
What used to be called 'the last word'. 'The ultimate' is, of course, always being changed and perhaps even improved, and for this reason, 'ultimate' may be translated 'the best we can do and you can buy at the moment', although prospective purchasers must never be encouraged to think this. 'The ultimate in a man's fragrance' (*New Yorker*, 13.9.76) is the best scent a man can buy for himself when he goes out shopping now, and 'The 3-bedroom penthouses are the ultimate in modern living' (*Sydney Morning Herald*, 28.2.76) will make a family quite comfortable for the time being, until somebody has better ideas in a year or two's time. 'Cloverleaf offers the ultimate in bathroom luxury' (Good Housekeeping, Feb 1977) is a rash claim. Anyone who had made it 50 years ago, before the days of heart-shaped baths, soft-carpeted bathrooms and elaborate mixer systems, could be made to eat his words now. And there is clearly more to come. The ultimate in bathrooms is never reached, and so, too, alas, with holidays, despite such announcements as 'world cruises, the ultimate in leisure' (*Vogue*, Jan 1977).

Ultra-modern
In an uncompromisingly modern style, with no echoes of yesterday's design. The word is used almost entirely by ignorant people, who have no real idea of what they are looking at, and certainly no means of telling if it is good or bad. It can sometimes come close to meaning 'simple', 'unfussy' and on other occasions it is perhaps best defined in terms of what it is not; mock-Tudor, mock-Jacobean, mock-Georgian or mock-baronial. It is a favourite among people who can think of no other adjective to use in the circumstances. 'Ultra-modern duty-free shops' (*D Tel*, 17.12.75) may mean that the shops have

good, practical fittings and equipment. 'The ultra-modern Fitzalan conference suite' (*High Life*, Dec/Jan 1975/6) probably looks as if a reasonably intelligent designer has tried to produce something suited to its purpose and to ignore irrelevant considerations. 'Ultra-modern' has, so far as furnishings are concerned, been largely replaced by 'contemporary' (q.v.), but it is still used a good deal by journalists, and by the travel trade, which confidently offers such temptations as 'a new experience in ultra-modern comfort' (*Vogue*, Jan 1977).

Unadulterated
Pure, nothing but, sheer. 'An organisation where unadulterated achievement is the only measuring stick for career advancement' (*S Times*, 4.4.76) is a context from which 'unadulterated' could be omitted with no harm whatever to the sense. The point that achievement is the sole criterion to be considered is already made perfectly well by 'only'. Assuming that 'unadulterated' is intended to mean something, however, we are bound to ask with what achievement might be 'adulterated'? Charm? Friendliness? Strength of personality? Impressive paper qualifications? Do such qualities really lessen the value of the achievement, to either the company or the individual? Is there really any comparison between unadulterated achievement and unadulterated milk or sugar? In short, does the writer have the slightest idea of what 'unadulterated' means?

Unbelievable
Remarkable. 'Choose from 7 unbelievable ski areas' (*Times*, 18.10.76). If the areas are really unbelievable, there is no point in the advertisement, which must at least attempt to make its claims credible.

Unblushingly
Without doubt or exaggeration. The correct use of the word is to be seen in such sentences as 'Muhammad Ali unblushingly said he was the greatest boxer the world had ever seen', i.e. no blush of shame came to his face as he said it. But only people can blush. The following is therefore ridiculous. 'Turkoman weavings . . . unblushingly functional, they seldom fail to achieve a forceful beauty' (*Apollo*, July 1966). A salesman might say, unblushingly, that these textiles are functional; the textiles cannot say it for themselves.

Uncommitted
Unenthusiastic. 'Had the two bands played to an uncommitted audience . . .' (*Melody Maker*, 29.1.77). A 'committed' audience is wildly enthusiastic; an uncommitted audience is presumably something less than that.

Uncomplicated
Suitable for anybody, no previous knowledge required. 'A wine of uncomplicated appeal' (*Times*, 6.3.76) is presumably one which can just be poured out and drunk with enjoyment, not even a quick look at the label being needed.

Unctuous
Smooth. The word is normally applied to people, in the sense of 'over-smooth'; a person's voice or manners can be described as 'unctuous'. To use it in connexion with wine, or any other drink, is both incorrect and unfortunate, since it implies that the wine is too smooth to be agreeable. 'A wine with a unique, unctious (sic), heady flavour' (1976 catalogue of Lay & Wheeler, Colchester).

Under-achievement
Doing worse than one theoretically should have done or was expected to do. An 'under-achiever' is someone who produces poorer results than he should, given his ability and intelligence. The traditional remark on a school report, 'Could do better', is now regarded as a value-judgement, and is only used nowadays in reactionary educational establishment. 'An under-achiever' is the modern form which is considered suitably objective and unhurtful. 'A reduction in under-achievement prediction errors was effected with several of the C.A.I. items' (*JER*, 61/9, May/June 1968).

Underprivileged
Poor. 'The underprivileged child in an underprivileged area' (Rubinstein & Stoneman, 1970). There is some confusion surrounding this much-used word, and its allies, 'privileged' and 'over-privileged', since there appears to be no agreement as to what constitutes the norm. If the base-line is 'privileged', i.e. having all the advantages to which a child is reasonably entitled, then someone with more than he needs is 'over-privileged' and someone with less is 'under-privileged'. 'Privileged' would then correspond roughly to 'middle-class',

'under-privileged' to 'working-class' and over-privileged' to 'upper-class'. But many writers use the terms as if the norm were intended to be somewhere vaguely between 'privileged' and 'under-privileged', so that both 'privileged' and 'overprivileged' children are regarded as having an unfair share of what the world has to offer. One cannot use a world like 'underprivileged' without making the other part of the comparison clear. 'Underprivileged' by comparison with whom? Used as an absolute it makes little sense.

Understated
Restrained, not showy or vulgar. A pair of shoes, for instance, can be described as possessing 'an air of elegance understated as never before' (*New Yorker*, 27.9.76) which is, of course, a considerable overstatement in itself.

Underwhelmed
Unimpressed. If 'overwhelmed', then why not 'underwhelmed', the logic seems to run. But to 'overwhelm' something is to cover and smother it completely, as a big wave does. 'Underwhelm' is a ridiculous back-formation, like 'beefburger', but with less meaning than 'beefburger'. 'Art Seidenbaum, columnist for the *Los Angeles Times*, was underwhelmed' (*Mus News*, Jan/Feb 1974).

Undirectional
Not pointing in any particular direction. It is a social science way of saying 'general' or 'vague' which, to people with a professional reputation to nourish and care for, would be too low and everyday to be safe. Something can therefore be referred to as 'having an overall undirectional effect of political significance' (*Educ & Soc Sci*, 1/3, Oct 1969), i.e. 'a general effect of political significance.

Ungainly
An 'ungainly' person is clumsy-looking, awkward. How a wine can be 'ungainly' is far from easy to understand but, nevertheless, 'the 1969s are, in my opinion, ungainly' (*Times*, 31,1,76).

Unique
Existing as a single example. The Parthenon is unique, and so is every human being ever born. Many things claimed to be unique are, however, nothing of the sort, and to describe anything or anyone as 'most unique' is to attempt to go beyond the limits of the possible.

The habit, even so, is widespread, with 'a most unique professional money management organisation' (*Times*, 22.7.76); 'beautifully expressive works of art presented in a most unique medium: Royal Doulton fine English bone china' (*Art in America*, Sept/Oct. 1976); 'the most unique collection of finest quality home furnishings ever assembled' (*Washington Star*, 17.10.76). All cities are necessarily 'unique', but there is some special quality 'that continues to make Atlanta one of the unique cities in the world' (*New Yorker*, 26.1.76) and, despite the fact that a house can be in only one place at a time, the opportunity has occurred to buy one in a 'unique position in lovely garden setting' (*S Tel*, 25.476). The prize for squeezing the last possible drop of value from 'unique' must go, however, to an article listing 'restaurants from the best to the most unique' (*Yellowbird*, 1972). Somewhere which is even better than the best certainly deserves a visit.

Uniquely

(a) Specially, as in: 'Old world charm recreated into uniquely exclusive landscaped units' (*Sydney Morning Herald*, 28.2.76). (b) Conveniently, as in : 'A luxury 681 bedroom hotel/conference centre, uniquely situated on London's Heathrow Airport (*D Tel*, 17.12.76). (c) No meaning at all, as in: 'Such uniquely maritime dishes as Solomon Grundy, Filet of Native Sole, Brown bread and Coupe Annapolis' (*The 4th Estate*, Halifax, 13.10.76). 'Maritime' means 'fish' but, whichever word one happens to prefer, something is either fish or it is not. 'Uniquely' does not change the situation in any way.

Unitary

Individual. One can have a 'unitary' system of counting or costing but, unless for some reason they are being regarded as mathematical units, people are thought of as individuals, not units. The psychologists and sociologists have other ideas, however, and see nothing odd in referring to the 'unitary treatment of students' (Solomon, 1963).

Unparsimonious

Generous. 'Generous' is, however, too warm a word for the social scientists and, in their search for something colder, they have come up with 'unparsimonious'. 'It would be psychologically unparsimonious to say that these associations are sometimes due to ethnic similarities' (Rokeach, 1960).

Unprecedented

Which has never happened before, unique in time. An action or a fact may well be unprecedented, so far as one knows, and the point can be worth making, but to make the same claim for a place is a waste of words. Every place is both unique and unprecedented. The estate agents think otherwise and offer us, for instance, a house which is 'occupying an almost unprecedented location in Kensington' (*S Times*, 23.11.75).

Untreated

When applied to a person, presumably means not having received psychological treatment, but an 'untreated' person gives rise to the wrong kind of associations. Sewage, for example, can be 'untreated', and so can a wound, or wood which has received no protection against decay or insects. Things, in short, can be untreated, people cannot, 'the low-popular children included untreated isolates' (*JEP*, 59/3, 1968).

Uplift

To raise, improve. The spirit is uplifted, a rock is simply lifted or lifted up. 'Uplifted' is, however, normally confined to spiritual matters and, although the Welsh are undoubtedly a deeply religious people, one cannot accept the appointment of 'a man or woman who will be capable of promoting and uplifting the image of the Welsh Craft Trade Industry' (*D Tel*, 20.1.77). 'Uplifted' and 'uplift' are in any case difficult words to use nowadays, since the brassière industry has publicised 'uplift' so extensively and for so long.

Urbane

Urban? An 'urban' person lives in a town, an 'urbane' person has polished, unrustic manners. It must surely be the first which is meant in 'the car for the urbane North American driver' (Toronto *Globe and Mail*, 9.10.76), although it is just possible that an exceptional motor manufacturer builds cars for drivers with outstandingly beautiful manners.

Urgent

Which forces one to pay attention, which brooks no denial? A common, trendy and rarely questioned critics' word. 'Reminscent of Munch, Nolde and Kirchner, he misses their fearful forebodings and urgent virility' (*Con*, Vol 165, May/Aug 1967); ' . . . and if that is not a misleading term for a performance of such urgent vivacity' (*Classical Music*, 20.10.76). In both of these cases, 'urgent' adds nothing to the meaning. 'Virility' and 'vivacity' are quite strong enough to stand on their own. The word can also be used as an absolute, meaning 'demanding immediate attention', 'with a message'. A comparison between two musical groups, for instance, can say: 'Whereas Gibbons was urgent, Be Bop seemed staid' (*Melody Maker*, 29.1.77).

User adequacy
Adequate to meet the needs of the user? The adequacy of the user? As with so many of these noun-noun compounds, the wilful and foolish omission of the preposition leaves the meaning in doubt. 'To participate in evaluating system performance for user adequacy' (*D Tel*, 20.1.77).

User-oriented
Thinking first and foremost of the needs of users? A car designer, for example, might just possibly think primarily of the people who are going to drive the car with which he is concerned, and, if he did, his work would be 'user-oriented', but what can possibly be meant a 'user-oriented investigation of the world around us' (*Mus News*, Jan/Feb 1974), since everyone must 'use' their environment, in the sense of live in it and by it?

V

Valid
Relevant, in one's own particular field? 'He is not only sensitive to current valid program content . . .' (*Mus New*, Jan/Feb 1974). This use of the word is curious and likely to confuse those who are accustomed to the more general meaning, 'in order', 'honest'.

Validated
Made valid, confirmed. Until recently only documents could be

validated, but now people as well can have a rubber stamp applied. 'It may help him (the student) feel validated in his academic competency' (Solomon, 1963).

Validity
Claim to be; right to consider oneself; merit. 'I still contest his validity as either a reasonable rock vocalist or composer' (*Melody Maker*, 29.1.77) contains the word in the third sense of 'merit'.

Value commitment
The academic world distinguishes between an approach with 'values', i.e. a willingness to believe that one thing is better than another, and an attitude which is 'scientific', i.e. collecting and assessing information solely on a basis of relevance and accuracy, without any feeling that one conclusion is morally superior to another. The distinction can often be observed only by indulging in considerable mental gymnastics. Many sociologists and historians would argue that values are built into their subjects, and educationists can refer to 'general studies with its value commitment' (*Educ & Soc Sci*, 1/1, Feb 1969).

Value-neutrality
Holding or expressing no view on good or bad. 'The conventional wisdom of value-neutrality' (*B J Soc*, June 1970). Cf. Value commitment.

Vanitory unit
An item of bedroom equipment, containing a washbasin built into a flat-topped fitment which is often continued to form a dressing table. 'Bedroom with vanitory unit' (*Times*, 30.4.76). An estate agents' selling point.

Vanity unit
A built-in piece of bedroom furniture, consisting of a dressing-table above and shelves or drawers below. Beloved of estate agents, who can see a ready market for the house containing '3 bedrooms, one with luxury vanity unit' (*SMJ*, 5.2.76). For the benefit of those not experienced in this terminology, a 'vanitory unit' (q.v.) has a washbasin, a 'vanity unit' has not, although the two are, alas, not infrequently confused.

Varietal
From a particular vineyard? Made from a particular kind of grape? 'None of your varietal whites with unpronounceable names' (*Nation Review*, 6/20, 1976).

Verbal encounter
A conversation or interview, not, as might be supposed, a quarrel. 'Face-to-face verbal encounters' (Pride & Holmes, 1972) are simply occasions on which one person is talking to another.

Verbal facility
Ability to write and talk with ease and confidence. 'Teachers in rural areas had verbal facility skills below the skills of urban teachers' (Corwin, 1974). The rural teachers were, to use plainer language, poor talkers and writers.

Verbal skills
Ability to read, write and spell? This is presumably what is required of candidates for a post demanding 'a science background with above-average verbal skills' (*D Tel*, 8.1.76), although it would not be tactful to say bluntly in print that many scientists are only semi-literate. One with 'above-average verbal skills' would be reasonably literate.

Vertical transportation
Lifts, elevators. One of America's leading manufacturers of lifts finds it possible to advertise 'an exclusive Otis technique that matches vertical transportation to your building's busy area' (*BB/NZ*, 1975), i.e. that it designs lifts suitable for the heavily used parts of your building.

Vibrant
Pulsating with life. Anything and anyone can qualify for this fashionable adjective nowadays. One can speak of a country 'where the economy is vibrant' (*D Tel*, 27.11.75), and of '15 vibrantly young, black Brazilian performers' (*Nation Review*, 6/20, 1976).

Vigorous
Full of strength and promise? 'The non-vintage is a vigorous, clean-cut wine' (*Times*, 19.6.76) suggests a public-school athlete rather than a wine, although one should charitably believe that the writer had

something appropriate in mind. 'A young, vigorous Company' (*D Tel*, 27.11.75) makes one think of a well-grown tree placed in good soil, and no doubt that is how this particular company sees itself. Industrial concerns are full of great romantics and their metaphors are with us to prove it.

Visceral

Guided by one's instincts and emotions, rather than by reason and intellect. 'Visceral', as anyone with a knowledge of Latin will know, properly means 'intestinal', and the present popularity of the word is only possible because so few people learn Latin nowadays. To say that someone is 'visceral' is not, perhaps, the most flattering of comments. 'Reagan is visceral; he's role-playing; he has a superb political instinct' (Miles, 1971).

Visibility

(a) Very similar to 'profile' (q.v.). Someone with 'high visibility' is in an important job. He or it has risen far enough above the rank and file to be noticed. One large firm can describe itself as a 'high-visibility corporate' (*Boston Sunday Globe*, 10.10.76) and another can announce that it has 'this high-visibility position with advancement potential' (*Boston Sunday Globe*, 10.10.76). (b) Record, presentation. 'Continuous visibility of suppliers' abilities to maintain deliveries' (*D Tel*, 5.8.76). All this means is that the suppliers' record of deliveries is kept up-to-date in some easy to understand form and supplied to senior managers whenever they ask for it.

Visitor theft

Theft of visitors or theft by visitors? The perils of omitting the preposition are never-ending. 'Heavy losses sustained by way of visitor theft' (Schlebecker & Petersen, 1972).

Vital

Essential, but more so. 'Arabic vital' (*D Tel*, 27.11.75). 'Our representatives from the vital link between Beecham Research Laboratories and the medical profession' (*D Tel*, 18.6.76). Something which is 'vital' is, in the strict sense of the word, a matter of life and death. A blood transfusion, for instance, could be 'vital' and so could a mountain rescue. A knowledge of Arabic might be 'vital' if one were trying to dissuade an Arab from making a murderous attack with a knife, but hardly for anyone trying to sell building materials or lorries. 'Vital' is also used in the sense of 'full of vitality'. One speaks of a 'vital person'. The two fashionable meanings, 'essential' and 'full of vitality' often appear to be mingled, so that it is impossible to decide what the writer has in mind. A band is described, for instance, as 'working on perhaps their most vital and immediate music of all' (*Melody Maker*, 29.1.77).

Volume producing
Able to sell goods in large quantities, not, as the following sentence suggests, to regurgitate them from one's own body. 'We require the services of two highly competent self-motivated volume producing salesmen to sell the full range of Ford vehicles' (*Sun*, 4.3.76).

Voluptuous
Sensuous in the most luxurious manner. 'Voluptuous' women have been with us since at least the beginning of civilisation. Elizabeth Taylor is popularly regarded as a living member of the breed – 'the voluptuous look, the stance, even the way she holds her glass, all bear the stamp of vintage Liz' (*Daily Express*, 31.1.77). 'Voluptuous' wines are, however, a comparatively recent idea. 'This rich fish needs a wine of character (some would say voluptuous) . . .' (*Times*, 2.7.76) means, perhaps, a wine suitable for a voluptuous person, a wine for Anthony or Cleopatra. 'A suite which is upholstered in discreetly voluptuous velvet' (*Good Housekeeping*, Feb 1977) may offer velvet in what is popularly considered a voluptuous colour, i.e. a colour to encourage voluptuous thoughts, or with a pile just thick enough to cause a thrill of expectation, but not so thick as to feel like a bearskin rug.

Warm
With no details omitted? Calculated to arouse the emotions of an audience? 'Luis Malles' warm story of incest' (*The Age*, 20.3.76) can hardly be 'warm' in the sense of cosy, friendly and reassuring.

Wax
Properly, to grow, become. Used only with a few adjectives, of

which 'eloquent' is the most common. The construction has to be: 'He waxes eloquent on the subject', i.e. 'he becomes eloquent'. There are now writers, however, who appear to believe that 'waxes' is a synonym for 'speaks', 'discourses'. One such illiterate can say, in a respected weekly journal, that the subject of women is one that a certain public figure 'waxes eloquently on' (*Spectator*, 31.1.76).

Wealthy

The upper middle class. There is and can be no absolute definition of 'wealthy'. How much capital or income does one have to have in order to deserve the label? It may be true, so far as England is concerned, that 'the wealthy have educated their young under the most intensive conditions possible, namely the secluded boarding school' (Rubinstein & Stoneman, 1970), but it is also true that many families who are far from 'wealthy' have made great sacrifices in order to give their children this type of education. There are strong hate and jealousy overtones to 'wealthy', which makes it a political, rather than a scientific word.

Weight

Impressiveness, solidity, authority. It is often difficult to decide if the word is being used entirely figuratively or not. In 'the subtle control of tempi, the meticulous balance of manners and themes, the sheer weight of the presentation' (*Fin Times*, 7.12.76) 'weight' is almost certainly wholly figurative; the presentation suggests authority. In 'The San Sebastian offers a little more weight' (1976 catalogue of Ellis Son & Vidler, Hastings and London), the sherry concerned is perhaps rather heavier than others, but it may also be more impressive.

Welfare

Arrangements made by the State to help people who are ill or in financial difficulties. 'Welfare' is not, however, a commodity, much as 'People want welfare' (*Soc Ruralis*, 6/2, 1966) may suggest this. 'People expect the Welfare State to look after them' makes sense, although one may not approve the sentiment. 'People want welfare', by analogy with 'people want bread' and 'people want a change of government', is a careless, woolly sentence, which is useful as a slogan, perhaps, but for nothing else.

Well-bred

Well-designed, well-made and expensive. 'Choose from our well-bred collection of co-ordinated sheets, petticoats and pillow-cases' (*Washington Star*, 17.10.76). 'Petticoat' is used here in the American sense of 'valance'.

Well-proportioned

Pleasing to look at, because the different parts are skilfully adjusted to one another. Applicable to furniture, people and racehorses, but hardly to wine. To describe a hock as 'discreetly well-proportioned' (*Times*, 27.11.75) is to leave the reader high and dry.

Well-rounded

Not narrow? With the sharp edges knocked off? 'It is important that the candidate be a well-rounded professional' (*D Tel*, 28.1.76) may mean that the person concerned has to be a 'complete professional', to use another jargon phrase, or that he has more to him than just his professional qualifications and experience.

Wiry

Hard, thin and strong? Jerky and staccato? A music critics' word. 'The quick movement is a system of three wiry figures' (*Times*, 12.11.76). The figures are not, one gathers, particularly warm or soothing, but what, in a positive sense, does 'wiry' mean here?

Wish

Want, should like. Traditionally, 'wish' is the polite word for indicating one's requirements, 'want' is more direct and less refined, and may also be intended to convey that the need is real and urgent. If a company tells candidates, 'we wish to make an appointment as early as possible' (*D Tel*, 9.12.75), how pressing is one to assume the matter to be? Does 'intend', 'must', 'are going', or 'should like' lurk behind the gentlemanly 'wish'?

Wondrous

Wonderful. The use of the old and largely obsolete word 'wondrous' implies that the remark is not to be taken completely seriously. 'Wondrous to relate', for instance, has slightly comic overtones, which surely cannot be intended in 'Time, plus common sense, produces wondrous results after surgery' (*The Australian Women's Weekly*, 7.1.76).

Word processing unit
Typing pool. The current Canadian government jargon phrase.
'Vacancies in the word processing unit' (Canadian government
circular, Sept. 1976).

Working-class
The noun is a synonym for 'members of trade unions', the adjective
for 'trade-union'. 'The output of the working-class movement'
(*TUC Report*, 1974).

Working people
People. Official trade union mythology divides society into trade
unionists and the rest. On suitably emotional occasions, however, it is
judged advantageous to drop the name 'trade unionists' and to
substitute 'working people'. To protect oneself against bewilderment
at such times, all one has to do is to translate 'working people' into
'trade unionists' every time one hears the term used. Examples are
frequent throughout the English-speaking world. On the Canadian
Day of Protest in October 1976, Joe Morris, President of the
Canadian Labour Congress, said the occasion 'marked a giant step in
the determination of the working people to gain a stronger voice in
the shaping of their own future' (*Montreal Star*, 16.10.76). The same
folklore is expressed in 'whenever working people have fought and
imposed advance' (*M Star*, 20.2.76) and, more aggressively and
threateningly, in 'I doubt whether working people will be willing to
go on making sacrifices of this nature for much longer' (*D Tel*,
19.1.77) (The Chancellor of the Exchequer, Mr. Denis Healey).

Y

Young
Below the age of 40. In the world of critics and impresarios, all
prominent musicians, especially soloists, have to be either 'young' or
'distinguished' (q.v.). The dividing line between the two can be
drawn at about 40, which is probably reasonable, since outstanding
musicians, like outstanding artists from other fields, tend to live
longer than other people. But, having read the advertisements, one

should not expect a 'young violinist' or 'young pianist' to look like an infant prodigy. He is most likely to be in his 30s. 'The young Russian pianist, Dmitri Alexeev' (*Times*, 16.10.75). Businesses and countries are also fond of describing themselves as 'young'. A 'young country', broadly speaking, is one to which industrialisation and opera houses have come late, a 'young company' did not exist 25 years ago. 'We are young in our culture' (*Queensland*, 1974) is another way of saying that our culture is still pretty raw.

Youth culture

Looking and behaving in a way totally at variance with anything one's parents and elders believe to be normal and right. 'Youth culture and all that it embodies; drugs, rock music, long hair and strange costumes' (Miles, 1971).

A NOTE ON SOURCES

A comparison between what is written in Britain, the United States, Canada, Australia and New Zealand suggests that the symptoms of linguistic disease are remarkably similar in all five countries and that, given the time and the stamina, every entry could be provided with examples from every country. Inspired and guided by what he find below, every reader, it is hoped, will compile his own lists of horrors and perils.

Many forms of jargon are now international, at least within those parts of the world in which English is spoken. Industry, management, the social sciences, music and art criticism, left-wing politicians and military men, for instance, tend to speak and write in much the same way everywhere, and a choice of examples is, in many cases, bound to be arbitrary.

Within these limits and given the aim of the *Dictionary*, to be illustrative rather than fully comprehensive, the sources cover a wide field. If the *Daily Telegraph* and the *New Yorker* seem at times to be receiving rather more than their fair share of attention, this is because no newspaper in the world carries, in the course of a week, as many advertisements for management posts as the *Telegraph* does, and no periodical matches the *New Yorker* for its reflexions of the snobberies, greed and inanities of the moneyed middle class. The wine-correspondent of *The Times* may also seem to receive more of the limelight than a single individual deserves, but she happens to work for a newspaper which gives a quite unusual amount of space to this subject in the course of a year and she herself has worked harder than most to create the kind of wine-poetry which such a noble theme clearly deserves. For the heavy concentration on the outpourings of the social scientists and psychologists of all breeds, no apology is required, since, together with the management business specialists, they are today's main polluters of English.

In order to make the *Dictionary* as useful and therapeutic as possible, particular attention has been given to today's symptoms of a disease which may well have existed in an acute form for twenty years or more. Striking and sinister examples from the 1960s have frequently been rejected in favour of what one hopes are equally impressive examples from the 1970s.

BOOKS

Allen   E. Elliston Allen *British Tastes* London: Hutchinson, 1968

Brubacher   John S. Brubacher *Modern Philosophies of Education* London: McGraw, 1969

Cardwell   J. D. Cardwell *Readings in Social Psychology: a Symbolic Interaction Perspective* Philadelphia: Davis Co., 1973

Cohen   Arthur R. Cohen *Attitude Change and Social Influence* New York: Basic Books, 1964

Competence   *Competence to Practise* London, 1976

Corwin   Ronald G. Corwin *Education in Crisis: a sociological analysis of schools and universities in transition* New York: John Wiley, 1974

Craft   Maurice Craft (ed) *Family, Class and Education: a reader* London: Longman, 1970

Cronin   Lawrence A. Cronin *The Transformation of the School: Progressivism in American Education, 1876–1957* New York: Vintage Books, 1961

Davis   Hunter Davis *The Creighton Report* 1976

Duhl   Leonard J. Duhl (ed) *The Urban Condition* London: Basic Books, 1963

Green   Arnold W. Green (ed) *Sociology: An Analysis of Life in Modern Society* London: McGraw, 1968

Havelock   Ronald G. Havelock *The Change Agent's Guide to Innovation in Education* New Jersey: Educational Technology Publications, 1973

Hooper   R. H. Hooper *The King Island Story* Sydney, 1973

Hoppe   Ronald A. Hoppe, et al. *Early Experiences and the Process of Socialisation* New York: Academy Press, 1970

Hyman   Herbert H. Hyman *Political Socialization: a Study in the Psychology of Political Behavior*

New York: Free Press, 1969

Jencks — Christopher Jencks, et al. *Inequality: a Reassessment of the Effect of Family and Schooling in America* New York: Harper Row, 1972

Lazarsfield — Paul F. Lazarsfield, et al. *Continuities in the Language of Social Research* New York: Free Press, 1972

Lipset — Seymour Martin Lipset *Rebellion in the University* Boston: Little, Brown & Co., 1971

Lowenthal — David Lowenthal *Environmental Structures: Semantic and Experiential Components* American Geographical Society, 1972

Mann — Michael Mann *Consciousness and Action Among the Western Working Class* London: Macmillan, 1973

Matthews — Betty Matthews *Britain and the Socialist Revolution* London, 1975

McLuhan — Marshall McLuhan *The Gutenburg Galaxy: the Making of Typographic Man* University of Toronto Press, 1962

Michelson — William Michelson (ed) *Behavioral Research Methods in Environmental Design* Stroudsburg, Pennsylvania: Hutchinson & Ross, Inc., 1975

Miles — Michael W. Miles *The Radical Probe* New York: Atheneum, 1971

Mueller — Robert E. Mueller *The Science of Art: The Cybernetics of Creative Communication* London: Rapp & Whiting, 1967

Mullard — C. Mullard *Black Britain* London: Inscape Corp., 1973. Reprinted 1975 under the title: *On Being Black in Britain.*

Nosow & Form — Sigmund Nosow and William H. Form (eds) *Man, Work and Society* New York: Basic Books, 1962

Perreault — J. M. Perreault *Towards a Theory for UDC* London: Clive Bingley, 1969

Pride & Holmes — J. B. Pride and Janet Holmes *Sociolinguistics* 1972

Rapoport — Robert N. Rapoport *Mid-Career Development* London: Tavistock, 1970

Rokeach	Milton Rokeach *The Open and Closed Mind: Investigations into the Nature of Belief Systems and Personality Systems* New York: Basic Books, 1960
Rubinstein & Stoneman	David Rubinstein and Colin Stoneman (eds) *Education for Democracy* London: Penguin, 1970
Ruddock	Ralph Ruddock (ed) *Six Approaches to the Person* London: Kegan Paul, 1972
Russell & Gablik	John Russell and Suzi Gablik *Pop Art Redefined* London: Thames & Hudson, 1969
Salzman	Eric Salzman *Twentieth Century Music: an Introduction* New York: Prentice Hall, 1974
Schlebecker & Petersen	John T. Schlebecker and Gale E. Petersen *Living Historical Farms Handbook* Washington DC: Smithsonian, 1972
Shrope	Wayne, Austin Shrope, *Experiences in Communication* New York: Harcourt, 1974
Solomon	Daniel Solomon, et al. *Teaching Styles and Learning* Chicago: Center for the Study of Liberal Education for Adults, 1963
Teodori	Massimo Teodori (ed) *The New Left: a Documentary History* London: Bobbs, 1970
Walker	John A. Walker *Art Since Pop* London: Thames & Hudson, 1975
Wörner	Karl H. Wörner *Stockhausen* ed. Bell Hopkins London: Faber, 1973

BROCHURES

(a) *Airlines*
Axiom: in-flight magazine of Eastern Provincial Airways
Delta Flightline Catalogue
High Life: in-flight magazine of British Airways
National Airlines Flight Amenity
Qantas brochure
sky: in-flight magazine of Delta Airlines
Yellowbird: in-flight magazine of North East Airlines

(b) *City information*
Australia Welcomes You, Australian Tourist Commission, 1976
Key, Dallas, Texas, USA
Metro Telecaster, Halifax, Nova Scotia, Canada
Panorama, Boston, Massachusetts, USA
The 4th Estate, Halifax, Nova Scotia, Canada
What's On in Ottawa, Ontario, Canada
WTOP, Washington D.C., USA

(c) *Hotels and restaurants*
Athenaeum Hotel, London, England
Boston Marriott Hotel, Massachusetts, USA
Copthorne Hotel, Gatwick, England
Good Times: House magazine of Trust House Forte hotel group,
    London
Howard Johnson restaurant, Dallas, Texas, USA
Magic Pan Crêperie, Boston, Massachusetts, USA
Marriott Essex House, New York, USA
Marriott Hotel, Dallas, Texas, USA
Marriott Motor Hotel, Chicago, Illinois, USA
Merrimack Valley Motor Inn, North Andover, Massachusetts, USA
Nova Scotian Hotel, Halifax, Canada
Royal County Hotel, Durham, England
Swallow Hotels Group (GB)
Trust House Forte, Coventry, England
Thurlestone Hotel, Devon, England
Wentworth Hotel, Sydney, New South Wales, Australia

(d) *Wine merchants*
Ellis Son & Vidler, Hastings and London
Lay & Wheeler, Colchester, England
Wine News: Hedges & Butler (GB)

(e) *Other*
BBC News, BBC 1, Radio 3
The British Road to Socialism, British Communist Party, 1977
Canadian Government circular
Catalogue of Woodeward and Lothrop's store, Washington D.C.,
    US, 1976
Communications course, Bristol, England
Hansard (GB)
Harvest shop, Bath, England

Report of the Annual Conference of the Trades Union Congress
(GB)
Report of National Conference on Degree Sandwich Courses,
University of Bath, England, 1976
Stone-Dri shop advertisement, Bristol, England

JOURNALS AND PERIODICALS

ABC Radio Guide, Australia
The Age, Melbourne, Australia
Air Travel Journal (US)
American Association of Museums Financial and Salary Survey (AAM)
American Journal of Psychiatry (Am J Psy)
Apollo (GB)
Architects Journal (Arch J) (GB)
Archives of General Psychiatry (Arch Gen Psy) (US)
Art in America
Art Journal (US)
Arts Canada
Australian Foreign Affairs Record (AFAR)
The Australian National University: Report (ANU)
The Australian Women's Weekly
BBC Radio Guide (GB)
Better Business, Auckland, New Zealand (BB/NZ)
British Journal of Sociology (B J Soc)
The Bulletin, Sydney, New South Wales, Australia
Business and Finance, Dublin, Eire
Business Horizons (US)
Classical Music (GB)
Comment: Communist Fortnightly Review (GB)
Connoisseur (GB)
Country Life (GB)
E.B. 75: Brochure of Commonwealth Educational Broadcasting
Conference, Sydney, New South Wales, Australia
The Economist (GB)
Educational and Social Science (GB)
Encounter (GB)
Federation of Australian Commercial Television Stations: Annual Report
(Aust CTS)
Good Food Guide (GB)

Journals and periodicals

Good Housekeeping (GB)
Harpers and Queen (GB)
Health: Journal of the Australian Department of Health
Hospital Administration in Canada
House Beautiful (US)
Journal of Educational Psychology (JEP) (US)
Journal of Educational Research (JER) (US)
The Listener, Auckland, New Zealand
Melody Maker (GB)
Mosaic: Journal for the Comparative Study of Literature and Ideas,
    University of Manitoba Press, Winnipeg, Canada
Museum News (US)
National Times: Australia's national weekly newspaper of business
    and affairs
Nation Review, Melbourne, Australia
New Society (GB)
New Statesman (GB)
New Yorker (US)
*OTC (Overseas Telecommunications Commission) Sydney: Annual
    Report* (Australia)
Handbook of Papua and New Guinea University of Technology
    (PNGUT)
Queensland Cane Growers' Association: 47th Annual Report, 1974
Radio Times: Programme guide of BBC, London
Saturday Review (US)
Scientific American
Signature: London edition of the magazine of the Diners Club
Social Work Today (GB)
Sociologia Ruralis (Netherlands)
Sociological Review (GB)
Sociology (GB)
The Spectator (GB)
Times Educational Supplement (TES) (GB)
Times Higher Education Supplement (THES) (GB)
Times Literary Supplement (TLS) (GB)
Vogue (GB)
Voice: Official Journal of the Australian Workers' Union, Shop
    Distributive Branch
Woman's Day and Australian Parent

NEWSPAPERS

Bath & Wilts Evening Chronicle, England (B & WEC)
Boston Sunday Globe, US
Bristol Evening Post, England
The Citizen, Ottawa, Ontario, Canada
Daily Express, London, England
Daily Telegraph, London, (D Tel)
Daily Telegraph, Sydney, New South Wales, Australia (DTS)
Financial Times, London, England
Globe and Mail, Toronto, Canada
Guardian, London, England
Herald Tribune, New York, US
Irish Times, Dublin, Eire
Montreal Star, Canada
Morning Star, London, England
New York Times, US
Observer, London, England
Shepton Mallet Journal, England (SMJ)
The Sun, Australia
The Sun, London, England (Sun GB)
Sunday Telegraph, London, England (S Tel)
Sunday Times, London, England (S Times)
Sydney Morning Herald, Australia
The Times, London, England
Washington Star, US